ISLAND TREASURES 2

Island Treasures 2

An Insider's Guide to Victoria, Vancouver Island and the Gulf Islands

❖

by Carolyn Thomas and Jill Stewart

Illustrations by Jim Wispinski

HARBOUR PUBLISHING

To our mothers,
Pat Stewart and Joan Zaruk,
with love and thanks.
❖

Copyright © 1990 by Carolyn Thomas and Jill Stewart

Published by Harbour Publishing
Box 219
Madeira Park, BC
V0N 2H0

Cover design by Roger Handling
Cover photo by Doug Nealy/Image Finders
Printed and bound in Canada

Canadian Cataloguing in Publication Data

Thomas, Carolyn.
  Island treasures 2

Includes index.
ISBN 1-55017-023-6

  1. Vancouver Island (B.C.) – Description and travel – Guide-books.
2. Victoria (B.C.) – Description – Guide-books.   3. Gulf Islands (B.C.) –
Description and travel – Guide-books.
I. Stewart, Jill.   II. Title.
FC3846.18.T56 1990   917.11′2′044   C90-091291-X
F1089.V3T48 1990

Contents

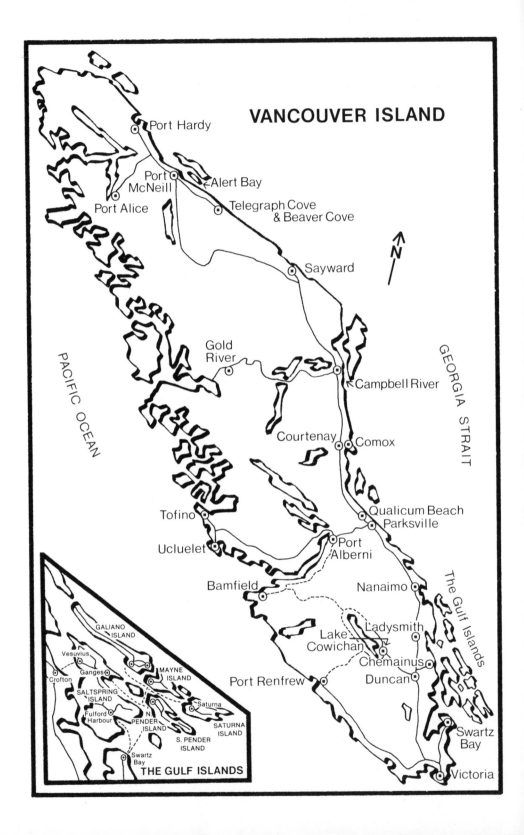

VANCOUVER ISLAND

PACIFIC OCEAN

GEORGIA STRAIT

Port Hardy

Port McNeill

Port Alice

Alert Bay

Telegraph Cove & Beaver Cove

Sayward

Gold River

Campbell River

Courtenay

Comox

Qualicum Beach

Parksville

Tofino

Ucluelet

Port Alberni

Bamfield

Nanaimo

Lake Cowichan

Ladysmith

Chemainus

Duncan

Port Renfrew

The Gulf Islands

Swartz Bay

Victoria

THE GULF ISLANDS

GALIANO ISLAND

Vesuvius

Crofton

Ganges

MAYNE ISLAND

SALTSPRING ISLAND

Fulford Harbour

N. PENDER ISLAND

Saturna

SATURNA ISLAND

S. PENDER ISLAND

Swartz Bay

Introduction

This is a guidebook with a difference.

We wrote the first edition of this book because it's the kind of book we wish we could find whenever we travel—one that can lead us to off-the-beaten-track neighbourhood secrets familiar to locals but usually unknown to visitors.

Like the original, this revised version of *Island Treasures* is a *selective*, highly personal guide. You may not agree with all of our choices, but we think you will find *Island Treasures* a useful starting point if you're looking for alternatives to those highly advertised tourist traps described in the glossy brochures. Although you will see an occasional well-known name in this book, we have deliberately sought the out-of-the-way and the not-yet-famous whenever possible.

As much as we would have loved to accept bribes (and certainly won't say no to generous offers from grateful establishments now!), all our sleuthing in the selection process was done anonymously, without financial constraints or obligations. Our theory was: if we, as average strangers off the street, enjoy a particular place or are treated well, then you, the reader, will probably do likewise. Whenever we were uncertain about whether to include any individual entry, our motto was: "The mediocre they can find for themselves!" We did have three major considerations to help us weed out the mediocre:

- entries had to be approved by both of us
- business establishments had to offer value for money
- other local residents had to rave about the entries

Two comments worth stressing here: for those travellers yearning to get as far off the beaten track as possible, our island is criss-crossed with logging roads open to the general public, except during periods of extreme forest fire hazard. Remember to check with local forestry company offices before you explore too far; a head-on meeting with a logging truck is bound to mean that the truck comes out on top. This is especially true for increasingly popular areas like the magnificent and controversial Carmanah Valley. Many forestry company offices will issue maps, route and campsite information to visitors, but the best time to travel the backwoods roads is on the weekends. Obey all posted restrictions.

Secondly, while we have done our level best to ensure that all information in this book is accurate at press time, we know that the way of the world is change. We were stunned after the release of the first edition of *Island Treasures* when we saw some of our personal favourites close up, burn down, retire, or move on! Expect some differences along the way, and please use the Reader Reply Form at the end of the book to tell us about your own favourites for future revisions of this guide.

This is not only another collaborative effort between two old friends (well, not *that* old!), but is also the result of the generosity of many others. We'd like to thank all the people who responded to our book-flogging appearances on radio talk shows all over the Island, Vancouver, and Washington State by sharing with us the inside scoop on "one more terrific place for your next book"; readers of the original edition who mailed in Reader Reply Forms whenever they discovered an island treasure of their own; all the members of the "Chemainus and Cowichan Valley A.M." group who invited us to speak at the breakfast meeting and subsequently shared a wealth of insider information with us; and reviewers near and far who loved our first book (even though they weren't related to either of us!) Particular thanks to Ron and Jean Way on Galiano Island, Gary and Julie McCaig in Port Alberni, and Harvey and Karen Henderson in Tofino for their specific and thoughtful local recommendations.

The delightful illustrations are, once again, by our favourite "poor, starving artist" Jim Wispinski, who translated our vague descriptions even better than we had hoped.

Last, but never least, we thank our children—Stephen, Raymond, Ben, and Larissa Jane—whose participation in this edition once more involved eating at countless unusual restaurants (not one of which was located under a pair of Golden Arches) and who each tolerated a mentally absent Mum more often than we like to admit while we were chained to the keyboard. Finally, special gratitude and love to our biggest fans, Colin Bowen and Tedd Wright, for their support, enthusiasm, and hugs.

Islands are magic places and the stuff of dreams. Vancouver Island, the largest island off the Pacific Coast of North America, is our home. It is also the destination of thousands of visitors each year from around the globe. We wrote this book to share with them the parts of our Island, and nearby Gulf Islands, that we love the most—our personal island treasures.

Jill Stewart
Carolyn Thomas

Victoria

We both moved here from Vancouver – and neither of us would live anywhere else. As far as we're concerned, Victoria is as close to Eden as possible, and we think that grumblers should just move back to Toronto and leave this charming city to those of us who appreciate its verdant beauty, its human scale and its relaxing rhythm. We invite you to explore some of the unique delights in Victoria and surrounding areas that have become our favourites.

What to See and Do

FUN OUTINGS

Outings, excursions, expeditions... call them what you will, they are what we like to do on holidays. Here's an assortment of enjoyable ways to spend your time in Greater Victoria. Some cost a small fortune, but most are downright cheap or even free. We hope that all will be the kind of outing you will remember well.

Craigdarroch Castle ❖ The castle is a treat for *Lives of the Rich and Famous* fans. Robert Dunsmuir, BC's first millionaire, built Craigdarroch for his wife Joan. The castle was finished in 1889 and it's a sumptuous example of what you get when you can afford to pay for it. The stunning stained glass and the masterful woodwork alone are worth the price of admission. Don't miss the panoramic view from the tower. As at the Art Gallery and the Royal BC Museum, proceeds from the gift shop help support the institution—so buy something. Admission fee for adults $3, seniors and students $2.50. In the heart of ritzy Rockland at 1050 Joan Crescent, 592-5323.

Dominion Astrophysical Observatory ❖ If you have an urge to examine the stars and planets at what seems like arm's length, don't miss a visit to this observatory. It features a giant telescope for public observation of the heavens, and during the summer, is open Saturday until 11 p.m. for even more impressive viewing. Located along a pleasant, winding stretch of country road, you'll drive right by if you take West Saanich Road out towards Butchart Gardens, Brentwood Bay or Sidney. At 5071 West Saanich Road, 388-0001. Free.

Gonzales Weather Station ❖ This weather station was built in 1914 and has the distinction of being the only facility of its kind in Canada to record an entire winter in which the temperature did not fall below 0° C. The meteorological displays inside include antique instruments and recorders. From the roof-top observation deck you can get a breathtaking view over the city and the Strait of Juan de Fuca. Free admission. At 302 Denison Road, off Fairfield—follow the hill up Denison, keeping to the right, 388-3350.

Limousine Services ❖ Expecting somebody special to arrive at the airport? Want to make an unforgettable impression for that special night on the town? An anniversary coming up for a couple that already has everything? Consider renting a limousine for a truly elegant effect. Victoria has several firms in the limo business: **VIP Limousine Service**, for example, has been renting out classics like their Cadillac and Silver Cloud Rolls Royce for over ten years. 1608 Quadra Street, 382-6805. Check the yellow pages for more businesses. Most firms have a minimum two-hour rental requirement, and the rates are pretty pricey—starting at $70 per hour—but what do you expect for a car with a bar?

Point Ellice House ❖ If you want a sense of what life was like for the upper middle classes during the latter half of the 19th century in Victoria, visit Point Ellice House. The house was bought in 1868 by Peter O'Reilly, an MLA, and most of the furniture and household items displayed were used by three generations of his family. The grounds are in the process of restoration to historical accuracy, thanks to the discovery of some garden notebooks kept by one of the O'Reilly daughters. Grounds open year-round, house open during the summer season. Look for the signs on Bay Street, near the bridge. We know, it looks as if you are in a junked car graveyard, but trust the signs. They will lead you to 2616 Pleasant Street, 387-5953.

Ravenhill Herb Farm ❖ We want to be reincarnated as the owners of Ravenhill in our next life. One visit shows why: a wonderful rambling house, a view to kill for, lambs, ducks and other livestock gambolling about the fields, and, best of all, a gently sloping sunny herb garden, full of enchanting scents and textures. The farm is open on Sundays from 1 to 5 p.m., spring through fall, when the owners offer potted herbs, dried bouquets and other garden bounty for sale. A 25-minute drive north of Victoria through scenic pastoral landscapes bring you to 1330 Mount Newton X Road, Saanichton, 652-4024.

Ross Bay Cemetery ❖ We had grave doubts about this entry. Would our cryptic remarks be understood? Would readers think we had captured the right spirit? Would there be the ghost of a chance people would visit the dead centre of town?

Yes! We want you tour Ross Bay Cemetery, 27.5 acres of prime south-facing waterfront real estate in Fairfield, a site which encompasses history, art, botany and sociology. The cemetery is an excellent example of 19th Century English cemetery landscaping with its winding roadways, attractive vistas and "appropriate" plants such as yew, holly and boxwood.

Paris's Cimetière du Père-Lachaise contains the grave of Chopin. London's Highgate has Karl Marx. Ross Bay, however, is no slouch in the famous last worldly remains department. Interred here are Sir James Douglas, founder of Victoria, renowned artist Emily Carr, and legendary Gold Rush character Billy Barker. Robert Dunsmuir, BC's first millionaire, lies at rest under a massive granite pedestal, embellished with cornice and pediment. The names on other monuments read like a *Who's Who* of early BC history—"hanging judge" Matthew Begbie, Premier Amor de Cosmos—and include many names found today on Victoria streets and landmarks.

Examples of cemetery art abound, from Celtic crosses to classical columns. The most unusual is a fireman's hat on a cushion, marking the grave of a city fireman killed on duty.

The Old Cemeteries Committee offers free guided tours, led by local historians, every Sunday at 2 p.m. Meet in front of Bagga Pasta in Fairfield Plaza, across Fairfield Road from the cemetery. Find out why Ross Bay Cemetery is so popular people are dying to get in.

MUSEUMS

We have a list of off-the-beaten-track museums to share with you, but first we would like to put in a good word—in fact, a good paragraph—for our own *Royal British Columbia Museum*. If you are the type who thinks all museums make you yawn, you really must visit our museum to clear that notion right out of your head. This is a living, working microcosm of our entire province. A first-rate Indian cultural display, a Victorian town at night (you can visit the local theatre for some silent movies, or peek through a kitchen doorway to smell apple pie baking) and fascinating dioramas of forest and seaside landscapes, make the Provincial Museum a must. Admission fee $5 for adults, discounts for seniors, students and youths aged 6–18, under 5 free. No admission fee on Mondays between October and April. 675 Belleville Street, 387-3014.

After visiting the Big Museum, you may proceed to the following charming small ones:

Canadian Scottish Regimental Museum ❖ Military buffs will enjoy a tour through this museum, which traces the history of the Canadian Scottish Regiment (the 16th Battalion). The display includes photographs, medals, uniforms, weapons and other militaria. This private museum is attached to the Officers' Mess and is open Thursday evenings 8 to 10 p.m., Saturdays 10 a.m. to 1 p.m. Special viewings available for groups on a pre-arranged basis. Call 388-3897 for information. Bay Street Armouries, Bay at Blanshard.

CFB Esquimalt Naval Museum ❖ The museum and archives are housed in two excellent examples of turn-of-the-century architecture. This is one of only two naval museums in Canada. (The other is in Halifax, Nova Scotia.) The museum is of interest to naval history buffs and displays artifacts, ship models and other memorabilia tracing West Coast naval history from British colonial days up to the present. Free admission. Open weekdays 10 a.m. to 2 p.m. Located at CFB Esquimalt on Admirals Road, half a mile north of the intersection of Esquimalt and Admirals roads. Ask the commissionaire at the gate for directions to the museum.

Fort Rodd Hill ❖ This is a National Historic Park, containing Fisgard Lighthouse, the first permanent lighthouse to shine on the west coast of Canada, and the remains of coastal defence gun batteries. There are acres of parkland, an information booth, a museum display, picnic sites and water views. Tours are available in the summer, and admission is free. Watch for deer! Located west of Victoria in Colwood. Turn off the Island Highway (1A) onto Ocean Boulevard at the traffic lights, and follow the signs to the park, 380-4662..

Maltwood Art Museum and Gallery ❖ This museum houses the Katharine Maltwood Collection of art, paintings, sculptures, glass, textiles, ceramics and furniture. It is located at the University Centre (follow the signs along Ring Road, which circles the campus). A second, contemporary part of the museum's collection is on display at the university's McPherson Library Gallery. 721-8298.

Maritime Museum of BC ❖ Those who agree with Ratty that there is nothing like messing about in boats, will not want to miss this specialty museum devoted to life on the bounding main. Located in one of Victoria's oldest buildings (it used to be the courthouse), it offers two floors of coastal maritime history in the form of artifacts, paintings, intricately-detailed scale models of ships and two actual vessels—the *Tilikum* and the *Trekka*—that sailed around the world. The second floor has special exhibits devoted to Captain Cook and to the Royal Canadian Navy. Enthusiastic and knowledgeable volunteers are happy to answer questions and give guided tours. The entry fee is $4 for adults, $3 for students. It's at 28 Bastion Square, 385-4222.

Metchosin School Museum ❖ This schoolhouse was built in 1872. Today it is home to an interesting collection of photos and pioneer items, including an archives department that traces the history of this rural area. 611 Happy Valley Road, no phone.

Regent's Park House ❖ This is a rarity among museums—a privately-funded one. The owner has filled—and we do mean *filled*—every corner of this heritage house with Victoriana from around the world. You could spend hours admiring the over-whelming clutter. An added bonus is the Canadiana costume collection, beautiful examples of fashions from Victorian and Edwardian days. Fun and fascinating! $3 admission fee. Open from the third weekend in May to Labour Day. Corner of Fort Street and St. Charles Street. Information at 479-5102.

Sidney Museum ❖ Somebody back in Sidney's pioneer days owned a Humane Mouse Trap, a bizarre metal cage which trapped (but did not kill) your rodent guests. Feeling as we do about mice—revulsion!—we found this fascinating but weird. This small, crammed building traces Sidney's roots as a bustling seaside town. Logging, farming and even washday displays are set up alongside Coast Salish Indian Relics and an authentic "Victoria Bedroom"—a bedsitting room as it used to be, com-plete with clothing, personal toiletries and the ever-present chamber pot. 2538 Beacon Avenue, Sidney, 656-1322.

Sooke Regional Museum ❖ This unique log building contains a fas-cinating display of artifacts telling the story of this region. Hay fever sufferers will be thrilled to know that the bright yellow broom plants covering the Island have all descended from one packet of seeds, brought to Sooke from Hawaii by the first permanent white settler. There's lots more to learn at this interesting museum at the corner of Phillips Road and Sooke Road, 642-6351.

Tod House ❖ Although Tod House is not open to the public (it's currently rented out to private tenants) you might want to drive or walk past this lovely farmhouse in Oak Bay. It's the oldest house in British Columbia—built around 1850. At one time it stood on waterfront acreage; today it is snuggled into a pleasant residential street, 2564 Heron Street, off Estevan, blocks from the sea!

NEIGHBOURHOODS

Greater Victoria has a number of distinctive neighbourhoods which locals call "villages," although you won't find a mayor's chain of office among them. Each is worth at least an hour's visit, and some are so enjoyable you will come back to spend the day. When you can't cope with any more "olde English charm," and feel the need to wander down tree-lined streets to rub shoulders with friendly Victorians on their own turf, try the following excursions.

Chinatown ❖ The first Chinese residents of Victoria arrived in the 1850s and lived in what was, at one time, the largest Chinatown on the continent, with a population of over 8,000. Most of the original Chinese immigrants were from the Pearl River Delta in South China, and their descendants speak the Cantonese dialect. Restaurants here serve mainly Cantonese food, although we do have a small number of Szechuan and Mandarin specialty restaurants.

Today's Chinatown is a far cry from its ancient ancestor. It has contracted to a two-block section on Fisgard Street west of Government, and you won't find the gambling clubs, brothels and opium dens which once flourished here legally (between 1862 and 1908 there were fourteen licensed opium factories here). You can stroll the narrowest street in Canada if you spot Fan Tan Alley—now an artists' enclave, but once rumoured to hold danger for any white person who dared to step into the dark alley. Chinatown shops are our choice for Best Browsing on a Rainy Afternoon. The fascinating little stores beyond the big red "Gate of Harmonious Interest" yield everything from pickled garlic to feather dusters, piled to the rafters in happy abandon. Bring the kids: Chinese restaurants here are crammed with families and you will feel left out without at least two children along.

A unique way to experience the authentic taste of our Chinatown is with **Les Chan** (Victoria's unofficial "Goodwill Ambassador of Chinatown") on one of his fascinating guided walking tours. Choose the day tour (includes dim sum luncheon), the night tour (includes a Chinese banquet dinner), or the innovative Cook's Tour for all us frustrated Chinese food chefs who need a crash course from an expert on shopping like a real pro. In addition, you'll visit the Chinese bean sprout factory, the rarely seen Chinese shrine, and hear intriguing tales (like the one about cavernous smugglers' tunnels which once led from Chinatown to the Empress Hotel.) All tours start at the Gate of Harmonious Interest; tour rates start at $15, with discounts for children and seniors. Ticket information from Tourism Victoria, 382-2127.

While in Chinatown, slip around the corner to visit the *North Park Studio* complex: a fine continental restaurant, *Larousse*; the *North Park Design Store* featuring uncommon pieces of home decor; and the second floor *North Park Gallery* which specializes in avant garde modern work. Housed in a tastefully renovated building at 1619 Store Street.

Cook Street Village ❖ This neighbourhood is near Beacon Hill Park, around the 300 block of Cook Street (named, of course, after Captain James Cook, the intrepid explorer and navigator who first sailed around our island in 1778). Serving the residents of surrounding Fairfield, it contains supermarkets and a secondhand shop with very reasonably priced stock, plus a tearoom and other quick bite spots along a shady stretch of Cook lined with tall trees. Stop on your way to the park for picnic fixings.

Estevan Village ❖ This is a one-block-long shopping complex, with just enough stores and services to make the neighbours glad they don't have to go any farther than around the corner. One of the finest restaurants in town is here, *Chez Daniel*, at 2524 Estevan Avenue. A bank, pharmacy, restaurants, and the only Stretch & Sew store in Victoria can also be found in this pleasant residential area of Oak Bay, on Estevan between Beach and Cadboro Bay Roads.

James Bay Village ❖ James Bay was the original suburbia of the old town of Victoria. It fell into decay earlier this century, but has been resurrected as a trendy place to renovate a character house. Much newer, and less well established than our other villages, it is in a district famous for close community ties and neighbourhood spirit.

The village's shopping and restaurant area is centred around the intersection of Simcoe and Menzies. Two highlights: Victoria's best butcher shop, *McColl's Meat Market*, downstairs at 230 Menzies Street, 382-1611; and the *Banana Belt Cafe* for absolutely enormous and satisfying breakfasts. Carolyn's favourite is the granola-topped pancake with *real* maple syrup, yogurt and fruit. 281 Menzies Street, 385-9616.

Market Square ❖ We couldn't resist adding this non-residential attraction to our list of neighbourhoods because it is such a great place to visit. A dreary block of decrepit buildings was extensively renovated some years back, and today Market Square could be in San Francisco or Montreal without missing a beat. Their three-day Jazz Festival features continuous live music by internationally-known artists in the garden courtyard outdoors. Plenty of benches and sidewalk tables provide a place to enjoy your lunch. Unique cosmopolitan stores and restaurants overlook the courtyard. The main entrance is through the imposing iron arch in the 500 block of Johnson Street. Parking is impossible on this route, however, so if you're driving, try the Market Square outdoor parking lot, around the block off Pandora. A free shuttle van service zips around town in the tourist season, but better yet, *walk*—this is a great area for exploring on foot and is an easy stroll from downtown hotels and the Inner Harbour, via Government Street.

Mattick's Farm ❖ Okay, okay, so this isn't exactly a "village" neighbourhood either, but this collection of markets and shops is certainly a great reason for a lovely drive in the not-too-far-away countryside, north along Cordova Bay Road.

Oak Bay Village ❖ We hesitate to mention this one because it's already *so* popular with Victorians and visitors who enjoy its Tudor-style architecture and the chance for a stroll "behind the Tweed Curtain." If you promise to take the *bus* out here (the Willows or the Oak Bay route from downtown), and leave the limited parking spaces for residents, we'll let you visit the outstanding shops here, several restaurants and the interesting *Athlone Court* shopping complex. *Monterey Mews*, another cluster of eleven shops hidden underneath and behind the

Blethering Place Tearoom, is a must. On Oak Bay Avenue between Monterey and Wilmot.

PARKS AND BEACHES

"Not far from the frenetic energy of Waikiki Beach is a small waterfront park favoured by residents of Honolulu. Tourists who accidentally stumble on this tiny park see a side of Hawaii that is well known to locals, but rarely experienced by visitors. Here, community-sponsored teams play evening ball games, elderly beachcombers wander the sand, and young surfers seek the Big Wave off the reef. Once you discover this pocket of quiet greenery, you remember it fondly for a long time."

This type of discovery we wish for visitors to Victoria as well. Grab your camera and your beach towel, and read on.

Regional Parks

We can't think of a better introduction to the natural heritage of this island than to visit our regional parks. Thousands of acres, representing a wide variety of environmental characteristics, have been preserved in the Greater Victoria region. These are some of our favourites.

Albert Head Lagoon Park ❖ This wildlife sanctuary is home to ducks, geese, and swans. There is a pebbly beach and a lovely view over the Strait of Juan de Fuca. Metchosin Road, off Old Island Highway.

Cole Bay Park ❖ A small, quiet park, surrounding a log-strewn cove, Cole Bay offers warm summer swimming and views of Saanich Inlet, as one travels the nature trails through the woods. Ardmore Drive, off West Saanich Road.

Devonian Park ❖ This tiny nature sanctuary was one of the first farms in the area. It features birdwatching, beachcombing along the cobble beach, wonderful views and short (fifteen to thirty-minute) woodland trails. The William Head minimum security prison is nearby, originally built in 1893 as a federal quarantine station to screen the health of Asian immigrants. William Head Road, off Metchosin Road.

East Sooke Park ❖ Allow one hour to drive out here. This park is the essence of the West Coast experience. Enjoy rock and shell collecting, Coast Salish petroglyphs at Alldridge Point, tide-pooling, whale-watching, fishing and hiking (both relaxed — to Iron Mine Bay — and strenuous — seven hours along the Coast Trail). A must-see. East Sooke Road, off Rocky Point Road, off Happy Valley Road, off Sooke Road.

Elk/Beaver Lake Park ❖ A huge freshwater lake, ringed by four beaches, is a sailboarder's paradise (rentals available). For the landlubber there are walking trails and bridle paths, picnic and recreation areas, plus open fields for team sports. The beaches are too crowded for our liking, but thousands of Victorians disagree. Off Pat Bay Highway.

Island View Beach Park ❖ The long sandy beach attracts beach-combers and swimmers, but also, alas, the ghetto-blaster set. Use the boat launch to escape, or do as we do and head to Cole Bay, a bit farther north. Island View Road, off Pat Bay High-way.

Lone Tree Hill Park ❖ A gnarled Douglas Fir stands alone on the rocky summit of this park, as it has for two centuries, and gives this park its name. The thirty-minute hike to the top is en-thusiastically recommended by our young hiker friends, Carl and Neil Erickson. The summit provides views of Victoria and the Olympic Mountains, plus lots of birdwatching oppor-tunities. Millstream Road, off Highway 1.

Mill Hill Park ❖ Hiking trails through cedar and fir forests lead to the summit of this park. Spring offers a bonanza of wildflowers and you can enjoy the view of Esquimalt Harbour all year. Atkins Avenue, off Millstream Road, at the new RCMP station.

Mount Work Park ❖ This beautiful park offers three lakes, arbutus forests, and waterfalls. McKenzie Bight is popular with scuba divers, tidepoolers and picnickers. Durrance Road, off West Saanich Road.

Portage Park ❖ Steps away from the busy Old Island Highway, forest trails lead to a shell-strewn beach. Our sons recommend swing-ing on the rope swing over this beach and exploring the E & N railway tracks just beyond the woods. There are picnic sites, and a fitness trail with five exercise stations. Craigflower Road at Four Mile House.

North Hill Park ❖ Trails past spring wildflowers and fall mushrooms lead to a hilltop park with lovely views over Satellite Channel and the Gulf Islands. Tatlow Road, off West Saanich Road.

Thomas Francis/Freeman King Parks ❖ These adjoining parks, six miles from town, offer very easy forest trails, including the Elsie King cedar boardwalk for the disabled. You can book a nature guide or reserve a wheelchair by calling CRD Parks Department at 478-3344. Prospect Road, off West Burnside Road.

Witty's Lagoon Park ❖ Nature trails, Sitting Lady Falls, bridle trails, a riding ring, sandy beach, and a Nature Centre make this a hit with locals year round. Metchosin Road, off Old Island Highway.

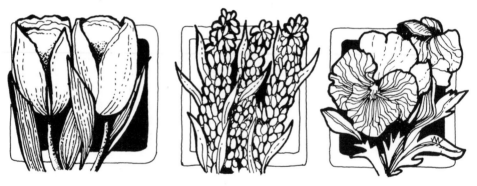

Barnard Park ❖ Jill stumbled on this park by accident when she lived in Vic West, and has visited it regularly ever since. From the road, you can see a playground and tennis courts; it's only when you get down to the lower level that you realize there is a walkway to take you along the water's edge—to West Bay Marina in one direction, towards downtown Victoria in the other. There are picnic tables at the marina end, and it's hard to imagine a more pleasant spot in which to soak up the sun. On Esquimalt Road at Sea Terrace.

Beacon Hill Park ❖ We know, we know—this is hardly a secret place, but we wanted to let you in on some little-known trivia about this beautiful park. An ancient Indian village once overlooked the ocean here. On the highest point of land blazed two fires, used to guide ships into the harbour. This hill was called "Mee-a-can," which means "the belly," because it was thought to resemble a reclining fat man. Take a look for yourself.

The park contains acres of gardens, walks, duck ponds, a farm zoo, a putting green (free), and areas for lawn bowling, picnics, and cricket (which is interesting to watch, if only to see if you can figure out what on earth the rules actually are). Free Sunday band concerts are held in the summer months. The local Horticultural Society sponsors a rock and alpine display garden, and the Mayors' Grove is a commemorative area of trees planted to honour Victoria's past mayors and other celebrities. Near the southwest corner of the park is Mile Zero of the Trans-Canada Highway and a cairn observing the 5,000-mile "Journey for Lives" of one-legged runner Steve Fonyo.

Bowker Creek Park ❖ When Carolyn pays her Oak Bay property taxes each year, she finds comfort in the knowledge that part of that money finds a home in maintaining this lovely little park. Bowker Creek looks like a drainage ditch in some areas of the city, as it meanders along on its way to the ocean. For a two-block section on either side of the 1700 block of Hampshire Road, however, it drifts through a full-fledged park setting. Several years ago the Bocking family sold a large chunk of their back, which bordered the creek, to the municipality. Resembling a Monet watercolour, the creek now widens into two duck ponds between granite-lined walls, with waterfalls, arched stone bridges and attractive gardens. It's possible to stroll from the picturesque Oak Bay Fire Hall all the way along the winding creek path to the Oak Bay Recreation Centre without battling street traffic.

This is a pleasant place to feed the ducks—and admire the fluffy babies if you happen to be here in May. A duck-feeding hint: when you're on your way to the ponds, drop in first at the Village Bakery, 2217 Oak Bay Avenue, and they'll load you up with free duck bread. Bring your own bag. And buy something, for heaven's sake.

Cairn (or Highrock) Park ❖ Where do Victorians take their out-of-town visitors to show off the best panoramic view in town? No, not Mount Doug. Not even Mount Tolmie. If you guessed Cairn Park in Esquimalt, you're absolutely right. Even native Victorians may have missed this one; we certainly would have had we not received a phone call after we were interviewed on local television about this book. The caller was an Esquimalt resident who said, "I hope you'll put Cairn Park into your book, because of its views and its pheasants." So far we haven't seen the pheasants, but he was correct about the views. At the top of the path is a stone cairn with mileage arrows pointing 360 degrees around you – from Beacon Hill, north to the Dominion Astrophysical Observatory, to Mount Finlayson on the west, then around behind you to Port Angeles, Washington, and back to the Inner Harbour.

Another interesting feature of this place is its accessibility for wheelchair visitors; they can travel right up to the summit, an elevation of 232¼ feet. A short, dirt path from the end of Cairn Street, where you will park, leads to the playing field where the path seems to end. Persevere, however, straight across the field, and you'll find a paved path up the hill. Off Cairn Street, which is off Old Esquimalt Road, in the municipality of Esquimalt.

Government House Grounds ❖ The Gardens of our lieutenant-governor's residence are open to the public all year, and are popular with Victoria brides for wedding-day photographs... for good reason. Exquisite formal landscaping and wide vistas of carpet-like lawns make Government House a real treat for frustrated gardeners like us. The grounds are included in the Art Gallery's walking tour. If you sign the guest book at the door (you can't go inside the building), an invitation to the famous Summer Garden Party will be mailed to you. This is your chance to don your finest hat and gloves and share goodies on the lawn with local gentry. You might even shake hands with the lieutenant-governor, the Queen's representative in BC. (Americans take note: we Canucks use the Oxford University pronunciation: "lef-ten-ant.")

Another opportunity for the public to drop in to pay respects, and the only chance to enter the interior rooms, is the annual New Year's Day Levee, when you can enjoy punch and sandwiches indoors. Government House is located along a beautiful stretch of residential homes, at 1401 Rockland Avenue.

Horticultural Centre of the Pacific ❖ We once heard gardening defined as "nine months of planning and three months of disappointment." Here at the new Horticultural Centre the planning is paying off every year, as development projects proceed and plantings mature. Set on 110 rolling acres framed by distant mountains, the Centre has a flourishing Demonstration Garden producing show-quality mums, glads and dahlias. Local gardeners have been generous with donations of trees, shrubs and cuttings to help this exciting showplace meet its goal. A special favourite, particularly with easterners, is the Winter Garden. It proves once and for all that Victorians can have blooms in their gardens every month of the year. Free admission October to May, $1 June to September, children free. Present entrance is at the intersection of Quale and Beaver Roads (off West Saanich Road), a fifteen-minute drive from downtown Victoria.

Playfair Park ❖ You could drive past the Playfair Park sigh on Quadra Street a dozen times and never be tempted to turn off to investigate unless you knew that Playfair holds a beautiful secret. If you time your visit during the spring or early summer, you will find an incredible rhododendron garden along this park border. Winding paths criss-cross the gardens so visitors can lose themselves among the native foliage. Lots of parking, a playground, and grassy fields complete this picture-postcard corner of the Saanich municipality. Off Quadra Street at Rock Street, watch for wooden signs on the east side of the road.

Royal Roads ❖ Where can you see an Italian garden, a rose garden and a Japanese garden? Butchart Gardens, right? Well, yes, but the entrance price seems to go up by leaps and bounds yearly.

No, when we have out-of-town guests to impress with Victoria's botanical bounty, we take them to Royal Roads. Formerly called Hatley Park, James Dunsmuir's castle and 650-acre waterfront estate now house a military college which boasts an expansive swathe of green lawn and the aforementioned gardens. To reach them, you descend a very impressive stone staircase guarded by stone lions. While on a smaller scale than Butchart's, the Royal Roads grounds have the overwhelming advantage of being free. Open to the public daily, 10 a.m. to 4 p.m., on Sooke Road about half a mile west of the Fort Rodd Hill turnoff, near Colwood Corners.

Salmon Spawning ❖ Fall means the annual migration of. . .no, not geese and ducks — schoolbus loads of children from the Victoria area to watch the salmon spawning.

23

Check your biology text for the lowdown on this miracle of nature, or better yet, pull on your rubber boots and join the kids as they march along the wet riverbank, looking for the grotesquely misshapen fish struggling gamely against the current to their birthplace. You'll learn everything you've ever wanted to know about salmon. For instance, did you know that after they reach sexual maturity and spawn, they die? Depending on the time of your visit in late fall, the rivers appear clogged with the red backs of dead or dying fish. Did you know that salmon waiting to spawn do not eat? They have enough accumulated body fat to live for months without food. These are but a few of the gems we have learned on our salmon-spawning visits.

The two best places to watch this spectacle are **Goldstream Park**, about twenty minutes north of Victoria on the Malahat Drive, and **Sooke River Potholes Park**, off Sooke Road, turn right onto Sooke River Road at the Milne's Landing Store.

Saxe Point Park ❖ We are amazed at the number of Victorians who have never heard of this park. We think it's one of the prettiest in Victoria, particularly in the spring when the raised flower beds are full of hyacinths, daffodils and tulips. You get an unsurpassed view of the Olympics, a rocky beach for poking around and some pleasant walking trails through the part of the park that has been left in its natural state. At the south end of Fraser Street in Esquimalt.

Swan Lake-Christmas Hill Nature Sanctuary ❖ It's pouring rain (actually, it rarely "pours here – it just mists heavily). Cheer up. As Victorians say, "At least you don't have to shovel it, ha-ha!"–and you can always go down to Swan Lake. This is one of the few spots which we like even better in the rain, so bring your rain gear and come for a wet walk. This park comprises almost a hundred acres of lake, marshes, fields and trails. A floating boardwalk rings the lake–you can feed the swans from the west side of the walk. On weekdays and weekend afternoons the Nature House is open to teach you more about the marshy environment. Tours are available if you call ahead. Easy to find, at 3873 Swan Lake Road, off Ralph Street, 479-0211.

UVic Rhododendron Garden ❖ The University of Victoria is one of Canada's prettiest campuses since many of the university's 381 acres are still naturally forested with West Coast ever-greens. The University Gardens features an exceptionally fine rhododendron collection. Both showy hybrids and more subtle, and rarer, species make an astonishingly beautiful display in May and June. (The garden perpetuates up to 150 different rhododendron species, sown from seeds.) On the south side of the campus, Henderson at Cedar Hill roads.

Beach Tours

You don't have time to drive all the way to Long Beach to see the Real Ocean, but you've had it with the crowds at local city beaches? Well, within an hour's drive of Victoria you can visit spectacular beaches that will impress even the most travelled beach bum. Our favourites are all west of Victoria, off Highway 1 towards Port Renfrew.

Whiffen Spit Beach ❖ Follow the signs to Sooke Harbour House on Whiffen Spit Road, off Sooke Road. This beach is accessible from the end of the road beside the parking lot. Great views, clam-digging, Indian artifacts.

Gordon's Beach ❖ Rockhounds and fossil fans enjoy this beach, but the pounding waves and walking trails are for everyone. Great views, clam-digging, Indian artifacts.

Sheringham Point Lighthouse ❖ While this is not exactly a beach, it is a super place to visit and admire the view. If you're lucky you might also catch a glimpse of whales from the rocky cliffs. On Sheringham Point Road.

French Beach ❖ There are campsites on this pleasant pebbly beach, a short walk from the parking lot. Thirteen miles past Sooke.

Jordan River ❖ Rated Number Two on the Pacific Coast, surfers visit Jordan River beach from September to May. Follow Sooke Road west to the townsite historically known as River Jordan and stop at Shakie's, just over the wooden bridge, for home-made fries and gravy.

China Beach ❖ We love this place! The wide open ocean beach is worth the fifteen-minute hike on steep trails from the parking lot, and the spectacular Pacific rollers give you a thunderous welcome. Three miles west of Jordan River.

Mystic Beach ❖ This beach offers a repeat of China Beach, but its trail will prove a challenge to all but dedicated walkers in good hiking boots. One mile west of China Beach.

Sombrio Beach ❖ Quite a bit farther down the road towards Port Renfrew. In fact, you're well past your hour's drive here, but that makes its discovery less appealing for the average visitor-you'll have more beach to yourself. A rough trail from the parking lot (allow half an hour for this hike) takes you to a wonderful beach with hiking trails along the river, a cave and even a makeshift sauna. At one time this was a haven for Back-to-Nature beach squatters.

Botanical Beach ❖ This is also known as Botany Bay. Not a beach for sand castles and sunbathing, but a fabulous tidepool area. Check tide tables before visiting (656-8371 during office hours on weekdays, or check the Weather section on page 2 of the *Times-Colonist*) so that you can plan for a low-tide visit when the potholes and intertidal hiding places teem with sea life. Take the three-mile logging road from Port Renfrew.

Prior Lake ❖ What's this? Nude bathing in Victoria? Turn right, just past the Island Highway underpass to Colwood and Sooke, and continue past the rifle range to the parking area for Little Thetis Lake (also a pleasant swimming spot). Keep going until you find a small parking area, at the bottom of a hill, and the sign that says "Prior Lake:No Nudist Bathing."

VICTORIA'S HANGING BASKETS

The hanging flower baskets symbolize Victoria to millions of visitors, although we actually stole the idea from Seattle. Every year since 1937, from June until September, these gorgeous baskets have hung from bright blue lamp standards around the downtown and Inner Harbour areas. Beacon Hill Park houses the birthplace of the baskets. In December the seeds are planted in the Parks Department greenhouses, twenty-five plants per basket. During the last week of May, just before display time, the public is invited into the greenhouses for close-up photography of Bloom City. Sometimes, late at night, you might catch workers carefully watering each of the 600-plus baskets with long-handled pipes connected to water-and-fertilizer tank trucks. When sopping wet, each moss-lined beauty weighs seventy pounds.

THEATRES

The major theatre chains are well represented in Victoria, and their offerings are heavily advertised in the Entertainment section of the *Times-Colonist*. The following theatres are more offbeat. Call to find out what's on next.

Belfry Theatre ❖ The Belfry, an old, restored church building, is now home to a variety of live stage productions. In the historic Fernwood neighbourhood at 1291 Gladstone, off Fernwood, 385-6815.

Central Library ❖ The library schedules Family Film Nights on Fridays, for ages 10 and up, and has 8- and 16-mm films for rent. 735 Broughton Street, 382-7241.

Cinecenta ❖ Buy a membership (non-members pay more) and enjoy cult films, old films, art films, children's films, and festivals. Call for a schedule. University of Victoria, Finnerty Road, 721-8365.

Langham Court ❖ This is a small, intimate theatre, home to the Victoria Theatre Guild's live productions. 805 Langham Court, off Rockland Avenue, 384-2142.

National Film Board ❖ The NFB shows free noon-hour films, from our award-winning filmmakers. They also provide a self-serve lending library and a small screening area, at 1412 Douglas Street, 388-3868.

Phoenix Theatre ❖ UVic's Phoenix is a showcase for the talents of theatre arts students. Some of the most exciting productions we have seen in Victoria have been staged at the Phoenix. The modest ticket price in no way reflects the calibre of performances. Look for the Phoenix sign on the right side of Ring Road, which circles the campus. Box office number is 721-8000.

Roxy Theatre ❖ This theatre screens offbeat Hollywood movies, cult movies, Canadian movies and arty movies. The Roxy also hosts the annual foreign film festival. Don't expect to see *Rambo XVII* here. Note for foodies: the Roxy has the best theatre concession in town, starring fabulous cookies and fresh coffee. 2657 Quadra Street at Hillside, 382-3370.

SPORTS

As you know by now, if you've been doing those things we all do on holidays – eat, sightsee, eat, lie on the beach and eat some more – the old waistline begins its slow but steady outward growth unless we throw in some regular exercise. For vacationers who think that fitness never takes a vacation, here are some easy and popular local places to check out when you're feeling energetic. (And for the not-so-energetic fishing enthusiast, we've thrown in a page for you too.)

Jogging Trails

Victoria has some of the most scenic jogging routes in the world. Local runners have their favourites: *Beacon Hill Park,* for instance, has a number of pleasant circle routes, including the two-mile perimeter of the park. Another popular, but windy, run is along the *Dallas Road waterfront.* You'll want to turn north up St. Charles Street, though, to avoid the killer hill at Gonzales Point. The Royal Victoria Marathon used to cover a double circuit from Mile Zero at Beacon Hill Park, east along the waterfront to St. Charles, north through Fairfield, east along the Oak Bay waterfront and back again. We once heard of a conventioneer, staying at a downtown hotel, who decided to go out for his regular morning jog before his conference sessions began. He bumped into hundreds of marathoners and decided to tag along as an unofficial runner. A little over four hours later he crossed the finish line at Mile Zero!

Runners who are looking for attractive places to run – without those marathon dimensions! – can look at the following trails:

Cedar Hill Recreation Centre ❖ This 2.2-mile chip trail circles the lovely Cedar Hill Golf Course. You can pick it up from several places, including the parking lot by the Tennis Bubble, next door to the Rec Centre at 3220 Cedar Hill Road.

Esquimalt Recreation Centre ❖ The Esquimalt Rec Centre doesn't offer a cedar chip trail, but the office at the swimming pool does carry maps with three jogging routes marked. All start from the centre and range in length from one to six miles. 527 Fraser Street.

Juan de Fuca Chip Trail ❖ This chip trail, located just west of Victoria, is actually two separate circuits. One is a bit more than half a mile long and includes five fitness stations, in case you get the urge to do a few dozen chin-ups. The other, longer trail is linked with this one and totals 1⅔ miles if you run the entire route. Lots of ups and downs, with the "ups" at either end. Behind the Juan de Fuca Recreation Centre, 1767 Island Highway. Look for the Start sign behind Centennial Pool.

UVic Jogging Trails ❖ The University is located on some very nice real estate, covering wooded areas as well as broad, open meadows. A maze of well-marked cedar chip trails covers the campus. The ½-mile Henderson Chip Trail is probably the easiest to start with, and this route hooks up with other trails, including the aptly-named Lung Buster. That one appeals to runners suffering from anaerobic oxygen deficiency, who want to climb the almost-vertical hill to the scenic lookout at Mount Tolmie. All of these trails, beginning with the Henderson Trail, are better in the early morning hours when traffic noise is minimal. Park at the Henderson Recreation Centre (2291 Cedar Hill Cross Road), and then cross Cedar Hill Cross Road at the Alumni Chip Trip sign.

Fitness Centres

These places all offer a drop-in rate for short-term visitors to Victoria, or for locals who want to try new places on for size before they buy a membership. In some cases priority is given to members, while drop-ins wait to see if there's room to sweat. All centres offer a wide range of aerobic classes geared from mild to intense levels of activity. Drop-in rates average $3–7.

Fit Commitment ❖ Co-ed classes and babysitting service, coupled with convenient downtown location, make the Fit Commitment a fitting centre. 1602 Quadra Street. 381-1554.

Fitness Dynamics ❖ Popular "no bounce" aerobic classes and weight training for women only are featured at this centre along with a babysitting service. 2040 Oak Bay Avenue, 595-3354.

Fitness Works ❖ Debbie Firestone's energetic staff offers women only and co-ed aerobic classes. These facilities close to downtown, provide a sprung floor and babysitting. 834B Johnson Street, 385-2348.

Henderson Park ❖ The Fitness Studio provides a Hydragym weight training circuit, free weights, sauna, and whirlpool. Women's and co-ed aerobic classes – plus babysitting services – are offered in a large bright gymnasium, by the municipality of Oak Bay. 2291 Cedar Hill Cross Road, 595-7946.

Nautilus Club ❖ This private club welcomes drop-ins if space is available. The Club provides babysitting service, weight-training equipment, squash courts, steam and tanning rooms, a licensed lounge, and a busy social calendar for the mostly young, single members. 1821 Cook Street, 381-0202.

Panorama Leisure Centre ❖ Drop in for co-ed classes, a 25-metre pool, tennis courts and limited morning babysitting. 1885 Forest Park Drive, Sidney, 656-7271.

YM-YWCA ❖ Best buy in town is the YM-YWCA $5 Day Pass, which gives you access to the pool, sauna, steam, weight-training facilities, rooftop running track, babysitting service and coffee shop. The YM-YW is close to downtown and welcomes drop-ins to women's and co-ed aerobic classes (included in the price of the pass). 880 Courtney Street at Quadra, 386-7511.

Racquet Sports

Tennis anyone? Or racquetball or squash? Here's the local scoop on where to get in a game or two around Victoria:

The best public tennis courts—no charge, just plunk yourself down on a bench beside the court you like—are probably the ones at *Stadacona Park* (near the Pandora and Fort intersection) and the three courts at *Beacon Hill Park* (by the Bowling Green on Cook at May Street). *Stadacona* courts are next to a lovely park, and two courts in particular have very good surfaces. For a minimal booking fee, you can reserve a court at *Henderson Park* (2291 Cedar Hill Cross Road, 595-7946) and even get in a night game under the lights. The public courts at *Windsor Park* (at Newport and Windsor in Oak Bay) have been recently resurfaced. Year-round, under-the-dome games can be reserved at the Tennis Bubbles at the *Cedar Hill Recreation Centre* (3220 Cedar Hill Road, 595-7121) or at the *Oak Bay Recreation Centre* 1975 Bee Street, 595-7946), where the porous cement surface—great for spin shots!—results in a very high bounce.

A slightly lower fee at the *Racquet Club* will let you play squash on one of their American or International courts. The six squash courts at the *Nautilus Club* are also available to visitors, *if* you can ever book one—the members keep this place busy. The *YM-YWCA* (880 Courtney Street, 386-7511) has both squash and racquetball courts open to visitors.

Fishing

Our collective fishing experience consists of one rainbow trout, caught by Carolyn's daughter Larissa out at Camp Thunderbird's Glinz Lake in Sooke. Watching a blood-crazed preschooler enthusiastically whacking a trout with the oar of your rowboat can really put you off your seafood. Still, we know that fishing is one of our Island's primary attractions. Well-known Victoria writer, editor, and sportsman Alec Merriman once wrote that some of the best salmon fishing in the world can be found within a 1½-hour drive of Victoria. We're taking Mr. Merriman's word for it.

If you'd like to give fishing a try, check in the Yellow Pages under *Boats-Charter* or *Fishing-Sport* for a long list of boat and licensed guide sources.

Golf

You've heard the old definition of a sportsman: a guy who gets tired standing all day over a hot golf course. Victoria sportsmen like to get tired on some of the most picturesque golf courses anywhere. Public courses are, of course, open to the public and are listed in the Yellow Pages. We've saved you the trouble of calling the private clubs. These are the ones which welcome visitors.

Glen Meadows ❖ This pleasant rural course has no membership restrictions, but does require two days notice to book your game. 1050 McTavish Road, off West Saanich Road, Sidney, 656-3921.

Gorge Vale ❖ Not many golf courses feature a military cemetery between the twelfth and seventeenth holes! Gorge Vale does. They also have a dress code, and require two days notice to book games for non-members. 1005 Craigflower Road, Esquimalt, 386-3401.

Royal Colwood ❖ This is a very scenic course, just west of Victoria. No membership restrictions, but they do require two days notice for a game. 629 Goldstream Road, Colwood, 478-9591.

Uplands ❖ The beautiful, oak-shaded Uplands course in this expensive residential area is pleased we welcome visitors on two days notice. However, no visitors on weekends, please. 3300 Cadboro Bay Road, 592-1818.

Victoria ❖ In order to play on these spectacular seaside links, you must have a membership in another private club, or be a guest of a club member here. Four days notice is required. 1110 Beach Drive, 598-4224.

Sports Shorts

Greater Victoria offers a smorgasbord of other sporting activities, too numerous to cover in this book. For more information on horseback riding, sailing, diving and sailboarding, or for watching events like baseball, hockey, cricket, lawn bowling or horse racing at Sandown Racetrack, contact *Tourism Victoria* at 812 Wharf Street in the Inner Harbour area,

382-2127. The helpful staff will load you up with brochures and info on just about any sport–participatory or spectator–that you have in mind.

TOURS, TOURS, TOURS

Tours can give visitors an inside view of the city that many locals miss. We recommend the following jaunts.

BC Legislature ❖ Call at Room 244 for reserved tickets to sit in on working House sessions (except on Opening Day). During summer, free guided tours, conducted in several languages, depart all day from the main foyer. Free. 501 Belleville Street, 387-3046.

Canadian Forces Base Esquimalt ❖ Free tours through this military base last 1½ hours; advance booking required. 380-4006.

Christ Church Cathedral Tours ❖ You can pick up a tour brochure at the front of the church, and a steward is usually on hand to answer questions. Christ Church, incidentally, is one of a handful of Canadian churches with *real* church bells. Bellringers must train for weeks in the 17th-century practice of "change ringing." You can hear them on Sunday mornings and during Tuesday evening practice sessions. Donations appreciated. Quadra and Courtney Streets. 383-2714.

City Hall ❖ Advance bookings are required for tours through this historic office building. Free. 1 Centennial Square, 385-5711.

Institute of Ocean Sciences ❖ Tours of this large modern complex of federal-government-run scientific labs overlooking Patricia Bay run on Tuesday and Thursday mornings. Advance booking is required. Free. 9860 West Saanich Road, 356-6518.

Lester B. Pearson College of the Pacific ❖ One-hour tours on weekday afternoons, October to April only, take you through the buildings and beautiful seaside campus of this world-famous college, one of a chain of United World Colleges offering 200 scholarships annually to students from around the world, who complete their final two years of high school here. Free. Pearson College Drive, off Highway 1A west. 478-5591.

Prairie Inn ❖ Take a walk through this cottage brewery to see how the end product, served next door, is made. Free. 7806 East Saanich Road, 652-1575.

University of Victoria ❖ The University of Victoria, situated on 35 parklike acres, which include a nesting field for English skylarks, is open to individual or group tours, geared to your particular interest. Free. Finnerty Road, 721-7636.

FOR NIGHT OWLS

To find out what's going on around town, visitors should do what Victorians do each Thursday: pick up a free copy of *Monday* magazine from bright yellow stands everywhere. Check the weekly "calendar" section for names, times, and locations. It is most helpful for lesser-known theatres and clubs, which rarely advertise in the daily paper. Our picks:

Bengal Room ❖ One of our favourite spots for an after-dinner drink in the utterly tasteful and newly renovated *Empress Hotel*. Bring lots of money or an expense account or be prepared to nurse your drink. Incidentally, the new lounge, beside the dining room on the main floor, has a great view of the Inner Harbour. 721 Government Street, 384-8111.

Cook's Landing ❖ This posh lounge offers live entertainment and one of the prettiest water-level views of the Inner Harbour. Laurel Point Inn, 680 Montreal Street, 386-8721.

Harpo's ❖ To hear top touring bands offering jazz to reggae to heavy metal, head for Harpo's, overlooking the Inner Harbour, upstairs at 15 Bastion Square, 385-5333.

McMorran's ❖ The swing and sway of the Big Band rhythm will encourage you to take a turn on the maple floor of the Seaview Room. 5109 Cordova Bay Road, 658-5224.

Oak Bay Recreation Centre ❖ A lounge operates upstairs from 6 p.m. on in the popular rec centre. (It is open all day as a restaurant for families). As you enjoy your drink and delicious sandwich, you can watch swimmers, curlers or skaters. Other entertainment includes big-screen television and frequent social mixers, 1975 Bee Street, 595-7946.

Prairie Inn ❖   This historic tavern, on the way out to Butchart Gardens, offers a good pub lunch and "Prairie Inn Lager," the product of the cottage brewery next door. 7806 East Saanich Road, 652-1575.

The Snug ❖   This great pub, in a great seaside hotel, is usually packed with local residents drawn by the views, fireplace and very good pub food. Oak Bay Beach Hotel, 1175 Beach Drive, 598-4556.

Spinnakers ❖   Victorians pack this pub for wonderful food, a fine view of the Harbour and beer brewed on the premises. 308 Catherine Street, 386-2739.

Upstairs Lounge ❖   We were refused admittance here one night because of our blue jeans, so wear something nice! This lounge features live entertainment and a tiny dance floor. The quiet table in the stairwell room is our favourite. Paul's Motor Inn, 1900 Douglas Street, 382-9231.

Victoria Jane's ❖   This quiet and elegant room is one of the most attractive lounges in town, with wood panelling and cozy wing chair room arrangements. Chateau Victoria, 740 Burdett, 382-4221.

Where to Eat

The best part of writing a subjective book like this has been the fun of picking our favourites. Ours may not be yours, but they do tend to reflect consistency, something that is not to be sneezed at when you are about to part with a considerable fraction of your wallet's contents. We have rejected more restaurants that you would believe, for reasons ranging from no toilet paper in the bathroom to indifferent service. We have built-in bias against places that don't serve their own desserts. (Not that we aren't crazy about Sara Lee cheesecake; we just object to paying $4 for a slice of it!) We check out bathrooms and front windows for cleanliness. They are a reasonable indicator, we think, of the care used in keeping salmonella at bay in the kitchen. We dismiss establishments, no matter how highly recommended by locals, for rude or sloppy service staff, but only after third-party confirmation.

SWEETS AND TREATS

We share a common philosophy about our Sweet Tooth, no doubt culled from our long association with **La Leche League,** a terrific volunteer organization which offers support to breastfeeding mums. La Leche encourages us to watch not only the baby's food, but also what the rest of the family eats. This attitude allows for family sweets and treats, of course, but always with the observation that if our kids are going to eat junk, we think it ought to be junk of the very finest quality. No dime-store jawbreakers, please, but keep passing those Rogers' chocolates! So if you plan to indulge, why not make it a truly gastrosensual sweet? Any of the following should put you into Sugar Heaven...

Casey's Bakery ❖ We like this bakery for a special reason: frozen croissants that will make your Sunday brunches famous, with almost no effort on your part. Casey's does all the work for you, and you take all the credit! Every month, owner Casey Boschma packages over 30,000 unbaked plain or cheese croissants into trays of ten. When you have brought a pack home, you can slip it out of the freezer at bedtime, place the skinny little blobs of dough on a cookie sheet, then go to sleep, knowing that the skinny blobs will puff into huge crescents overnight. After twenty minutes in the oven, they are ready to serve, and your family or guests will go wild. The croissants are the genuine, flaky, European-style pastry, with twenty layers of dough, and taste as good as they smell. Casey's also offers ready-baked croissants and a variety of other frozen foods that you can bake yourself: cornish pasties, meat pies and fruit tarts. Prices are very reasonable, and this is one of the few places in town that sells Hovis bread. At 2032 Oak Bay Avenue, just east of Foul Bay Road, 598-2712.

C'est Bon Croissant ❖ These people offer very bon croissants in their two tiny establishments. Try plain ones, enhanced with savory fillings like spinach and feta, or sweet, centred with chocolate. Don't miss the herb-flecked foccacie bread or the crusty baguettes either. Eat in or, in summer, outside at 10 Bastion Square, 381-1461, or get some croissants-to-go in the Oak Bay Village's Athlone Court, 114A-2187 Oak Bay Avenue, 598-5415.

Coco's ❖ The smell of chocolate wafts out from Coco's, driving passing pedestrians mad. Belgian chocolate is cunningly fashioned into baskets which can be filled with enticing chocolates chosen individually from the display case. There are creams spiked with liqueurs – Grand Marnier, Frangelico or Kahlua – or molded into unusual shapes like mice and escargots. Located in the pedestrian walkway between Fort and Broughton, at 722 Broughton Street, 384-2262.

Dutch Bakery ❖ This is the place where Real Victorians hang out! At the front of the shop you can buy mouthwatering artistic pastries on the right-hand side, and equally enticing Dutch chocolates on the left. The Thomas children believe that this is the only source of birthday cakes on earth – one day's notice, please! The back half of the store is a coffee shop where, if you're lunching alone, you will probably be asked to share a table. You could end up with two thirteen-year-olds spending their babysitting money or an elderly lady who will regale you with tales of pre-war Victoria. The food is cheap and good. Save room for the mocha cake. At 718 Fort Street, under the purple awning, 385-1012.

English Sweet Shop ❖ Jill's mother is addicted to Turkish Delight – the result of a dissipated childhood back in England when she used to squander her allowance on the stuff at every opportunity. Jill was happy to find this reliable source of the genuine article, handmade by a Vancouver confectioner. The same candy maker also supplies hand-dipped chocolates, marzipan figures, and such old fashioned treats as aniseed balls, molasses humbugs, and horehound sticks. Expatriate Brits might like to note that the store imports such English chocolate bars as "Bounty" and "Curly Wurly," normally unheard of here in the colonies. And lest you think that penny candy has gone the way of the

5-cent cigar, be assured that the English Sweet Shop has a children's section where your kids can blow their money, just like Jill's mother did. At 738 Yates Street, 382-3325.

Fairfield Bakery and Deli ❖ Such a common name for such an uncommon bakery. Their peach pastries are a triumph of the baker's art and the showcase holds other enticing delicacies with a decided Italian influence – like ricotta pastries. Giant peanut butter and chocolate ship cookies find favour with kids and huge cheese buns make a nice change from sandwiches in lunch bags. You can also pick up sliced meats and other deli items here. In the Fairfield Plaza, 1564 Fairfield Road, 598-6113.

Italian Bakery ❖ Happiness is . . . waiting inside the Italian Bakery at 10 a.m. for the first trays of fresh, hot croissants to come through the swinging double doors from the back kitchen. The Italian Bakery croissant is the standard by which all others are judged, as in: "These are not as flaky as Italian Bakery's." After the croissants, out come the first batches of long thin baguettes of French bread. No other bread sold around town can match the hard crusty shell and the fresh chewy inside bites. Ditto the sourdough loaves here. So once you've cornered the market on croissants, baguettes and sourdough, what else is there? How about Italian Easter bread, heavy with eggs and fruit? Or the handmade chocolate eggs, each with a small gift inside? Or the fantastic French cream-filled pastries lining the side cooler? There is little in this fine place that resembles your average shopping centre bakery – no brownies, doughnuts, or muffins. The European influence, combined with quality ingredients like honey, sea salt and unbleached flour are what draw the faithful from far and wide. Highly recommended! At 3197 Quadra Street, off Tolmie, 388-4557. Closed Mondays and most of August.

Rising Star Bakeries ❖ Even if you don't visit the Rising Star's retail outlets, you will probably sample their breads, croissants or cakes at several restaurants around town, as they are now in the wholesale business as well. In the mid-1970s, when we first discovered them in untrendy quarters in Vic West, they were what is now called a "granola kitchen." Dare we say we miss the old days, when you knew that what you bought for your children at the Rising Star was oh-so-good for them. Our suspicions grew some years ago when we spotted genuine Nanaimo Bars here, without even a pretense of tofu, whole-grain flour or anything resembling wholesome ingredients. The new products are indeed yummy, and you can still buy their nutritious peasant loaf, loaded with seeds, nuts and dates. Two locations: 1320 Broad Street, 386-2534 and Hillside Market, 598-3515.

Rogers' Chocolates ❖ Why are we including this famous Government Street landmark in a book about off-the-beaten-track treasures? The first reason is to invite non-chocoholics (and we've heard that these people actually do exist) to step inside the shop to admire this wonderful example of turn-of-the-century architecture. Rogers' has leaded art glass, golden oak panelling, Art Nouveau light fixtures, and mosaic floor tiles. It is worth a visit, even if you are not planning to purchase (although how you can resist these hand-dipped delights is beyond us).

The second reason we want to mention Rogers' is to tell you "How to Eat a Victoria Cream." Over the years we have noticed that out-of-towners (and even the odd Victorian) can be spotted along Government Street actually trying to eat one of these gigantic chocolates in a single sitting. This, my dears, is simply not done: A Victoria Cream is designed to be shared by at least two and preferably four chocolate lovers, so that each tantalizing bite can be properly appreciated. Rogers' classic creations can be purchased individually or boxed, and mail orders are always welcome. Since 1885 at the same address: 913 Government Street, 384-7021.

Tudor Sweet Shoppe ❖ The Tudor Sweet Shoppe, located in the heart of the Oak Bay Village shopping area, recently added genuine Rogers' chocolates to its stock, thus saving locals a long trip downtown for the real thing. The store also sells all the conventional bulk candy your dentist warns you against, as well as ice cream cones in the summertime. We like shopping here for fresh coffee beans and bulk teas. Service is prompt and courteous, as you'd expect from this old-fashioned store. At 2228 Oak Bay Avenue, 598-2911.

Champs Elysées ❖ When we're up at the north end of the downtown core, doing something dreary such as paying parking tickets or property taxes at City Hall, we like to cheer ourselves up by dropping into the Champs Elysées. True, it's not in Paris, but the elegant pastries in the showcase taste, in true Gallic tradition, as good as they look. You can take a mouth-watering selection home, or just treat yourself to a coffee and calorie break at one of the little tables. 1680 Douglas Street, 383-0833.

DAYTIME DINING

Take a break halfway through a busy day to discover some of the following delights in daytime dining. Most are open during limited business hours for coffee, lunch, and afternoon tea. Some are open a bit later for an early dinner. All are special to us for one reason or another, and we invite you to stop in where the locals lunch.

Back Alley Deli ❖ We love the location of this deli; it's one of many springing up beside, beyond or behind exercise clubs. In this case, after a sweaty Standing Cardio class at Fitness Dynamics in the Oak Centre, you can replace those ounces you've worked off at the Back Alley Deli. As the name implies, it really is in the alley behind the Centre, with free parking in the lot out back. The absolutely irresistible tarts at this place will force you to a lifetime of aerobic punishment as compensation; the best are the apple tarts with cheddar-cheese-flecked pastry. There is also a nice variety of the usual meats, salads and deli stuff. Decor is Early Kitchen Table, nothing fancy, and the staff is very friendly. Treat yourself to a coffee and something fattening after your next workout. Near Foul Bay Road, at 2052 Oak Bay Avenue, 595-5311.

Barb's Fish & Ships ❖ No, it isn't a typo – that's actually what the sign on this little waterfront take-out place says!

Not being fans of the typical greasy deep-fried batter found at most fish-and-chip spots around town, we had almost resigned ourselves to omitting this most English of meals from our book on this most English of Canadian cities. Then we remembered that Barb's, down at Fisherman's Wharf, draws raves from the most skeptical critics. What more appropriate location to enjoy ever-so-delicately battered halibut and homemade fries (with the skins on, and smacked with brown malt vinegar, just the way they like them "over 'ome")? A couple of picnic tables on the wharf are available, but we prefer to take our dinners, neatly tucked into their newspaper cocoons, up the ramp to grassy Fishermen's Park. From here you have a super view of the fishing fleet and of the Inner Harbour, with its busy marine traffic. How could you ever eat fish and chips at a shopping mall after this? Look for the brightly-multicoloured roof from the Fisherman's Wharf parking lot, off Kingston. Cash only.

The Demitasse Coffee Bar ❖ The Demitasse is even a surprise to long-time residents, who drive by its noisy location on Blanshard and wonder how such a tiny hole-in-the-wall can survive. Well, there's more to this place than meets the eye, including a charming room at the back of the restaurant with a fireplace and cozy atmosphere that is much quieter than the bustling coffee bar out front. Take your pick, depending on your mood. Rumoured to have the best Nanaimo Bars in town, the Demitasse also serves unusual luncheon specials: rollmops on toasted bagels with cream cheese, for instance. There are terrific fresh salads and, of course, coffee, coffee, coffee. If you like what you're drinking you can buy a bag of beans to enjoy at home. Non–coffee drinkers should try a "Foamachino," which is basically the thick milky bubbles from hot cappuccino, mixed with grated chocolate. Try to plan your visit for after 1:30, when you might actually be able to get a table. At 1320 Blanshard Street, near the corner of Pandora, 386-4442.

Dunlop House ❖ We bet that few Victorians will recognize the name Dunlop House, but if we said "That Big House on Camosun College Campus," we would get enlightened nods. From September to April, with a long break over Christmas holidays, the second-year students of Camosun's Hotel and Restaurant program practise their hospitality on members of the public. Hours are extremely limited and reservations are required well in advance. This is a tremendously popular spot; the College staff alone could fill this room, and they often do. Prices are only marginally higher than eating at home – and the students do all the work. They're being observed and graded on everything from presentation to clearing away the plates. An insider's tip: best to wait until late October, to give students a few week's at the beginning of semester to warm up. Look for the charming beige house on the north side of Lansdowne Road, between Richmond and Foul Bay. For reservations phone 370-3144.

Eugene's Snack Bar ❖ Go early or late for lunch at Eugene's. From noon until 1 p.m. this place is *packed* with nearby workers and downtown shoppers. The reason is simple: wonderful Greek food at rock bottom prices. We like the messy but delicious gyros-donner and the souvlakis, with a side of Greek salad, but the spanakopita and tiropita are close runners-up. 1280 Broad Street, 381-5456.

Gazebo Tea House & Gallery ❖ Yes, there is a gazebo in the corner of the pretty garden, but you don't have tea in it. The gazebo functions as a mini art gallery and you can browse through it before or after your meal. Teas, light lunches and early dinners are served in the cozy dining room; in warm weather customers spill out onto the expansive deck overlooking the garden. Fresh and wholesome are key adjectives to describe the food: hearty soups, fresh-made sandwiches on brown bread and homemade desserts such as hazelnut torte and cheesecake. We like to stop in here to fuel up before a tour of Butchart Gardens. 5460 Old West Saanich Road, 479-7787.

Lunn's Pastry, Deli and Coffee Shop ❖ When Mr. Lunn opened his bakery on Sidney's main street some years ago, he planned to sell only his award-winning breads, with maybe a cup of coffee and a sweet on the side. Today, having expanded the original to include the former health food store next door, Lunn's is a crowded coffee shop on one side and a thriving bakery and deli on the other, The locals certainly like it here: we suggest coming very early for lunch, or much later, after the Sidney office crowd has returned to work. The homemade soup is famous. One regular told us, "I would kill for their cheese soup!" Now that's loyalty. Cheese soup is the special on Thursdays only. A nice, old-fashioned, small town favorite. At 2455 Beacon Avenue, Sidney, 656-1724.

Pepper's Cafe ❖ We like this little cutie for a morning or afternoon break of cappuccino and homemade muffin or a fast lunch of gourmet pizza by the generous slice and fresh juice. The pizzas are fresh-made all day, the toppings change regularly and the homestyle crust is first-rate. There are little tables against the wall or you can perch on a bar stool at the window counter and watch the world go by at 783 Fort Street, 383-8838.

Mary's Coffee Bar ❖ Alas, the original Mary is no longer with us, but her name lives on in this diner near the airport. Customers include regulars who have been coming here for breakfast or lunch for years. Mary's is neat as a pin inside and out, decorated with aeronautical memorabilia—our sons like the display of propeller blades on the wall. Best of all, the food is good. Nothing pretentious—plain sandwiches, burgers served on whole grain buns with *real* fries on the side, Four-Alarm Chili and an inexpensive breakfast special each day. There are lots of newspapers to browse through as you finish your coffee, too. Give yourself an extra hour before your next flight out of Victoria International and visit Mary's first. Follow the signs to the airport off McTavish Road, but bear right at the In-dustrial Area sign, to 9535B Canora Road, Sidney, 656-9343.

386-DELI ❖ High praise, well-deserved, abounds for this diminutive delight where Judith Stuart and her dedicated staff offer im-aginative seasonal cooking. The menu changes daily so check the chalkboard to discover what's offered, from soup to pasta to dessert – all homemade, of course. Lunches are divine; dinner is on Fridays only and reservations are mandatory. Across from the Royal Theatre at 1012 Blanshard Street, 386-DELI.

Willows Galley ❖ This fish and chips cafe, a longtime favourite of Carolyn's children, is conveniently sited a short stroll from both Willows Elementary School and Willows Beach. Jane's recommendation: "Real French fries, nice and hot – not like those places where they sit under the red lights." Ben's vote goes to the great hamburgers. Try this neighbourhood landmark for a take-out lunch or dinner on your way to the sandy shores of Willows Beach. 2559 Estevan Avenue, 598-2711.

FROM BUDGET TO BIG SPENDER GOURMET

The following restaurants belong in the "Every Town Has One" category; the kind of place that is a permanent fixture on the locals' list of favourites. For instance, Montreal has *Ben's*, Winnipeg has *Junior's*, Inuvik has . . . well, never mind. You get the picture, we know: a cross between a coffee shop and a late-night diner. Most are open for dinner, but not too late. Value for money – here's the cream of our crop. . .

Barley Mow Inn ❖ This Tudor-style restaurant only *looks* as though it's been here since Captain Cook's day. It is actually a recent addition to the restaurant scene, and one that was an instant hit with the university crowd nearby. If you suspect that's because it's cheap and good, you are absolutely right. The extensive menu runs from nachos to the Barley Burger; daily lunch and dinner specials are chalked on the board near the entrance. This is a no-reservations, casual spot. We feel obliged to add that casual is a word that can often be applied to the service as well. If you're in a hurry, we suggest you tell your server at the outset. Worth a trip to 2581 Penrhyn Street, off Cadboro Bay Road, 477-4412.

Carrington-Wyatt ❖ While it is true that from the outside the Carrington-Wyatt in Sidney lacks cachet (it's hard to disguise that ex-airplane hangar look), inside it's done up very prettily, with Laura Ashley wallpaper and lace tablecloths. The menu is remarkably free of culinary cliches. Innovative seafood dishes include a prawn and mussel salad, and the kitchen also produces a very good curry, complete with condiments. The desserts are terrific. 9732 1st Street, Sidney, 656-1822.

The Cultured Cow ❖ The sandwich you get here is like Mum used to make for you before she got healthy and started spending all her time at aerobics class. It comes on wholesome whole-grain bread and the hamburgers come on brown buns. The tomatoes are organically grown by the owner, and there is a preponderance of sprouts everywhere. The original frozen yogurt is served for dessert. You'll never guess what kind of meat is served inside the Buffy Burger! The restaurant is noisy, lively, informal and deservedly popular with Victorians. There are outdoor tables on the sidewalk terrace. 801 Fort Street at Blanshard, 386-6000.

Goodies ❖ Goodies is for people who like big — make that gigantic — breakfasts, especially the omelets that have been famous for years among Victoria omelet experts. You can choose from weird and wonderful combinations like "Banana, raisin and sour cream" or "Avocado, sprouts and tomato." There is a dollar off each omelet from 7 to 9:30 a.m. weekdays. Standard breakfast items, like our favourite, eggs Florentine, are all tasty. Huge deli sandwiches, in addition to the omelets, are made to order for lunch. Instead of home fries, try the fresh salad with Goodies' own dressings (our favourite is the cucumber yogurt).

Tuesday through Saturday, from 5 p.m. on, Goodies goes Mexican. What they advertise is "Home-cooked California-style Mexican dinners." For a place so far north of Redondo Beach, you get a pretty good meal, albeit in a more subdued environment that Californians would recognize. Have a jumbo margarita and a half-order of nachos while you decide on one of the substantial entrées. Upstairs at 1005 Broad Street, 382-2124.

Grand Central ❖ Contemporary fare with a Cajun and Creole twist is the specialty at Grand Central. Cheerful young servers, dishes ranging from black bean soup to Key lime pie, and in warm weather a flower-filled patio to dine on, make this place a winner in our book. At the end of a passageway in the sensitively restored heritage site at 555 Johnson Street, 386-4747.

Herald Street Caffe ❖ One of Carolyn's favourite places and a regular stop in her monthly Night Out with three other women. For years they scouted around, trying to discover the best restaurant in Victoria. The scouting stopped when the Herald Street Caffe was found.

The decor here is inviting – a peach-and-grey colour scheme with masses of fresh flowers everywhere, including really outstanding arrangements of glads, bird-of-paradise and such on the central bar. The pasta is fresh and half-orders are available, so that you'll have room for Black Bottom Pudding. (Don't even think about coming here without trying it.) We also recommend the spinach salad (best in town) and the veal with lemon. You can't go far wrong with whatever you order from the menu or the daily chalkboard. Come very early for dinner because no reservations are taken and lineups start by 7 p.m. You can enjoy live piano music occasionally. Tucked in next door to Sager's Maple Shop at 546 Herald Street, off Government Street, 381-1441.

John's Place ❖ The following note was found one morning stuffed in the mail slot:

> Carolyn:
> You might want to check out my favourite place for your book. Basic fare, well prepared. Great music on the jukebox. Best fries in town. Often live music on weekends – dancing on Saturday nights. Eclectic clientele, from punkers to yup-pies. Free newspapers (in abundance) in the mornings.
>
> Peter R.
>
> P.S. Poached eggs on corned beef hash – yum!

This restaurant sounded as if it deserved a visit! And another. And another. The breakfast menu is extensive, cover-ing quick, early morning snacks like the "Eat on the Run" special (guaranteed no longer than five minutes from chef to you) or the "Sleep-In Breakfast" offerings available until 3 p.m. If you like sweets for breakfast, you'll love the Belgian waffles with cream cheese syrup. The lunch menu includes homemade soups, hamburgers buried under fried onions, luscious des-serts – everything is made here except the whole grain and sourdough breads. And yes, those fries are as good as we expected. Thanks, Peter! Just east of Douglas at 723 Pandora Avenue, 389-0711.

Metropolitan Diner ❖ When we were researching this book, we had dessert lovers from as far away as Duncan write to recommend Chocolate Bags from the Metropolitan. They are just what you'd expect: a bag-shaped container made of dark chocolate and filled with white chocolate mousse, raspberry sauce and fresh fruit. Pricey, but meant to be shared by at least four people. That is, if anybody has any room left after dinner here.

We like the Met for numerous reasons. First, we like the mini loaves of bread, from white studded with chilis to whole wheat with sunflower seeds. Second, we like the eclectic range of dishes offered: Indonesian sate, Italian calzone, California pizza toppings. Third, we like the daily fresh fish options, which are either pan-fried with ginger and lime or baked in parchment. Fourth, we like the imaginative way restaurant standards are made uncommon – for example, the spinach salad topped with a mango chutney dressing. Fifth, we like the soup...but a taste is worth a thousand words. Try The Met for yourself. In an otherwise completely undistinguished block at 1715 Govern-ment Street, 381-1512.

Mom's Cafe ❖ We don't know about playing cards with a man named Doc, but we do know that Nelson Algren was wrong about never eating at a restaurant called Mom's. Mom's Cafe in Sooke has a definite homey ambience right down to the rummage-sale knicknacks. The food is hearty, wholesome and good. And cheap! You will find big, fat, messy hamburgers that squirt out the other end when you bite them, heartwarming homemade oxtail soup that you'll never find in any French restaurant, thick milkshakes in *metal* containers and, you guessed it, Mom's apple pie. The kids get placemats to colour and you get to go home with almost as much money as you came in with. Turn right a block past Sooke Corners and look for the blue building at 2036 Shields Road, 642-3314.

Pagliacci's ❖ At first we weren't going to mention Pag's because we assumed that everybody already knew about this famous Victoria restaurant. Popular demand, however, has forced us to include it for the benefit of visitors who may be unfamiliar with the Siegel family. Lest we be accused of nepotism, we'll let Victorians themselves tell you how crazy they are about this restaurant. *Monday Magazine* cited Pagliacci's in its annual "Best of Victoria" readers' poll in the following categories:

Best Downtown Lunch Spot
Best Desserts
Best Late Night Restaurant
Best Restaurant for People-Watching
Best Place to Be Rowdy

The "rowdy" part we can vouch for: if you're lucky, you'll be stuffing yourself with fabulous New York cheesecake while resident nutbar and television star Howie Siegel is on hand to mingle with his guests. A quiet, intimate spot this is not – just great food, live music weeknights and fun. So come on in already. Between Fort and Broughton at 1011 Broad Street, 386-1662.

Stonehouse Pub ❖ On your way out to Swartz Bay to catch a ferry over to the mainland? Consider extending your last few hours on our Island with a stop at the Stonehouse Pub. It's a new neighbourhood pub in an old Tudor building, complete with cottage garden. You'll find reasonably priced pub fare for lunch, afternoon tea or dinner, plus darts, croquet and horseshoes for the sporting set. And it's certainly a step up from the cafeteria on the ferries! Just outside the BC Ferries terminal, at 2215 Canoe Cove Road, Sidney, 656-3498.

Vegetarian

Gwen's Health Foods & Light Meals ❖ Years ago, Carolyn brought her sister Catherine (from the Big City) to Gwen's for lunch on the way out to Butchart Gardens. It was such a hit that Gwen's became a compulsory stop during Catherine's future visits — even those that didn't include a trip to Butchart's. Seems the Big City lacks anything quite like Gwen's. What distinguishes this little place is a charming couple who have run their rural establishment long enough for it to qualify as an institution among Victorians. Try a smoothie, made with whatever fresh fruit is in season — sometimes the luscious blackberries growing out in the back yard. Then order a bowl of homemade vegetable soup and any kind of sandwich. If you're not too full, finish up with a piece of homemade pie. It's got flaky whole-grain pastry and a dollop of soy creme (that's like ice cream for healthy people) on the side. It adds up to a wholesome lunch that gives credence to the theory that the more apple squares you eat at Gwen's the healthier you become. Open Friday through Sunday only at 6002 West Saanich Road, 652-3132.

Blue Peter Pub & Restaurant ❖ Carolyn and Tedd are long-time fans of this Sidney waterfront eatery, whether they're looking for a) excellent, elegant fare served overlooking the marina next door, or b) excellent pub fare served overlooking the marina next door. Whichever half of this off-the-beaten-track restaurant you choose (and sometimes a long wait at the dining room side prompts a decision to pop in at the pub instead), you'll be impressed. The view, the seafood, the little dinner rolls served warm from the oven, the chowder...we could go on and on. Try for a table outdoors on the deck (either side) if possible. 2270 Harbour Road, Sidney, 656-4551.

Four Mile House ❖ It's worth a drive in the country to see the fine stained glass windows added as part of the renovations at this historic roadhouse. The interior is bright, the menu suitably pub-like and the table service is cheerfully efficient. West of Victoria at 199 Island Highway, 479-2514.

Six Mile House ❖ The Six Mile used to be a welcome resting place for nineteenth century travellers heading west of Victoria. Today, it's equally popular with diners looking for excellent food at miserly prices. The menu changes daily and options range from steaks and roast beef to lighter pastas and seafood. When weather permits, we like to take our meals outside onto the sheltered patio. 494 Island Highway, 478-3121.

Fore & Aft Cafe ❖ Here's an out-of-the-way little restaurant that is well worth the scenic drive to Brentwood Bay. The Fore & Aft seems to grow from its waterside moorings, overlooking the beautiful bay. Carolyn recommends their "world famous Fore & Aft omelettes, special Sunday brunch and the luscious homemade soups such as tomato-sorrel or leek and potato." For dinner, try the salmon done in phyllo pastry with shrimp and crab or the brie and walnut quiche. Hours vary according to the season; closed January and February. Summer hours range from 9:30 a.m. to 9 p.m., Sunday dinner served until 7:30 p.m., closed for dinner on Monday. 899 Marchant, Brentwood Bay, 652-2799.

WHERE ARE THOSE TEA ROOMS?

By now you've probably noticed we've neglected to mention that great Victorian tradition of Afternoon Tea. This is not because we don't love an afternoon cuppa ourselves – in fact, we spent one enjoyable winter on a weekly Tea Room Tour. Teatime is a standard feature of a visit to Victoria: the time for a quiet sit-down with goodies and a hot beverage between 2 and 5 p.m. Most tea rooms do a very acceptable job of providing tea service. Some, like the *Empress Hotel*, have made teatime an institution with an institution. Many visitors would never dream of leaving town without taking tea at the Empress. The venerable old girl's recent multi-million dollar facelift has resulted in separate tea and reception lobbies so you no longer have to worry about passing herds of tourists dropping cameras on your cucumber sandwiches.

We would like to recommend a few tearooms which are typical of the kind of places locals take their out-of-town guests. One favourite is *Point No Point*, an hour's drive west of Victoria and worth the long trip, even in stormy weather. This isn't as odd as it sounds; this simple wooden building is perched over a stretch of rocky, driftwooded shoreline, and the crashing waves are even more spectacular on a rainy November day than in the summer. The tea here includes walnut date bread, cinnamon fruit buns and an assortment of cakes and cookies, but the real appeal for us is the sea air and enthralling vista. Teatime daily form 1:30 to 5 p.m. Point No Point is 40 miles west of the city on Highway 14, R.R. #2, Sooke, 646-2020.

From May to October we like to go to *Margison House* for light lunches and afternoon tea in a charming home full of antique furniture and pretty decorative touches such as baskets of dried hydrangeas. Fresh flowers decorate tables and plates – there's even a bloom with your bill. Good hot scones and homemade jam. Open noon until 5 p.m., Thursday to Sunday at 6605 Sooke Road, 642-3620. (Watch the driveway, it's very steep.)

Closer to home, in tweedy Oak Bay, we have three favourites. The *Blethering Place*, festooned with Toby jugs and Royal Family memorabilia, serves a proper tea with little sandwiches and cakes. Hearty eaters may prefer to tuck into the very good, dinner-plate-sized cheese or raisin scones. The Bethering Place is a popular local institution so be prepared for long lineups – or else arrive very early or very late for tea. 2250 Oak Bay Avenue, 598-1413.

Alternately, head down the diminutive *Maddie's Restaurant and Tea House*. Afternoon tea is served upstairs and down in a couple of charming, cozy rooms. You can have a healthy fruit plate with yoghurt and toast – or forget the diet and go for the chocolate layer cake with raspberry sauce. 2540 Windsor Road, just off Newport, 595-3135.

Finally, as a change from the Empress lobby, try tea in another time-honoured institution: *The Oak Bay Beach Hotel*. The hotel is suitably Tudor-like, complete with half-timbering and mullioned windows, and the spacious lobby is full of comfortable arm chairs and sofas. Throw in a sea view, a fireplace, and an elegantly presented tea tray with some of the best pastries in town, and you've got an afternoon tea to write home about. 1175 Beach Drive, 598-4556.

THAT SPECIAL EVENING OUT

Some entries here are so expensive that you may be able to afford them only when your rich cousin is picking up the tab; others are surprisingly good value but are so elegant that meals qualify for that "special occasion" label. Reservations always recommended.

Bon appetit!

Camille's ❖ Camille's is the kind of intimate, romantic place with wonderful food at fair prices we're always hoping to find. The fare is West Coast contemporary: seafood, imaginative pairings such as chicken with apricot and ginger sauce, and intelligent use of the fresh herbs which are grown in the kitchen. Presentation is one of the restaurant's strengths, with edible flowers decorating plates and strewn over salads. Don't miss the Chocolate Venus for dessert. Dinner only, Tuesday to Saturday, downstairs at 45 Bastion Square, 381-3433.

Chez Daniel ❖ Flipping through the Yellow Pages in an effort to decide on a really good restaurant is absolutely no way to guarantee a fine meal. Making reservations at Chez Daniel is.

Chef Daniel Rigollet opened his small Oak Bay restaurant years ago, in a tiny neighbourhood shopping block well off the beaten track. The combination of simple but tasteful decor, a handful of evenly-spaced tables and award-winning cuisine has earned the restaurant a steady stream of loyal customers, augmented by visitors to Victoria who have been lured here by rave reviews. We like the pork medallions with—of all things—prunes, preceded by coquilles St. Jacques. Presentation is picture-perfect, and those sauces...! Desserts are delicate and just enough after the elegant entrées: tiny meringues with fresh strawberries, for instance. There is also an extensive wine list, some selections in the three-digit price range. Pricey, but a reliable spot for the finest in French food. At 2524 Estevan Avenue, 592-7424.

Chez Pierre ❖ This was one of the very few culinary oases in the gastronomic wasteland that was Victoria in the early seventies. Seventeen years later, satisfied diners are still beating a path to the door, knowing they will enjoy personal service and an unhurried, first-rate meal. 512 Yates Street, 388-7711.

Deep Cove Chalet ❖ The result of our *Island Treasures* "Best Restaurant in which to Blow Your Entire Paycheque" contest would be a three-way tie among Chez Daniel, the Latch and this place on the waterfront in Deep Cove. To watch the sunset from a window table here, while savouring one of Chef Pierre's dinners, is to be able to die happy. The beauty of the location can't be exaggerated: lawns sweep down to the sea and expansive gardens adorn the huge property. If you can, come for lunch out on the terrace. This is where we take frostbitten easterners if they happen to visit on a sunny spring day—they go mad overlooking the water, surrounded by rhododendrons in full bloom. Victorians can be cruel that way.

We hasten to throw in our observation that Pierre's own paté is the best in Victoria, and the Sunday buffet is a seafood lover's dream. This is not the groaning-board buffet that the Empress offers, but a smaller selection of fresh shrimp, smoked salmon, whole prawns, crab legs, exquisite salads and several hot non-seafood entrées. Very expensive, very attentive service, very elegant—and yet, when we have taken our children for lunch here they have been warmly welcomed. Reservations mandatory. In Sidney at 11190 Chalet Drive, off West Saanich Road, 656-3541.

Larousse ❖ A subtle and understated decor and a small but well-balanced menu add up to a restful meal. Emphasis is on the best aspects of nouvelle cuisine, such as inspired use of herbs and uncommon pairings. Located on the street level of the North Park Studio complex at 1619 Store Street, 386-3454.

The Latch ❖ A wonderful waterfront location, a classic old home, casual elegance and fine food—all the ingredients for a very special night on the town are combined in the Latch. Built by famous Victorian architect Samuel Maclure as a summer residence, *Miraloma*, the restaurant continues the old tradition of gracious entertaining. Seafood specialties are offered, depending on the fresh catch, and there is a selection of dishes which are changed regularly. For lunch we recommend "The Breakwater." It's not on the menu, but the kitchen has always obliged us when we ask for it. Private rooms are available if you have a group getting together. After dinner you're invited to enjoy coffee upstairs in one of the charming fireplace lounges. You'll feel like a guest at the original summer residence! At 2328 Harbour Road in Sidney, 656-6622.

La Petite Colombe ❖ This cozy charmer continues to be our favourite place for celebrating birthdays, anniversaries and toher landmark occasions. The kitchen combines French classicism, contemporary tastes and Japanese artistry in a highly individual and always rewarding culinary experience. If your budget can't handle dinner, try the excellent and reasonably priced lunches. 604 Broughton Street, 383-3234.

Sooke Harbour House ❖ Sooke Harbour House's kitchen has become one of *the* places for aspiring young West Coast chefs to train, in the same way that Californian chefs make a pilgrimage to Chez Panisse. Food writers – and gourmets – from all across North America have raved about the original cuisine at Sooke Harbour House. Local seafood is a specialty, and herbs and flowers from the extensive gardens are incorporated into all the imaginative dishes. The dining room itself is a visual but completely unpretentious delight with seashells sharing mantel space with wooden ducks, and expansive sea view and a comfortable seating area around a big fireplace. Reservations mandatory. As Sooke Harbour House is also a small hotel, we've included accommodation information in our Where to Stay section. 1528 Whiffen Spit, Sooke, 642-3421.

ETHNIC DINING

When Jill moved to Victoria from big sister city Vancouver in 1969, Victoria was a virtual gastronomic wasteland, with only hotel dining rooms and Chinese restaurants available for the local gourmand. By the time Carolyn rolled in five years later, things had improved a lot. Since then restaurants have been opening (and sometimes closing again) with dizzying speed. While Victoria, because of its scaled-down size, does not have the same kind of ethnic mix to draw on as, say, Toronto does, we do have a respectable number of eateries turning out cultural favourites from tandoori chicken to tortillas. We offer here a quick tour of our personal picks.

Chinese ❖ First up is the ubiquitous Chinese food restaurant. Our favourites in Chinatown include *Foo Hong's*, a Victoria institution, long a popular spot among celebrities, politicians and just-plain-folks with their kiddies. No decor, no fawning service, just a place that's jam packed with devoted fans. Best place in town for take-out meals, too. 564 Fisgard Street, just west of Government, 386-9553. Nearby is **Wah Lai Yuen**, which offers that rarity in Chinese establishments, the pastry shop. The wonton soup is our favourite. 560 Fisgard, 381-5355.

For visitors who feel uncomfortable in the arborite-table atmosphere of most Chinatown eateries, we recommend **Ming's** and the **Chinese Village**. They provide the same excellent fare, but in rather more sumptuous surroundings—at a higher cost, of course. The Chinese Village is run by affable Randy Lee, who took over this lovely restaurant from his father Jack. For years the Lees have sent forth satisfied diners, replete with egg rolls and butterfly prawns. Located in the interesting oriental building across from Mayfair Mall at 755 Finlayson Street, 384-8151. A dramatic carved dragon leads into Ming's spacious dining room. The kitchen staff does an excellent job with the various permutations and combinations of ingredients in Chinese cookery. Break out of the dinner-for-four rut and order something from the extensive a la carte menu. At the corner of Quadra and Johnson, 385-4405. Unlike their China-town cousins, both of these restaurants recommend reserva-tions for dinner.

Our final Chinese favourites: the **Szechuan Restaurant** for lovers of that regional cuisine's hot and spicy taste (853 Caledonia, near the arena parking lot, 384-0224); the **Hunan Village** for the other hot and spicy Chinese regional cuisine, featuring smoked meat specialties—the onion tart is a must-eat (546 Fisgard Street, 382-0661); and the **Jade Palace** for its famous dim sum luncheons. Dozens of tiny delights are wheeled to your table for sampling (560 Johnson on the second floor of Market Square, 381-3833).

Greek ❖ In a Mediterranean mood, we like **Eugene's** (see **Daytime Dining**) and **Periklis**. Jill would kill for Periklis' dolmades, and the cheese pie is pretty good too. A disreputable friend once tried to get Jill to stuff a dollar bill down the pants of a Greek dancer here; if you're into this kind of thing, they have belly dancers in the evenings as well. 531 Yates Street, 386-3313.

Hungarian ❖ Continuing around the globe, Carolyn, whose Uk-rainian background makes her our Eastern European/Slavic expert, gives the nod to the **Hungarian Village** for goulash, schnitzel and other rib-sticking fare. The helping are huge, the prices are reasonable and homemade specialties, like their poppyseed cake, make this a longtime favourite with locals.

1550 Cedar Hill Cross Road, just west of Shelbourne, 477-3023.

Indian ❖ Jill drools like a Pavlovian dog at the mere mention of Indian cuisine, and still laments the passing of the late, great *Shah Jahan* restaurant. Rising phoenix-like from the same location, however, is *Da Tandoor*, specializing in tandoori-style cooking. Don't miss the nam, unleavened bread baked in the tandoori charcoal oven. 1010 Fort Street, 384-6333.

The *Taj Mahal* is another winner, with two house specialties – chicken tandoori and lamb biriyani particularly recommended. 679 Herald Street, 383-4662. The *India Curry House* turns out a wonderful chicken tikka and excellent samosas. Oddly located behind a gas station at 2561 Government Street, 384-5622.

Japanese ❖ We have two suggestions for Japanese food devotees: for a quiet and serene lunch or dinner, impeccably served and so inexpensive you'll suspect an error in your bill, try the *Yokohama* (980 Blanshard Street, 384-5433). For an entirely different Japanese experience, bring the whole family to the *Japanese Village* – especially on a Sunday night when magician Tony Eng performs his tableside tricks after your meal. The real show at this place is the chef at each table. There's a lot of cleaver juggling and fancy chopping as the business of creating your delicious dinner turns into a performance. In spite of all the hoopla, the food at the Japanese Village – which has branches in three other Canadian cities – is fresh, terrific and you'll have as much fun eating it as you will have watching its preparation. Downstairs at 734 Broughton Street, 382-5165.

Mexican ❖ When we have a hankering for Mexican food, we head for *El Rancho* to down the house enchiladas. Jill thinks their refried beans are better than the ones offered in Mexico. Dinner from 5 p.m. is worth the long drive to 1600 Bay Street, 595-7422. We also like *Goodies* for Mexican nights, Tuesday through Saturday (see *Budget Gourmet*) and the funky little family-run *Las Flores* for homestyle Mexican cooking at prices almost as cheap as making it at home yourself. Authentic live entertainment on Sunday evenings. 536 Yates Street, 386-6313.

Pizza ❖ We're still on a quest for the perfect pizza. So far, the best bets for "gourmet" pizza with unusual toppings are *Peppers Cafe* and the *386-Deli* for take-out or eat-in pizza by the slice, and *The Metropolitan Diner* or *Southside* for an uptown lunch or dinner ambiance. (Southside at 608 Yates Street, 383-6273. See our Daytime Dining and Bugdet to Big Spender sections for directions to others.)

If we're feeding several ravenous teenagers we think the best of the chain establishments is *Boston Pizza*. We like the outlet at Blanshard and Hillside for a reasonably upscale atmosphere, good nachos and good-sized individual pizzas, thus avoiding nasty topping arguments among siblings. Among homegrown pizzerias, *Romeo's Pizza* consistently tops *Monday Magazine* and CFAX radio polls as the best in Victoria. Four locations: downtown at 760 Johnson, at 1581 Hillside, in Langford at 2945 Jacklin and at Quadra and Mackenzie.

Vietnamese ❖ If you think Vietnamese food is much like Chinese, you're in for a surprise. Since the first edition of *Island Treasures*, two Vietnamese restaurants have opened in Victoria and we recommend both of them.

Le Petit Saigon is consistently good, has an extensive menu and offers value for money. The hot and sour soup is a standout, as are the dipping rolls. 1010 Langley Street, 386-1412.

As a reminder that Vietnam was once a part of French Indochina, *Mekong* offers French dishes such as rabbit in red wine sauce along with the Vietnamese specialties—and all-Canadian hamburgers! We like the Vietnamese dish called "nem": rice paper wrappers enclosing spicy ground pork meatballs, lettuce, bean sprouts and pickled onion, with a side of peanut sauce for dipping. Think of it as a Vietnamese taco. 1515 Cook Street, 384-9012.

Thai ❖ Siam, Victoria's only Thai restaurant, recently opened its doors and we were there, forks in hand and jaws ready. As in Chinese dining, the best idea is to order one dish per person, plus a bowl of rice. Thai cooking shares some ingredients with Chinese cuisine too—lots of vegetables, rice, noodles—but the treatment is quite different. Lemongrass and basil are frequent seasoners and some dishes can be highly spiced. All the ones we've sampled have been delicious. 1314 Government Street, 383-9911.

FOLK FEST

The last week of June send Victorians into a frenzy of culinary anticipa-
tion. That's when Folk Fest rolls into Centennial Square for its annual
celebration. Several kiosks, representing nationalities from our ethnic
communities, are set up around the fountain in the Square. You can eat
tostados from the Mexican kiosk, holubtsi from the straw-thatched Uk-
rainian hut, or giant langos – or elephant ears, as we call them – from the
popular Hungarian stand. We know Victorians who plan dinner here
every night for the whole week of Folk Fest, enjoying a different cultural
treat each evening. There's more than just the best food in town, though.
Free entertainment is provided continuously from mid-morning until dark.
This is a never-fail crowd pleaser, and a must if you're in town in late June.
Centennial Square is located behind City Hall, at Douglas and Pandora.

Where to Shop

ANTIQUES, COLLECTIBLES, AND JUNQUE

A great idea for a souvenir of any visit anywhere is a little treasure picked
up while browsing through antique shops. Carolyn has a brass cow bell,
circa 1855, hanging against a brick wall to remind her of a sunny New
Brunswick day spent at a country auction. Every time the kids give the
bell a clung, memories of that day surface again. Besides, antiques and
collectibles look much better in your home than those dreadful salt-and-
pepper shakers shaped like little mounted police. And *please*, no more tacky
imitation totems! For a one-of-a-kind gift or memento, plan a visit to any
of the outstanding sources of antiques and almost-antiques in Victoria.
Remember, too, that items over 100 years old are duty free if certified as
such by bona fide antique dealers.

Antique Row ❖ Antique hunters will discover a wealth of prizes in
the three blocks of upper Fort Street between Blanshard and
Cook, known to locals as Antique Row.
    The highlight of the 800 block – a treasure trove of small
shops containing china, furniture, stamps, and coins – is *William Dennis and Son Gallery*, specializing in nineteenth
century prints – engravings, lithographs, and woodcuts. Botanical prints are particularly noteworthy.
    As you walk east along Fort, on your way to the 900 block,
peek through the gates at number 848, an office building
housing government services, for a glimpse at one of the

prettiest garden courtyards – complete with a fish pond – that you're likely to see anywhere.

The 1000 block is richly endowed with shops for the serious collector. Polished silver, from coffee services to frames, is at *Jeffries and Co. Silversmiths.* Discover militaria at *Hibernia,* and fine furniture in the quaint, Tudor-style building at *Domus Antica. North by West Gallery* is the place for cartography buffs seeking antique maps and prints. On the other side of the street, *Vanhall's* offers excellent hallmarked silver and fine china. If you love old jewelry and clocks, don't miss *The Golden Cameo* and *Sands of Time,* both sharing the same building.

Relocated to lower Fort Street is *David Robinson Antiques.* The antique furniture and decorative pieces are beautifully displayed throughout several rooms in a heritage building. Look for the green building at the corner of Fort and Langley, entrance at 1016 Langley, 384-6425. Happy hunting!

Aladdin Antiques ❖ The ads for this store used to say: "We have male and female strippers." (This is the furniture variety, of course!) Victorians have known Aladdin's for years as the place to restore and refinish old wooden furniture – Carolyn has even had old doors stripped down here. The store recently moved to expanded premises where they continue their restoration work, and also sell quality older pieces. It is worth the trip out here just to see the etched glass front doors of the shop and the tasteful arrangements of upholstered and oak furniture. There is a limited selection of refinished work, but our favourite spot is upstairs in the warehouse. This is where they stash the "before" items: dusty and scratched, they pile higher and higher until it seems just like somebody's abandoned attic. Prices up here, naturally, are considerably lower than you'd find if you waited until Aladdin's restored the fine woodgrain finish for you. At 545 John Street – walk along Bay Street west of Government until you see the large sign, 383-2533.

Attica Historic Home Supplies ❖ Looking for that whatzit for your old clawfoot bathtub? That funny piece for your Depression glass light fixture? Attica is a gold mine of stuff for the most determined (and fussy) junque shopper. They used to specialize in demolition materials, but slowly added more and more interesting bits and pieces, as well as beautiful furniture, from the insides of the homes they were knocking down. It's still the place to find recycled building material, plumbing supplies, windows, doors, and even wooden flooring, but the casual browser will love Attica for the fascinating array of old brass, stained glass, and antiques. Carolyn's matched set of pressed-back kitchen chairs – just like your grandmother had – came from here. There's lots of free parking, in an interesting old part of town, at 2027 Store Street, 383-7373. While you're in the neighbourhood, plan to stay longer to take in Capital Iron and the Second Hand Sports Centre.

Auctions ❖ Does the world "auction" conjure up the image of sunny summer afternoons at backyard estate sales, where every piece of furniture, every jar of thumbtacks and every other item unwanted by the family of the deceased is dragged out to the lawn? Victoria, alas, rarely offers backyard bidding like this, but we do have two fine auction houses in town: *Lund's* and *Kilshaw's*, both on Fort Street.

We like Kilshaw's for uniformly better-quality furniture, but the dealers like it here too, so prices tend to go higher than they might for the same piece at Lund's. Kilshaw's sale is on Friday evening at 7 p.m., with previews all week during office hours. Lund's has two weekly sales, both on Tuesday: at 1 p.m. is what we used to call "Lund's Junk Sale" – with apologies to the Lund's staff who might disagree – at which the serious bargain hunter can wade through all the used appliances and boxes of garden tools to uncover some real gems. Carolyn bought a pair of mint-condition brass headboards here one afternoon for $50; later that same week she saw the identical set at a downtown store for $140 *apiece!* On Tuesday evening at 7 p.m. you can bid on better quality modern and antique furniture, art, and miscellaneous.

A helpful hint from seasoned auction regulars: both Lund's and Kilshaw's will accept advance or absentee bids if, for some reason, you must miss the fun of attending in person. Just stop in at the office before sale time to indicate the item number and your top bid. At Lund's you do it yourself with a small pad of advance bid paper; at Kilshaw's you tap on the glass wicket to have your bid recorded on Mr. Kilshaw's clipboard file. Lund's is at 926 Fort Street, 386-3308, with Kilshaw's just a few steps away at 1115 Fort, 384-6441.

Sidney Antiques ❖ Even for browsers who are not captivated by antiques, the six large rooms at Sidney Antiques are worth a long look. From the finest quality antiques down to new brass, jewelry, and crafts, this shop has something to intrigue just about everybody. The owners have amassed an impressive collection of china and stoneware, beautiful silver pieces, and even a room full of old tools and kitchen implements. Trade a few nickels for old English pennies at the desk, then try out the mechanical scenarios in glass cases – tiny figures leaps to life as they illustrate the evils of drinking, or a burglary in progress. A German music box fills the store with tinkling, turn-of-the-century melodies. This is part store and part museum, a real bonus for your next visit to the town of Sidney, en route to the ferries or airport. Don't miss it at 2372 Beacon Avenue in Sidney, 656-3621.

Faith Grant The Connoisseur Shop ❖ Close to the more densely populated Antique Row but, appropriately, higher up the hill, Faith Grant's is located in a white character building on Fort Street. The aristocrat of antique shops in Victoria carries extremely expensive, but extremely fine-quality merchandise. Many years ago we asked the owner whether she would be participating in a community centre's Antique Fair, and can still remember the regal way in which she stiffened and said, "My dear, that would be like going into a fashion show with the Salvation Army!" You'd have to look hard to find a shop more tastefully set up. Faith Grant's, 1156 Fort Street, is worth a stop when you're at Antique Row. 383-0121.

The Island Gallery ❖ We like this tidy but jam-packed corner of Oak Bay Village, which offers a wide variety of lovely antiques, interesting older collectibles, and reproductions – from Chinese bamboo trays to beautiful estate jewelry in perfect condition. There is always an interesting assortment of porcelain and bisque dolls, fragile christening gowns, and children's toys from long ago, as well as brand-new wing chairs covered in the fine leather that looks better and better as it ages. The Island Gallery also sells modern reproductions of classic antique furniture, mostly in mahogany. You can have any of your purchases packaged and shipped anywhere in the world. Don't miss the lovely flower arrangements, an ever-changing display of local flowers that decorates the shop twelve months of the year. They are all done by the shop's owner. At 2184 Oak Bay Avenue, 598-5534.

Waller Antiques ❖ Jill's sister Hilary, a Big City Sophisticate, treks regularly from Vancouver to Victoria just to shop for antique jewelry at Waller Antiques. (Jill is hoping to outlive her and inherit the collection.) Co-owner Myra Waller, a graduate gemmologist, is extremely knowledgeable about the history of jewelry; each beautiful piece in the store comes with a carefully researched write-up. The Wallers also carry silver, porcelain and other objets d'art to grace your home as well as your person. Added bonus: behind the shop is an enchanting pocket-sized garden. It displays the Waller's stock of traditional English country garden ornaments, guaranteed to drive passionate gardeners into a buying frenzy. 828 Fort Street, 388-6116.

BOOKS AND RECORDS

Our personal feeling about books and records is that they should be chosen with care from knowledgeable store owners who are discriminating about the kind of stock they buy. Chain stores are okay for the latest Sidney Sheldon novel or Corey Hart album, but you don't go to them when you want a special volume of poetry for your one and only, or to find that obscure Hoagie Carmichael record. In this category, we like personal attention and a passionate interest in the subject on the part of the seller.

Au Coin du Livre ❖ Si vous pouvez lire cette page, vous allez aimer cette librairie, Au Coin du Livre. Ici, on peut acheter des livres francais, des jeux, et beaucoup d'autres choses interessantes. La Société Francophone de Victoria, 423-1207 Douglas Street, 383-5335.

Bolen Books ❖ One of the best places to find books outside the downtown core, Bolen's offers a great selection of general interest and fiction titles. Also check for art books and a marvellous range of calendars at Christmas. Hillside Mall, 595-4232.

Everywomans Books ❖ There's one version of the fairy tale *Snow White* that is guaranteed to annoy feminist mothers. In it, our heroine is asked if she will come to live with the seven dwarfs so she can "cook, and clean, and sew, and spend her days taking good care of" those messy little slobs. Role models like this won't be found within the pages of books at Everywoman's. This specialty bookshop sells titles by and for women of all ages and personal persuasions. There are books on current issues, from pornography to childbirth, as well as the classic feminist writings, and histories (or is that *her*stories?) of women pioneers in many fields. There may even be a Snow White, in the carefully selected, non-sexist children's section, who tells those dwarfs a thing or two about shared domestic duties. Everywoman's is at 641 Johnson Street, 388-9411.

The Field-Naturalist ❖ Jill found a wonderful book on Botanical Latin in the Field-Naturalist. If you think this sounds exciting, not weird, then you too will like the stock here. It's geared to gardeners, hikers, bird-watchers (owner Bruce Whittington writes a regular birding column in the *Times-Colonist* news-paper) and others who appreciate the wonders of nature.

Besides the books, there are posters, binoculars, jigsaw puzzles, cards and lots of outdoorsy stuff for kids. 1241 Broad Street, 388-4174

Griffin Books ❖ We visit Griffin Books regularly in search of off-beat volumes on gardening, cooking, antique jewelry, art and other specialty interests. We also like Griffin's excellent selection of blank journals, with themes for travellers, gardeners, diarists, and others who value the written word. On the east side of Market Square, 168-560 Johnson Street, 383-0633.

Island Fantasy ❖ Intrigued by the arcane mysteries of *Dungeons and Dragons?* Island Fantasy is a D & D fan's paradise. The store also specializes in examples of the art of cartooning. There are collections of Donald Duck comics, and works devoted to the best of the late, great Walt Kelly's creation, Pogo (including all the words to that old Christmas carol, "Deck the Halls With Boston Charlie"). Comics are bought and sold—everything from Asterix to GI Joe is lined up alphabetically on central display tables. Now aren't you sorry you traded your Little Lulu collection for a used softball mitt? The posters are an eclectic lot: fantastic unicorns, a puckish Alfred Hitchcock, a fluffy-haired Albert Einstein... At the west side of the court-yard level in Market Square, 560 Johnson Street, 381-1134.

Munro's Books ❖ Munro's is truly addictive for the hardcore book-worm. Such a wonderful selection! It's easy to while away a whole morning in this lovingly restored heritage building—one of the few bookstores to take over a bank! The excellent children's section holds pint-sized chairs for browsing book wormlets. There's a strong emphasis on CanLit, along with an extensive range of British and American titles. The reference section is particularly fine, as is the huge collection of fine art calendars that appears at Christmas time each year. At 1108 Government Street, 382-2464.

Sri Atman ❖ Locals have either never heard of this place or they think it's the best bookstore in Victoria. If you lean towards the holistic healing/metaphysical thoughts/vegetarianism/astro-logy/yoga end of things, this is your book shop. You'll come out feeling less frazzled because soothing meditation music plays softly in the background (This music—on tapes or records—is for sale.) Cards, crystals, and incense round out the gift section. At 1308 Government Street, 383-3032.

Tanner's Books & Gifts ❖ This Sidney bookstore looks like a small-town corner bookseller from the outside; once you're inside you will be surprised at how the place seems to go on and on. It has everything from cookbooks to books on British Columbia history and travel. For visitors arriving by ferry at nearby Swartz Bay, Tanner's is a perfect first stop. Pick up some local maps, magazines, the daily paper, and something for the children from the large toy department. At 2436 Beacon Avenue, Sidney, 656-2345.

Yates News & Books ❖ This place carries an exhaustive selection of magazines, North American and European, plus a number of leading newspapers from around the world. At 736 Yates Street, 383-6634.

Earth Quest Books ❖ Readers with itchy feet will want to walk them into Earth Quest Books, specialists in travel books. Volumes are grouped according to geography, so whether you want to go trekking in Nepal, shopping 'till you drop in New York or eating your way around the south of France, you'll find a guidebook here. Maps—country and city—are also on hand. 1286 Broad Street, 361-4533.

The Nautical Mind ❖ One of the nice things about living in a bookish city like Victoria is the number of specialty bookshops which exist here. Newest of these is The Nautical Mind, sellers of marine books and charts. Find non-fiction books ranging from sailing techniques to naval history; fiction with a nautical theme is also stocked. One set of bookshelves is devoted to an array of nautical videos—William F. Buckley Jr. tells you how to navigate by the stars and Alec Merriman advises you how to catch salmon. #101 19-25 Bastion Square, 388-6367.

Secondhand Books

Bain's Books & Militaria ❖ Exceedingly friendly staff, free homemade cookies and lots of chairs for browsers make Bain's a winner for militaria bibliophiles. Open noon to 5 p.m., Monday to Saturday downstairs at #1 – 1111 Blanshard Street, 380-9880.

Cyril Alexander Books ❖ Militaria is a specialty of Cyril Alexander, but they have a good range of general titles as well, mostly hardcover. 915A Fort Street, 388-9984.

The Haunted Bookshop ❖ Bibliomaniacs beware! Going into the Haunted Bookshop is akin to dropping an opium eater into a poppy field. It's dark, a bit musty, and filled with used books, virtually all hardcover, many of them antiquarian, with some first editions. The range is general; prices are very low. It's fun to spend several hours ensconced in one of the comfy chairs, poring over an early edition Jane Austen that is carefully inscribed with the original owner's name in the meticulous penmanship of the day. Almost all of Carolyn's turn-of-the-century gardening book collection came from these shelves. It's at the courtyard level, south side, of Market Square, 560 Johnson Street, 382-1427.

Poor Richard's Books Ltd. ❖ There's a private club air to this bookstore – we always feel as if we've intruded on a conversation between members. However, we continue to shop here because the stock (mainly used hardcovers) is varied, interesting, and well-arranged, and we like the resident cat. Located in a lovely brick heritage building at 968 Balmoral Road, at the corner of Vancouver Street, 384-4411.

Snowden's Book Store ❖ Now you know what happens to old *National Geographics* – they end up at Snowden's, along with such upscale mags as *Gourmet* and *Architectural Digest*, and specialty publications dealing with hot rods, guns and ammo, and other such interests. Paperbacks abound: romance readers can OD on Harlequins; sci-fi fans are well-served; and there are lots of war/adventure/mystery books for the bloodthirsty. Upper brows will find plenty of Good Literature, too. At 619 Johnson Street, 383-8131.

Curious Books & Comics ❖ Our sources (sons Ben and Raymond) assure us Curious Comics is THE place for comic aficionados. Desperate parents, trying to vacuum around piles of comics decorating teenage bedroom floors, might like to note Curious Comics stocks LARGE cardboard boxes designed to keep collections dust-free and tidy. Downstairs at 559 Johnson Street, 384-1656.

Bookends ❖ Other general bookstores to visit are *Hawthorne Books*, 1027 Cook Street, 383-3215; and *Village Books*, 3826 Cadboro Bay Road, 477-1421.

Used books can be found at *Burnside Book Bin*, 106 Burnside Road West, 384-4021; *Oak Bay Books*, 1964 Oak Bay Avenue, 592-2933; and *Pickwick Books*, 1610 Island Highway, 474-2042. Other used bookstores include *A to Zee Books*, 1820 Government Street, 386-1534; and *Babbling Books*, 965 Kings Road, 386-1331.

Chains are represented by *The Bay*, 1701 Douglas Street, 385-1311; *Classic Books*, Mayfair Shopping Centre, 381-2700, or Tillicum Mall, 381-3034; *Cole's*, Victoria Eaton Centre, 361-9744; *Eaton's*, Victoria Eaton Centre, 382-7141, or Tillicum Mall, 384-2211; *WH Smith*, Harbour Square, 386-1391, CanWest Shopping Centre, 478-3543, or Town and Country Shopping Centre, 380-9488; and *Woodward's Stores*, Mayfair Shopping Centre, 386-3322.

We would also like to draw your attention to often-overlooked sources of specialty books. The *Maritime Museum of BC* (28 Bastion Square, 385-4222) carries nautical tomes and *Crown Publications* offers an excellent range of books about BC, 546 Yates Street, 386-4636. Gift shops at the *Royal British Columbia Museum* (675 Belleville Street, 384-4425) and the *Art Gallery of Greater Victoria* (1040 Moss Street, 384-4101) also stock a variety of books.

Finally, the bookstores at the *University of Victoria* and *Camosun College* are not devoted solely to dry texts with the look of Required Reading. You will find volumes on everything from bringing up baby to the language of flowers. UVic Bookstore is on campus off Finnerty Road, 721-8311. There are two Camosun Bookstores, main branch at Lansdowne campus, 3100 Foul Bay Road, 570-3080; Interurban campus branch, 4461 Interurban, only open 8 a.m. to 12:30 p.m., 370-3386.

Records, Records, Records

Lyle's Place ❖ We have it on good authority from our rock experts (our children) that Lyle's is *the* place for punk/New Wave/ Heavy Metal. There are new and used records and tapes, with emphasis on hard-to-find British imports. If you're a fan of a particular group, you can buy band-name T-shirts, buttons, flags, and key rings with which to proclaim your allegiance, plus a poster to decorate your bedroom wall. All this and record rentals too. At 726 Yates Street, 382-8422. Second location at 711 Goldstream Avenue, 478-9272.

Sinfonia ❖ When records are on our Chopin Liszt, we keep coming Bach here because the owners really have a Handel on the needs of classical music lovers. Clearly marked sections arrange tapes and records alphabetically by composer, by instrument, by performer, or, in the case of opera, by name. The tenor of the store is low key; relax in wicker seats while you listen to music or read through back issues of music magazines. They stock a super series of tapes (Burton reading Thomas, Glenda Jackson reading classic fairy tales), some enchanting old music prints, and state-of-the-art compact discs. Would we string you along? At 45 Market Square, 560 Johnson Street, 383-5211.

Sweet Thunder ❖ Sweet Thunder is the kind of place that makes you wonder why you ever buy records at a department store. A wicker-furnished listening area—with free coffee yet—is set up at the back of the store so you can sit and enjoy the music before you start browsing through the classics by Jelly Roll Morton, Chick Corea, or George Winston. This is a jazz/ blues/classical store, and the world needs more independent record retailers with such an eclectic selection. At 575 Johnson Street, 381-4042.

CLOTHING

While Victoria has its fair share of chain and department stores, we also boast a number of specialty boutiques that offer out-of-the-ordinary clothing. We've tossed some of our favourite budget-minded places in here too, for those of us with more taste than money.

Baden-Baden Boutique ❖ There are plenty of ladies' wear stores providing us with British and American imports. Only one specializes in German fashions, but that one is certainly giving the others a run for their money. The fabrics (including an irresistible leather lookalike) are first rate, and the designs have that unmistakable European chic. At 667 Fort Street, 386-5252. Second location at the Conference Centre Plaza, 712 Douglas Street, 386-1912.

British Importers ❖ When we're rich (which we will be when all you people reading a library copy of this book go and buy your own) we will buy presents for the men in our lives at British Importers. We will buy genuine Harris tweed jackets and silk Giorgio Armani suits, Scottish cashmere sweaters and Sea Island cotton shirts, Bally shoes and Sherlock Holmes deerstalkers. Then we'll stock up on handmade crêpe de chine ties and Italian leather belts and, just to round out the package, Hardy Amies toiletries and Porsche folding sunglasses. We won't even gasp at the pricetags. A superlative men's store, with very unsnooty staff, at 138 Victoria Eaton Centre, 386-1496.

Cardin's Fashions ❖ For years we avoided this place, scared off by the thought of all those dollar signs implied by the name. When we finally did stop in, we were pleased by the variety of quality clothes here: nice detail work like double-stitched seams and pleated tucks mark the difference between department store sportswear and interesting designer merchandise. We like this store—especially at sale time! The staff is friendly, and a sewing machine is set up for immediate alterations. At 103-1841 Oak Bay Avenue, 595-2222.

Carnaby Street Boutique ❖ There is nothing else quite like Carnaby Street in Victoria. We recommend a visit, even if your wardrobe wouldn't normally include the exotic and unusual clothing found in this exotic and unusual shop. The interior is dark, smelling faintly musky, with strange, bell-tinkling music in the background. The stock ranges from Bolivian wool sweaters to Indian cottons. As well as men's, women's, and children's clothing from all over the world, there are unique items like mirrored festival jackets, copper cookware from Syria, jewelry from Tibet and North Africa and rugs from Afghanistan. You could spend hours in the quiet, cool corners of this store and forget you were actually in staid old Victoria. At 538 Yates Street, 382-3747.

Extra's ❖ There are other accessory shops around, but we think Extra's is extra special. The jewelry is really unusual and the pantyhose, belts, and handbags are all up-to-the-minute and guaranteed to change that little basic black dress from boring to brilliant. 1010 Blanshard Street, 380-1003.

Fashion 8 ❖ The owner's of Fashion 8 try to offer designer wear to fit a working woman's budget—and usually succeed. Prices are quite reasonable for the kind of designer names found on the labels, and the stock is varied and interesting. 606 Johnson Street, 361-9575.

Francine's ❖ This whole place has a bargain basement ambience. Merchandise on mismatched hangers is jammed onto racks, and people try things on over their street clothes rather than bothering with dressing rooms. As in most discount houses, you have to search through lot of polyester kitsch, but you will unearth plenty of respectable brand names—LA Seatcovers, Sweet Baby Jane. Head for the back to find the real cheapies. We like Francine's for summer cottons and for the kind of general, knocking-about clothes that you wear at home and don't mind the baby drooling on. Upstairs at Harbour Square Mall, 910 Government Street, 384-2911.

Gibson's Ladies Wear ❖ A trip to Gibson's is not for the faint-hearted middle class. It ranks with the most expensive shops anywhere, and for years has been synonymous with good taste and big bucks. Clothing at Gibson's leans towards elegant, classic styles; clientele here see purchases as investments. Designer labels predominate and the store carries everything from chic sportswear to knock-'em-dead after five ensembles. At 708 View Street, 384-5913.

John McMaster's Men's & Ladies' Clothing ❖ Incongruously situated in the middle of Antique Row is this very sedate, utterly untrendy store, which looks like it should be called a haberdashery. This is definitely a shop for conservative dressers – the Harris tweed/navy blazer/cavalry twill/grey flannel trouser set. There are bargains to be had at annual sales – like the $250 wool suit that Jill's husband bought for $50 one year. There is also an in-house tailor shop for customizing, and a ladies' wear division which is conservative in the extreme. At 1012 Fort Street, 384-4712.

Marc Downs ❖ Check this discount centre regularly because stock turnover is rapid. Merchandise is attractively displayed and currently fashionable – which is not always the case in knockdown houses. It helps to be a small size, and the emphasis is on separates – pants, skirts, blouses – suitable for either casual or office wear. 769 Fort, 383-2251.

Nushin, Nushin Boutique and Anthony James ❖ The name has changed and the premises are bigger but Nushin is still the place to find a knockout of an outfit for a special occasion, or a dress-for-success suit which is authoritative but not boring. The expanded size of the store just means you have more European designer fashions to choose from. Also expanded are the sections devoted to some really smashing accessories and eye-catching jewelry. Nushin is at 606 Trounce Alley, 381-2131. Around the corner is Anthony James, owned by the same family and stocking distinctive European designed menswear as well as imported fashions for women. 1225 Government

Street, 381-2152. The Nushin Boutique in Oak Bay carries casual chic for women from Esprit, Jones New York and Ralph Lauren. 2250 Oak Bay Avenue, 595-2223.

Kettle Creek Canvas ❖ Normally we don't include chains in *Island Treasures*, but we're making an exception for Kettle Creek, an all-Canadian success story. The company began as a cottage industry in southern Ontario, and today has stores in most major Canadian cities. Victorians embraced Kettle Creek's clothes immediately because they're perfectly suited to casual West Coast lifestyles: dirndl-style denim and cotton skirts, bush shorts and pants, jumpsuits and jumpers, shirts and sweatshirts. Shorts, pants, and most tops are unisex, and the material is a wonderful cotton which just gets softer and softer with each washing. Two locations: Victoria Eaton Centre, 134 Fort Street, 384-2155 and Hillside Centre, 595-2213.

Polo Ralph Lauren ❖ We can't afford to actually *shop* here, we just like to drop in to torture ourselves by looking at wonderful designer clother we can't afford for either ourselves or our men. We also like to admire the absolutely superlative job done on transforming this turn-of-the-century bank into a very classy boutique. The building was designed by egocentric architectural genius Francis Mawson Rattenbury (creator of the Legislative Buildings and The Empress Hotel). We think he'd approve of the renovation which incorporates fireplaces, woodwork and other design details in a series of handsomely appointed rooms. Mr. Lauren himself apparently rates the Victoria store fourth most beautiful in his world-wide chain of boutiques (after New York, Paris, and Rodeo Drive, if you must know.) So go and have a look. You might even be able to afford something. 1200 Government Street, 381-7656.

Starboard Jeans ❖ Are you outfitting several kids—or even just one!—in the ubiquitous dress of the latter half of the twentieth century? Yes, we're talking about jeans, ex-working apparel of cowboys and now designer wear. Without designer labels but perfectly fine are the jeans stocked at Starboard, a discount hous. There are black, stone-washed and ordinary jeans here, starting at pre-schooler and working up to adult sizes. Prices are amazingly cheap. The money you'll save on your own jeans will offset the designer prices your teenaged offspring will continue to insist on. 1817 Douglas Street, 383-2717.

Silks for Men ❖ Luxurious undies for gents are the specialty of this unusual boutique. Treat your man to silk boxer shorts, jockey briefs, nightshirts or a smoking jacket. (Even if he doesn't smoke, he can still look like a model from GQ.) 616 Trounce Alley, 380-1555.

Victoria Originals

How about a one-of-a-kind designer original to remind you of your visit to Victoria for many fashion seasons to come? Local clothing designs rival Big City creations for style and flair, but they don't come close to the pricier numbers where your wallet is concerned. Try the following shops for their collections by local designers.

Maresa Boutique ❖ Here you will find a number of Victoria and Vancouver originals, plus hand-crafted jewelry, batiked and hand-painted silk scarves and eelskin accessories. 2227 Oak Bay Avenue, 592-1412.

Off the Cuff ❖ Representative fashions by Nancy George, some very funky jewelry and an eclectic assortment of pre-owned clothing are found at 589 Johnson Street, 386-2221.

Footnotes

Ashley James ❖ This is where ladies with aristocratically narrow, expensive, Italian feet fit them in aristocratically narrow, expensive, Italian footwear. The store offers a range of sizes from 4 to 11, and fittings from 4A to D. And if you thought Victoria was two years behind the Continent in terms of style, look again. Owner Penny Ridyard travels to Europe twice a year so she can personally order up-to-the-minute styles and colours. She also picks out matching handbags, hats, silk scarves, gloves, panty hose, and handmade belts to complete the accessory picture. In the Bank of Commerce Mall at 105-1175 Douglas, 385-2345.

Roots ❖ The whole family can march into Roots to be outfooted in high quality, Canadian-made leather shoes and boots. We particularly like the boots here—trust Canadian designers to come up with good looking yet practical footwear for out winters! Styles are often unisex; some may be worn pulled up or cuffed down for a versatile look. We also approve of Roots' soft leather baby booties (Rooties?). They sport a non-slip suede sole and a diagonal closing zipper. Junior will have some trouble trying to get out of them! Dad and Mom can also get leather vests, jackets, handbags, and briefcases. At 1010 Broad, 383-4811.

Volume Shoes ❖ In our never-ending desire to get more for our money (some have been so unkind as to describe us a cheapskates), we found Volume Shoes, a discount house for ladies' footwear. Don't look for atmosphere. There isn't any. Just find your shoe size on the wall signs and start checking for bargains. The tables in the middle of the store contain markdowns of markdowns all jumbled together so don't miss them. We've bought $70 leather boots here for $25, and there are similar bargains in shoes. Good hunting. 727 Yates Street, 381-3868.

Classy Consignments

We both became experts at tracking down bargains as young brides married to poverty-stricken students. We did it out of necessity then; now that it's chic to haunt garage sales and second-hand stores, we find that we weren't penny-pinchers. . . merely avant garde. Here is our personal guide to the best of the previously-owned. One warning: you may go and find nothing for several visits. Don't give up. In second-hand shopping it's the luck of the draw that separates the hard-core bargain seeker from the dilettante.

Elan Fashion Collections ❖ The owner of Elan is very picky about what she takes on consignment, and you, budget-minded reader, reap the rewards of her selectivity. Lots of the stock is new—samples and line ends. Jill's favourite dress had an original price tag of $185 still on it when she bought it from Elan for $55. Carolyn has picked up gorgeous angora sweaters, a classic linen suit, designer blouses and more. It's rare for us to visit and walk out empty handed. The address is 102-1841 Oak Bay Avenue, but the entrance is actually around the corner on Chamberlain, 598-5331.

Gisela Studios ❖ Have you ever wondered where rich people take their expensive clothes when they clean out closets? ("My dear, I've already worn it *twice* and just everybody has seen it!") We discovered the final resting place of good little ultra-suedes and silks when we found Gisela's (pronounced with a hard G). Incidentally, if you're the kind of practical bride who blanches at the idea of spending megabucks on a dress for one day, no matter how special, check Gisela's supply of once-worn bridal gowns for sale or rent. Carolyn bought a raw silk blazer here for $70, and a snakeskin shoulder purse for a mere $18. Everything on the racks is of the finest quality, but a department store prices. The shop is tucked away downstairs at 104-2250 Oak Bay Avenue, 598-2412.

House of Savoy ❖ House of Savoy has some of Victoria's best buys in women's (and men's) pre-owned fashions. Of course you take your chances when you visit: some days you strike it rich; other days there's not a thing that fits. Still, we like the variety and turnover of stock so well that we're betting you find something on your first try. Owner Marion Savoy has an unusual collection of unique beaded sweaters from the '50s, wedding dresses for sale or rent, and a display of men's wear too. But the real appeal for us is in the discovery of a very high-quality, reasonably priced garment every so often – the Holt-Renfrew, Albert Nipon, and Ports labels keep popping up between the polyester sportswear. Somewhere out there is a perfect size 8 who is squandering money buying retail when Marion has half a store of designer clothes waiting, at practically giveaway prices. At 1869 Oak Bay Avenue, 598-3555.

The Olde Fashion House ❖ Carolyn's working wardrobe boasts several designer outfits from this stylish consignment boutique, all bought at a fraction of the original retail price. New and next-to-new fashions of uniformly excellent quality, a spacious interior and gracious staff make this shop a must for those of us with more taste than cash. Closed Mondays. 1971 Oak Bay Avenue at the corner of Foul Bay Road, 598-9932.

Phase II Fashions ❖ Here is another in the growing number of women's consignment shops around town – and one of the handful of regularly reliable stops for the smart consumer. We like this store because quality is good to excellent, with the odd bonanza thrown in – like the Rouie silk dress at $40 we once saw there. Shoppers, you can't buy polyester at that price! If you're lucky, you'll find your own goldmine among the neat, colour-coordinated racks of fashions. Near the Italian Bakery, at 3185 Quadra Street, 382-6155.

Vintage Clothing ❖ Remember starched crinolines under poodle skirts? Marabou feather boas? Little hats with perky feathers on the brim a la Lucy Ricardo? Three little shops that specialize in these fashions of bygone years at *The Bay Window, Still Life,* and *Off White.* To be honest, few people in *our* social circles actually wear the clothes these shops carry, but somebody must; each is doing very well selling the offbeat, the forgotten, and the newly-rediscovered. The Bay Window has delicious vintage evening wear plus some terrific jewelry. 587 Johnson Street, 384-4547. Still Life offers both men's and women's styles from the forties and fifties. We particularly like the men's hats (wear it again, Sam.) 551 Johnson Street, 386-5655. Aside from dated treasures such as beaded evening tops, Off-White is noted for its wonderful selection of rhinestone costume jewelry, sparkling in the back showcase and watched over by a chatty parrot. 1318 Government Street, 381-2533.

GIFTS, HANDICRAFTS AND EVERYTHING ELSE

Please, we beg you, do not squander your hard-earned cash on the ersatz souvenirs ranged on shelves in one of the tourist traps on lower Government Street. Before you make any decisions on Inuit or Indian art we suggest you visit Gallery of the Arctic, Arts of the Raven, and Nunavut Gallery to look at the genuine article and get a feel for what is good. The stores in this section were selected because they offer unique items not generally available, or one-of-a-kind Canadian handicrafts.

Alcheringa ❖ Imports from Down Under are the specialty here, and bloody find ones they are too, mate. Sheepskin products hold centre stage; handsome yet serviceable coats and vests for men and women are the key performers. You can dress up your car with sheepskin seat covers, your baby's bed with a cozy lambskin sleeper, your feet with slippers, or your cleaning cupboard with a longhandled duster. Wooden tribal jewelry is displayed in glass wall cases and a cluster of stuffed koalas and other wildlife are grouped at the back. Genuine Aussie hats and long raincoats give you the complete Crocodile Dundee look; the stylish leather coats and dynamic bathing suits are a reminder that Australia has a thriving fashion industry. At the very back of the store is a Tribal Art Gallery. Alcheringa owner Elaine Monds has personally amassed this extraordinary collection of primitive art via yearly trips to Papua New Guinea. It's a must-see. 665 Fort Street, 383-8224. Second location in Hillside Centre, 595-2505.

Amandla ❖ Enchanting Amandla stocks unique items from Africa: art, clothing, jewelry and baskets. Definitely worth a look when you're in Sidney. 2385 Beacon Avenue, 655-3121.

Arts of the Raven ❖ The raven is a major symbol in the cultural heritage of West Coast Indians. If you want to add to, or start, a collection of Indian art, go no further than this gallery that bears his name. Quality is uniformly high whether you're looking at a carved mask, engraved silver jewelry, or a limited edition silkscreen print. Renowned artist Tony Hunt is artistic director; on permanent display are many of his family's cultural artifacts, such as potlatch gear, creating a mini-museum. Don't miss the pottery, a non-traditional medium which incorporates traditional motifs in a creative fusion of the old and the new. If you budget is limited, the art cards are an inexpensive way of commemorating a visit. At 1015 Douglas Street, 386-3069.

Balloon Madness ❖ After Carolyn's surprise birthday party, it became a game to observe just how long the dozens of balloons decorating the house would last. After almost two months—yes, two whole months—they finally began to wither and shrink, and were taken down in the same sad spirit that accompanies removal of the Christmas tree corpse each year. During those two months, however, balloons cheered up every visitor to the Thomas home, a testimonial to the true value of balloons in the world. Balloon Madness offers shiny, metallic Mylar, or conventional rubber balloons, plain or helium filled. You can celebrate a birth (It's a Girl!) or a birthday (Over the Hill). You can find something for children (Care Bears or He-Man) and for your sick relatives (Get Well Soon). If you can't find the balloon you have in mind, Balloon Madness will custom print it for you. There are delivery people who dress up in costume for crazy deliveries of "balloon-a-grams." . At 503 Yates, corner of Wharf, 384-4531. Second location in the Market at Hillside, 598-2676.

The Bombay Company ❖ If, through lack of foresight in choosing your ancestors, you lack a houseful of antique furniture handed down through several generations, head for the Bombay Company. They specialize in good quality, reasonably-priced reproductions of occasional pieces and accessory items. One of their winged butler's tables graces Jill's living room, and her husband has his eye on the English officer's portable bar (ideally, one should also have a batman to set it up and take it down). In the Hillside Mall, Hillside and Shelbourne, 598-1522.

Capital Iron ❖ We heard a great story about a friend's father who, on his rare visits to Victoria from his home in Ireland, preferred Capital Iron to any other tourist destination in town. We don't know whether we'd pass up Butchart Gardens, but we do suggest this wonderful old store for anybody fascinated with obscure collections of you-name-it. Capital Iron is a general store spread out over several buildings, selling kitchenware, paints, hardware, plumbing and electrical supplies, camping and fishing gear, shoes, and clothing. The basement, though, is what keeps visitors returning. Here the intrepid collector can find military surplus (just the gas mask you've been searching for!), electronic stuff, Japanese glass floats, chains and pulleys of all sizes and purposes, fishing nets, handcuffs, and other esoterica so dear to the male heart. When your mate announces, "I'm just going down to Capital Iron for a few minutes . . ." you can be sure the guy's gone for the day. Get him to take the kids with him—there is a terrific playground just outside the entrance to the Garden Department. On historic Store Street at number 1900, 385-9703.

Century Cameras ❖ Impecunious photographers should head to Century Cameras to find quality used photographic equipment, sold by knowledgeable and helpful staff. Jill bought a second-hand telephoto lens for her husband's Pentax for a (relatively) mere $190 last Christmas. Other lensed gear includes microscopes, binoculars and telescopes. 1410 Broad Street, 388-5522.

The China Cupboard ❖ If you've smashed one of Grandmother's prized Limoges plates and are about to be disinherited, hurry off to The China Cupboard, where owner Jan Montgomery will search through her collection for a replacement. If she draws a blank at matching your treasure, she will take the particulars for her registry in case it appears at an estate sale. Jan's specialty is discontinued lines of china; her store is a fascinating repository of odd pieces, attractively displayed on splendid old buffets and tables. She also offers an eclectic selection of Victorian collectibles, and keeps a registry of these as well. If your passion is anything from Toby jugs to thimbles, hie on down to 2183 Theatre Lane, behind the 2100 block Oak Bay Avenue, phone 598-3858.

'*Chosin Pottery* ❖ If the roadside sign says "Open," turn in to the driveway and visit the showroom at the left side of the house, situated in a sylvan garden of delightful naturalness. Here the work of renowned potter Robin Hopper, and that of partner Judy Dyelle, is displayed. Jill has been collecting Robin's stuff for years and has a houseful of his attractive and functional bowls, mugs, and casseroles. Robin's beautiful larger bowls and wall-hung plates definitely fall into the art category. In contrast, Judy Dyelle creates charming, decorative pieces with subtle, pastel glazes. Worth the drive to scenic, rural Metchosin; look for 4283 Metchosin Road, 474-2676.

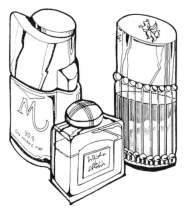

Crabtree & Evelyn ❖ One of Jill's favourite shops, Crabtree & Evelyn is the place to go when you start murmuring, "What can I buy for this impossible person?" We guarantee you will walk out with the perfect gift. The shop stocks European toiletries: lotions, shampoos, and more varieties of soap, includ-ing shaving soap, than we would have believed possible. The fragrance in the air wafts from a display case holding a variety of loose potpourri which may be purchased by the scoop. Another showcase holds grooming implements, from moustache combs to badger-bristle hair brushes. The front of the shop is devoted to food: liqueur-spiked preserves, specialty mustards, chutneys, oils and sauces, English and French candies, and, for children, Peter Rabbit biscuits. 137 Victoria Eaton Centre. Look for the dark blue exterior on Fort Street. Phone 381-6344.

Dig This ❖ Unearth some treasures at Dig This, a must for gardeners. Giftware for growers includes herb-filled potholders (these smell wonderful when you put your teapot on top), big-pocket aprons for gathering fruit, and clay pots pre-filled with soil and seeds for windowsill gardens. Serious gardeners will want to check out the English equipment that's guaranteed to last for a lifetime of digging. There are pots of porcelain from France, and of unglazed clay from Portugal. We like the unique accessories: colourful wooden row markers shaped like vegetables, and art cards with flower designs. It's down a short flight of stairs on the south side of Bastion Square, number 45, 385-3212.

Fan Tan Gallery ❖ You are definitely not in the mood to shop if you can leave this store empty-handed. We think it's one of the best sources in town for really unusual gifts: rustic, handwoven reed baskets (from shopping to firewood sizes), African woodwork, basketry and jewelry, and a whole roomful of country style folk art from pewter candlesticks to terra cotta wall decorations. A gem of a store, right in the heart of Chinatown at 541 Fisgard Street, 382-4424.

Gallery Shop ❖ Behind the reception desk at the Art Gallery of Greater Victoria is one our favourite gift-buying spots—the Gallery Shop. The emphasis is on handicrafts; distinctive pottery, enamelled and silver jewelry, silk and wool scarves, handwoven ties, and wood sculptures. The children's corner contains stuffed animals, books, wooden toys, and felt mobiles. Art cards, prints, and books round out the selection. Prices are very reasonable, and your money goes to support the Gallery, so you can feel virtuous about your spendthrift habits. 1040 Moss Street, 384-7012.

Gallery of the Arctic ❖ Stunning, museum-quality Inuit sculpture and prints, chosen with an eye for excellence, are the hallmarks of this gallery. The staff are well-versed in the various aspects of the media, from differences in artists' styles to the source of the soapstone to what the mythological figures represent. We are confident that once you view the awesome pieces in here, you won't look twice at the poor imitations being flogged elsewhere. Adjoining The Quest at 611 Fort Street, 382-9012.

The Handloom ❖ Proving that Canadians are more than hewers of wood and drawers of water. The Handloom offers distinctive Canadian crafts: jewelry of singular design, some very fine examples of the potter's art, unusual wall hangings, handmade silk scarves, woven stoles, and wood sculptures. The price range is wide enough that you can find something for everyone. At 641 Fort Street, 384-1011.

International Knives ❖ Serious cooks, serious fishermen, serious campers—anyone, in fact, who demands the best in cutting instruments, will love International Knives. Whether it's a Swiss Army knife for your Scout, or a Scottish skean dhu for your sock, this place has it, along with related sharp and pointy items like darts and scissors. They also carry various sharpening stones or, if you're a complete fumble fingers, let them do the sharpening for you. At 1306 Government, 383-2422. Second location at Tillicum Mall, 383-0012.

Irish Linen ❖ To step into Irish Linen is to be transported back in time. The interior is dark, the wooden floor creaks, and the merchandise is ranged on shelves behind the counter and in glass showcases. But what merchandise! Owners Maura and Bar-

bara Lamb travel to Ireland regularly to seek out the work of cottage craftspeople. The result is goods of an extraordinarily high quality. This is the place to find that crisp damask table-cloth for special occasions, hand-tatted lace cloths for the tea tray, fine lawn handkerchiefs to grace a jacket pocket, and earth-tone woven placemats to complement pottery tableware. They also sell napkins in every colour of the rainbow, embroidery fabric by the yard, and a wonderful, heat-proof material called "No-Mar" to protect your table from heat marks and rings. At 1019 Government Street, 383-6812.

Leafhill Gallery ❖ Leafhill is a well-established gallery offering visitors and residents alike an opportunity to view the best work of mostly BC artists. Themes range from coastal seascapes to up-country Western landscapes, and quality is uniformly high. At 47 Bastion Square, 384-1311.

The Lighthouse ❖ If your taste runs to the modern—and even if it doesn't—you will like The Lighthouse. As you would expect from the name, the store carries a wide selection of contemporary lamps and lighting fixtures. There's lots more, too: myriad candles and holders, unusual jewelry, uniquely-shaped glass vases, and other objets d'art for your house, most sporting the unmistakable clean lines of Scandinavian design. P.S. Don't forget to look at the mobiles hanging from the ceiling. Upstairs in Harbour Square Mall, 910 Government Street, 383-6633.

Meacham's ❖ The world of jewelry is fraught with traps for the unwary; that is why we appreciate honest, trustworthy John and Victoria Meacham. The Meachams are extremely knowledgeable regarding gemstones and you'll find a number of unusual gems, often in remarkable settings. Victoria's specialty is custom design work (she created a stunning wedding ring for Jill). As well, the Meachams carry estate — or as Victoria delicately phrases it, "previously enjoyed" — jewelry, and quality costume pieces. Appraisals, cleaning and repair work are also offered, and the service is low pressure and personal. 1031 Fort Street, 385-3521.

Mexican and More ❖ The thing Jill appreciates about this shop, after taking a classic "gringo beating" in the mercado at Merida, Yucatan, is that all the best of Mexican handicrafts are here for you to view without being a) hot and sweaty; b) nervous; and c) at the mercy of the Berlitz Spanish-English phrase book. Onyx, in all its many-hued glory, is here, fashioned into chess and backgammon sets, bookends, and ornaments. Leather products — handbags, belts, wallets — woven and cotton goods, pottery, and silver and turquoise jewelry are also on hand. All this and you won't get Montezuma's Revenge either. Across from the Bay at 1702 Douglas Street, 385-1118.

The Museum Shop ❖ Want to buy an original Han dynasty bronze horse from 200 BC? If you said yes, you obviously have a Donald Trump sized bank account. We keen but impoverished art lovers head for the Museum Shop to find exquisitely crafted replicas of the real thing at a fraction of the cost. The shop specializes in distinctive reproductions of statues, jewelry, and historic curios held in major museums around the world. The Museum Shop's facsimiles come with cards delineating the history of the object. The children's section has old-fashioned books and neat stuff such as wooden rulers listing all the British monarchs from Roman Britain to Elizabeth II. Art cards, stationery, jigsaws, gorgeous calendars and posters round out the selection in this interesting store. 1011 Fort Street, 381-5553.

Nunavut Gallery ❖ The emphasis at this gallery is divided approximately half and half between Inuit art and contemporary Canadian works. The owners lived in the North for a number of years, and both are familiar with Northern art and artists. They have soapstone sculpture, exquisite bone carvings, and prints—both Inuit and Indian. Contemporary art runs from sculpted ceramic animals to marine watercolours. The gallery also has a custom framing service, some nice gift items like silk scarves with Inuit designs, and art cards. 2188 Oak Bay Avenue, 598-1344.

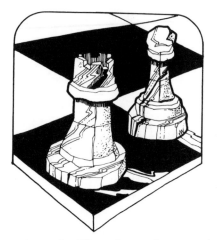

Old Morris Tobacconists ❖ This shop takes you back to the time when ladies were banished after dinner while the gentlemen lingered over brandy and cigars. Housed in a wonderful example of Romanesque Revival architecture, complete with the original mahogany fittings, Old Morris boasts a special room where temperature and humidity are strictly controlled to keep cigars in perfect condition. There are Havanas, of course, plus Dutch and Brazilian cigars for anti-communist smokers. All other accoutrements of the addictive weed are sold, from lighters to pipes, and (cough, cough) specialty cigarettes. At 1116 Government, 382-4811.

Out of Hand ❖ We first came across this shop when they had their Bird Bath Show. Intrigued, we found a little ceramic bathtub with a little ceramic bird lounging in it, and an azure blue, two-level pottery bath for a Zen garden. These are typical of the out-of-the-ordinary crafts found here, contributed by crafts-people from all over the Island. Contemporary woodwork and outstanding pottery share display space with hand-painted silk scarves and unusual handcrafted jewelry. 566 Johnson Street, 384-5221.

The Quest ❖ We recommend The Quest for anyone who wants a genuine Canadian craft piece to take home as a memento. Owner Joan Bomford travels across the country to choose items for the store, and you can trust her impeccable taste. Stock ranges from Suttles and Seawinds fabric products from Nova Scotia to exquisite hand-crafted jewelry, and includes an excellent selection of first-class Canadian pottery. The price range is quite wide, so even if you're on a limited budget you can still find something. Adjoining the store is the Gallery of the Arctic, a must for collectors of Inuit art. The Quest is at the corner of Fort and Government, 382-1934.

Robertson & Hovey ❖ We have a weakness for shops like this. Botanical prints adorn the walls, dried flowers fill baskets and potpourri supplies line the shelves. The owners are the makers of pure herb and flower scented soaps and candles as well. Enjoy. 618 Broughton Street, 386-2171.

Royal BC Museum Gift Shop ❖ The justly-renowned Museum boasts a worthwhile gift shop. Everything in the shop relates to the museum in some way. You can find excellent Indian artwork, locally crafted jewelry featuring BC gems, and a host of botanically-inspired goods, from art cards to pressed-flower bookmarks. The book selection is first rate, ranging through local and natural history, horticulture, and art. It's the child-ren's section, though, that is particularly outstanding, with educational volumes on everything from dinosaurs to rocks. On the main floor of the Provincial Museum, 675 Belleville Street, 384-4425.

Specialty Guns ❖ This is not our field of expertise, but if you like things that go boom, our resident firearms expert (Jill's husband) says this is the place for aficionados. The selection of firearms, ammunition (particularly hard-to-get obsolete stock), and associated gear is large, and the prices are competitive. This, by the way, is a "man's store." The staff, although always polite, have a slight air of surprise when Jill accompanies her husband here. A word of warning, too, for American visitors who want to take some of this stuff home with you: customs regulations tend to be complex. Best to check before you buy. At 576 Yates, 383-1044.

The Spirit of Christmas ❖ "My Visa card starts to quiver when I walk in here," said one of our friends. Ours too. It's impossible for even the hardest hearted Scrooge to maintain a Bah Humbug attitude in the Spirit of Christmas. Decorated trees line the middle of the main floor; surrounding alcoves and showcases are full of stuffed animals, Disney figures, miniature lighted village scenes, and tree and house decorations galore. Upstairs, the mezzanine floor displays nativity scenes, dolls, more trees and a seemingly endless assortment of ornaments. Don't miss it, any time of year. 1022 Government Street at Fort, 385-2501.

Surplus City and General Store ❖ This cavernous warehouse falls into our Everything Else category. On the main floor, you pick your way through new dining room suites, umbrella stands, occasional tables, rugs, bookshelves....Toilets, doors, light fixtures and other demo specials are ranged along the west wall. Up a rickety staircase are kitchen and bathroom cabinets; at the back of the main floor is a room with kitchenware galore. If you like poking through dust-filled nooks and crannies in search of a bargain, this place is for you. 517 Herald Street, 388-7172.

SPECIALTY FOOD SHOPS

We all have days when 5 p.m. finds us racing through the local supermarket, throwing packaged convenience stuff into the basket.

This section is *not* for those days.

This section is for when you have lots of time to plan or cook for a special occasion—when you can enjoy browsing around and picking up little gourmet goodies for your family or guests.

Bagga Pasta ❖ From humble beginnings stocking homemade pasta and sauces, Bagga Pasta has blossomed and expanded to two locations. They still have excellent pasta (try the smoked salmon and dill ravioli) and neatly packaged sauces to take home, but the stock now includes Italian gelati, olive oils, tomatoe paste (sensibly packaged in tubes), fresh herbs and non-edibles such as cookbooks. Pick up a montly newsletter for pasta recipes and new product tips. Enjoy a cappuccino and warm muffin at one of the little tables at the Fairfield location on the west side of Fairfield Plaza, 1516 Fairfield Road, 598-1153. Oak Bay location at 2000 Cadboro Bay Road, 598-7575.

Benny's Bagels ❖ This here's yer Noo Yawk style bagel, see. You can buy them individually or by the baker's dozen to take home — or choose your favourite, from poppy seed to raisin cinnamon (Carolyn's choice) to take into Market Square, slathered with cream cheese for lunch, or with jam for breakfast. You can also perch on a stool by the window and watch the passing world. Coffee is available, and the cooler holds juice, pop, and milk. Rhoda would love it. At the Johnson Street bridge side of Market Square, 132-560 Johnson Street, 384-3441. Second location in the Market at Hillside, 598-4353.

Italian Foods Import ❖ The spicy aroma that surrounds you when you step in the door of this deli sets your mouth right up for the taste treat of fresh phyllo pastry (that's their own home-made spinach and feta cheese pie), pure olive oil, European cheeses, meats, and specialty sausages. All the imported canned goods you'll ever need for Mediterranean dishes — from Italian plum tomatoes to anchovies to dark olives — are crammed onto the shelves, too. The little seating area is a good spot for a cappucino break. At 1114 Blanshard Street, around the corner from Fort, 385-7923.

Okanagan Estate Cellar ❖ Civilization comes to Victoria in the form of the Okanagan Wine Cellar, where you can actually taste the stuff before you buy. The store carries the full product lines of five BC estate wineries. If you're use to the meagre selection of estate wines in the government liquor stores, you're in for a surprise. The staff opens a variety of wines each day so you can sip, browse, and make a choice based on taste rather than luck. Fine oenophilic accoutrements like glasses, corkscrews, and books are sold, and non-alcoholic products include

Okanagan fruit leathers and mineral water. In the Hillside Mall, 595-6511.

Self-Heal Herbal Centre ❖ We haven't the foggiest idea what you do with powdered lobelia, but if it's on your shopping list you can find it down at Self-Heal Herbal centre. Same goes for slippery elm bark, Labrador tea, or organic chickweed. If you share our ignorance of the uses for these fascinating items, the Centre's knowledgeable staff can educate you about everything lining the walls of this pleasant shop. Aside from the standard health food store stock, Self-Heal sells a good variety of books on nutrition and holistic health. There's even a shelf full of natural pet supplies. At 1106 Blanshard Street, 383-1913.

The Wooden Shoe ❖ Jill first discovered this place when she was researching an article on specialty foods one Christmas, and promptly fell – teeth, jaws, and palate – for all the Dutch delicacies here. Dutch chocolates are sold, naturally, but so are biscuits and crackers and cheeses and meats (including such exotica as horsemeat and jellied eel). The shelves of Indonesian foods are a reminder that the Dutch had a strong presence in the East Indies. At Christmas-time the store is practically bursting with special Dutch Yuletide treats like the ginger button cookies strewn by Sinter Klaus' helper, Black Peter. At 2576 Quadra Street, 382-9042.

Gourmet Take-outs ❖ There are some weeks which call for special Friday night pampering: buy a bottle of Scotch, rent a movie, pick up some food and pull up the drawbridge. The brand of Scotch and the choice of movie we leave to you, but we have two suggestions for food. Pizza or Chinese take-out won't do, what you need is a proper meal with three courses and plenty of vitamins, minerals and protein. Try either *Complete Cuisine* or *Cheryl's Gourmet Pantry* for appetizers, entree with side dishes, and dessert. The prices are a lot cheaper than dining out, and the taste is homemade. Complete Cuisine is at 1824 Oak Bay Avenue, 595-3151, and Cheryl's Gourmet Pantry is 2017A Cadboro Bay Road at Foul Bay, 595-3212.

KIDSTUFF: TOYS AND BOOKS

We're assuming you're not looking in a book like this to locate run-of-the-mill department store toys. If you want anything heavily advertised between Saturday morning cartoons, you already know where to find it. If, on the other hand, you're searching for an abacus, a Steiff teddy, or a wooden train that refuses to break, no matter how many babies smash it against your furniture, then you might want to pop into some of our favourites. We have also included bookstores that cater primarily to children – as writers we believe in catching them young!

Apple Jo ❖ Tucked away next to Peter Pan, this tiny delight is run almost singlehandedly by Nona Appleby. The shop specializes in Sasha dolls, which are ranged around the walls. There is also an unending supply of doll clothes, puppets, and clown dolls, all hand crafted by Nona and members of her family. 1322 Government Street, 383-0512.

Children's Book Fair ❖ Call Larry or Marty Layne for the perfect book for any child on you shopping list. Both former teachers, the Laynes personally select each book for positive, family-oriented content. The Layne children are the test market – they'll help you select your books based on which ones they like the most. Prices are exactly what you'll find in the department store maze, but the personal service isn't. The Laynes operate the business from their home at 2160 Ferndale, 477-0173.

Foxglove Toys ❖ Unusual, imported toys and craft items, kites and puppets, art supplies and plenty of low-priced novelties encourage the kids to part with their cash. On the Pandora Street side of Market Square, 560 Johnson, 383-8852.

Kaboodles Three ❖ Anyone who's been to Kaboodles Vancouver locations on West 10th or at Granville Market knows what to expect in the Victoria store: nifty games and toys, party stuff, cards and wrap. The playthings are both fun and educational and lots of the stock is priced within reach of children's allowances (and parental budgets.) This is definitely the place to shop for birthday party decor and favors, unusual stocking stuffs and presents for your favourite child. (Harried mums: there's a little play area for tiny tots.) 1320 Government Street, 383-0931.

Playfaire Alternative Toys and Books ❖ A former teacher owns this tiny shop which is crammed with creative toys and well-chosen books. Especially helpful are the signs, which offer knowledgeable recommendations for every age group. In the Fairfield Plaza at 11-1594 Fairfield Road, 595-7444. Second location in the Saanich Centre, Quadra at MacKenzie Avenue, 727-7191.

Primary Playthings ❖ This enticing toy shop stocks such old-fashioned delights as humming tops, wooden mosaic puzzles, and gyroscopes. Pre-school and baby toys are a specialty, but older kids are not ignored. They will find plenty of games, science kits, and intricate colouring books, 631 Johnson Street, 384-2936.

Storyline Books ❖ This family-oriented bookstore features parenting, cookery, and "lifestyle" books, but also stocks a good selection of Canadiana, and a number of popular paperbacks if you just want a quick read for the ferry. What we really like, though, is the children's section, carefully chosen for literary merit (lots of Caldecott and Newberry award winners here) and, as often as possible, for Canadian content. You will find a number of French language books too, for children in French immersion. Many of the classics (*Heidi, Alice in Wonderland, Black Beauty*) are available on long-playing tapes, a good way to interest a non-reader in books. 1019 Douglas Street, 385-3343.

Teacher's Corner ❖ This is *not* your average toy shop! Educational, classroom-oriented material predominates, but there are lots of really different ideas for your own child's play in the way of stickers, art supplies, and books. 2014 Douglas Street, 385-5977.

The Toy Shop ❖ The Toy Shop receives regular visits from us at birthday and Christmas time. We appreciate the range of quality imported toys, dollhouse furnishings, art supplies, and stuffed animals. There are also inexpensive small items suitable for stuffing birthday loot bags and Christmas stockings. 1834 Oak Bay Avenue, 598-3832.

Clothes for Kids

Are you one of those ambitious parents who take a sewing course in the evenings to learn how to make adorable T-shirts for your children – until you discover that children's consignment shops sell perfectly good ones for 99 cents each? Once you visit these great little stores, it's hard to swallow retail prices again, considering the speed with which children seem to grow out of their gear.

Abra-kid-abra ❖ Abra-kid-abra is a good example of a shop that sells high-quality used children's wear, sizes infant to 14. We dare you to sew you own children's stuff for less – we don't think it can be done. Carolyn bought a "Polly Flinders" hand-smocked dress here, for under $7. Another visit yielded boys' rugby pants at $5 each, and a Pierre Cardin dress shirt, including natty clip-on tie, for $4. The shop is light and airy, with merchandise well-displayed. There is a kiddies' play table to keep little ones happy while you're bargain hunting. (And could somebody tell us the reason that *every* store can't provide a children's corner like this?) Abra-kid-abra also sells new clothing and craft items, and rents baby furniture, high chairs, and car seats – they are mandatory in BC – a handy service for those with visiting babies. At 2024 Oak Bay Avenue, 595-1613.

Caledonia Market ❖ With apologies to all other church rummage sales, we present the Caledonia Market. This parish fundraiser is held for only part of the year, on Thursday mornings. Even though it's a hit-and-miss target, we invite you to stop in for real bargains. Like all rummage sales, the Market sells mountains of miscellaneous stuff, but it's the supply of children's clothing that has kept our interest since we spotted near-new boys' grey flannel dress pants here for a quarter. The advantage of rummaging is that there is no overhead and no staff to pay, so prices are downright ridiculous. The atmosphere is pleasant; the friendly ladies of the church chit-chat with you as you browse. Call to check if the Market is on before visiting the basement of St. Mary's Church Hall at 1701 Elgin Road, off Oak Bay Avenue, 598-2212.

Marks & Spencer ❖ If Marks & Spencer is good enough for genera-tions of British parents, it's good enough for us, too. Here's some British trivia, by the way: did you know that the company's Marble Arch location in London regularly makes the pages of the *Guinness Book of World Records* because it has the fastest turnover of stock on earth? The Victoria branch of this British institution is no threat to that record, but it is the place to find uniformly high-quality children's togs at fair prices (they do have adult sizes too, but we like the children's "St. Michael's" line best). The imported clothing has that sturdy appearance that makes you think even *your* kids can't wear this stuff out. All those Britons can't be wrong. At 1212 Douglas Street, 386-6727.

Perfect Playgrounds

The best playgrounds around Victoria, according to our consultants and experts (our kids!) are:

Juan de Fuca Playground ❖ This will make you wish you were eight
years old again! Huge logs make up this adventure playground,
with slides, swings, tunnels, and wild rides on a flying cable.
Nearby is the **Tom Thumb Safety Village** where your five-
to eight-year-olds can pedal tiny cars around the "town" while
learning about road and pedestrian safety. Open classes are
held in the summer months at 10 a.m. and 1:30 p.m. No charge.
For more information, phone 478-9584. Behind the Juan de
Fuca Recreation Centre, 1767 Island Highway, Colwood.

MacDonald Playground ❖ Here is another super adventure playground, complete with swinging bridges, rope ladders, under-
ground "caves," and the same kind of cable ride you'll find at
Juan de Fuca. At MacDonald Park, in James Bay at the corner
of Oswego and Simcoe. The James Bay Community Centre,
around the corner at 140 Oswego, has a coffee shop and
washrooms.

Gyro Park ❖ Where else can you ride an ugly sea serpent, scale a
leaping salmon, or battle a ferocious octopus? All gigantic and
completely safe because they're not real, of course. These
imaginative climbing structures are desperately in need of a
paint job, but our kids don't care a bit. Best of all, Cadboro Bay
Beach, a sheltered, sandy swimming beach, is right here, too.
It's crowded on the weekends, but a popular spot for generations of Victoria children. At the foot of Sinclair Road, Cadboro
Bay.

Where to Stay

As a tourist mecca, Victoria has plenty of hotels downtown. Motor hotels
and motels are scattered along Douglas Street and line both sides of Gorge
Road. Most of these are advertised widely, so you or your travel agent
can easily find them. What we have selected are out-of-the-ordinary
places where we would like to stay because of the location, amenities, or
little personal touches. We have also included a couple of spots – the Y
and UVic – for the budget-conscious.

The Beaconsfield ❖ "An Edwardian Inn" is what the small sign outside the Beaconsfield discreetly announces. If your idea of a
fine hotel includes antique furniture, canopy beds, goose-down
comforters, and fireplaces, you'll like this 1905 converted man-

sion. It's located on a quiet residential street within easy walking distance of downtown. Room rates—from $90—include a full breakfast. At 998 Humboldt at Vancouver, 384-4044.

Abigail's ❖ Sister establishment to one of our other favourites, The Beaconsfield Inn, Abigail's offers the same kind of upscale B & B ambiance. Look for down quilts, jacuzzis, fireplaces and wonderfully satisfying breakfasts in this tastefully restored turn-of-the-century mansion within easy walking distance of downtown. Doubles from $90. 906 McClure Street, 388-5363.

The Bedford ❖ Jill's picky sister Hilary staying in, and approved of, the elegant Bedford. It's in the style of small European hotels with emphasis on personal service and lots of luxuries such as down quilts and jacuzzis. The Red Currant dining room is in the capable hands of Anne Milne (late of Cafe Splash and Bishop's in Vancouver), and the little Garrick's Head Pub tucked away on the Bastion Square side of the hotel is handy for light meals. Double room rates start at $135. 1140 Government Street, 384-6835

Holland House ❖ Here's a hotel with a difference: original art hangs on the walls and musical soirees occasionally take place on Sunday afternoons. We've had sophisticated guests from Toronto be impressed with the ambiance, with includes four poster beds and fireplaces. Adults only, no smoking. Gourmet breakfast included in room rates which start at $100 couble. 595 Michigan Street, 384-6644.

Point-No-Point Resort ❖ This is one of Victoria's well-kept secrets: the seaside hideaway, close to town and yet a million miles away, that is perfect for those who are looking for privacy and relaxation without crowds, traffic, or television. Simply-furnished housekeeping cottages line the waterfront, overlooking half a mile of private beach. (Our very favourite cabin is the beautiful new one, with a glassed-in sun porch, right at the ocean's edge.) Just bring your groceries, everything else is supplied—including wood for your evening fire. Lunches and afternoon teas are served in the Tea House seven days a week (see *Where to Eat*). About forty miles west of Victoria on Highway 14, R.R. #2, Sooke, 646-2020.

Sooke Harbour House ❖ Perched on the edge of the water at the end of Whiffen Spit Road, Sooke Harbour House is a romantic's dream come true. Jill spent her wedding night here, in this perfect West Coast setting. The food in this combination hotel and restaurant is superb: imaginative, artistic, and delectable. Cosmopolitan owners Sinclair and Frederica Philip use the freshest ingredients possible, including herbs and vegetables from their own garden, seafood from Sooke fishermen, and meat from local farmers.

The charming rooms upstairs in the original building are furnished, like the restaurant, in homey country style. A new building, adjacent to the original and blending sympathetically with in, contains the newer rooms, each decorated in a nautical theme (mermaid, octopus...). One room is wheelchair accessible, several sport hot tubs, all have private patios or balconies and ocean views. Room rates – doubles from $95 – include breakfast and lunch. 1528 Whiffen Spit Road, off Sooke Road, past the village of Sooke, 642-3421.

University of Victoria ❖ Check into the academic circle, for one night or a whole summer, and enjoy a student's-eye view of this beautiful campus. Rooms here tend to be spartan, as you'd expect in a place that is designed for students, but you won't find much to complain about in these modern, attractive surroundings. Rates are attractive too: singles run about $22, including a full breakfast in the residence dining room; doubles are about $34, with breakfast. The university is located in the Gordon Head area of Victoria, with frequent bus service to downtown and back. Enter via Ring Road, which circles the whole campus, from Finnerty Road or Henderson Road. Call the UVic Housing and Conference Services for reservations: 721-8395.

YM-YWCA ❖ Our recommendation for women travellers is one of the thirty-one rooms at the Y. Single or double rooms are available—singles are $23 plus a refundable $4 key deposit; doubles are $39 plus two key deposits. You have to pad down the hall to the common bath, and the rooms are very basic (bed, chair, table, closet)... but the coffee shop is right downstairs, everything is clean and shiny, and you're not paying Hilton prices. Best of all, you get to use the Y facilities, including the pool, at no extra charge. Summer visits are limited to two weeks, but in the winter you'll find some long-term residents. Book well ahead as this is a popular place with smart tourists who want good value and a convenient, close-to-everything location. 880 Courtenay Street at Quadra, 386-7511.

BED AND BREAKFAST

Now a word about Victoria's bed and breakfast establishments. *Tourism Victoria*, at 812 Wharf Street (382-2127), has a small mountain of information about private and commercial bed & breakfast places. These range from modern homes in the northern subdivisions of town, to turn-of-the-century heritage buildings right downtown.

Central Island

The Cowichan Valley

We used to think of the Cowichan Valley as a mere pitstop along the highway—a long strip of gas stations and fast food joints. It was only when we began research for this book that we discovered the *other* Valley: the charming communities that are well worth a scenic drive up in the morning for some interesting small-town shopping (we like **Kenneth and Station streets** in Duncan best), lunch with the locals at the **Red Rooster** or the **Arbutus Cafe**, and a stop at the **Cobble Hill Herb Farm** on the way back. A super day trip, and only a pleasant hour's drive from Victoria or Nanaimo.

We also recommend a side trip east of the main highway, on **Cowichan Bay Road** which winds beside the water and through picturesque farmland. Stop for a leg-stretching break at the little strip of marinas, restaurants, and shops lining the road at **Cowichan Bay**, and walk out on the wharf to admire the boats and the view of the Bay, Separation Point, and Saltspring Island.

In the other direction (south and west) is **Shawnigan Lake**, a popular summer vacation area for Victoria residents. You can drive all around the lake (keeners can bike this fourteen-mile length of road) with a stop at **The Galley** for snack. The lake offers water recreation—swimming, boating, sailboarding, and fishing—and the surrounding countryside is the site of cross-country skiing in winter. (Check with local Visitors Information Centres for specifics.)

Chemainus, just north of Duncan, is a must-see. In fact, we're so crazy about this little town that we've given it its own sub-heading at the end of this section.

Welcome to the Cowichan Valley.

What to See and Do

Art Mann Kin Park ❖ On the way to Maple and Genoa Bays, just east of the town of Duncan, you might like to scoot down Indian Road to Art Mann Kin Park. Facilities include picnic tables, playground equipment, and boat launches, but the real reason to come is to admire *Quamichan Lake*, where swans and geese float about and small children fish enthusiastically from the banks.

Bright Angel Provincial Park ❖ There's an enchanting "Wind in the Willows" quality to this park. The first thing your kids are going to love about Bright Angel is the suspension bridge spanning the Koksilah River (which, at this point, is little more than a creek). They can terrify their parents by making the bridge swing crazily; they can add more grey hairs by leaping out over the river on one of the rope swings tied to the trees on the bank. Trails wind along most of the 1,500 feet of river frontage, and continue throughout the covered picnic shelter and, of course, toilet facilities. To get there: turn west off the Trans-Canada onto Allenby at the traffic lights south of Duncan, then turn left immediately onto Koksilah Road. You'll drive through a pretty pastoral landscape – watch for the Bright Angel sign.

British Columbia Forest Museum Park ❖ While not exactly off the beaten track (it's situated right on the Trans-Canada Highway just north of Duncan), we have included the Forest Museum because it's a *must!* If you were intrigued by the logging exhibits in Victoria's Provincial Museum (and if you haven't been there, turn right around and go back) this Museum Park will tell you even more about trees – and then some. The very reasonable admission fee ($4 for adults, $3.50 for students and seniors, $2 for ages 6 to 12, under 6 free) allows you to ride the steam train around the hundred acre site, past a farm homestead and logging camp, through natural forest, and over a trestle spanning Somenos Lake. Alight at North Cowichan

Station and tour the Log Museum, a fascinating display of old photos, artifacts, and beautifully-executed diaramas that trace the history of man and the forest. There's a hands-on activity area with giant logs to gape at and a hand car to ride, as well as a picnic area and snack bar. The kids will love it, and we think you will, too. Open daily from May to late September. Look for the signs along the highway, 746-1251.

Cowichan and Chemainus Valleys Ecomuseum ❖ The Ecomuseum is an interesting concept. It is, in effect, a 400-square-mile "museum without walls." Ladysmith marks the northern terminus, Mill Bay the south, the Vancouver Island shoreline the east and the Nitinat Triangle the west. Instead of a building housing artifacts, the Ecomuseum is a distinctive geographical region, and the "collection" is everything—from birds to mills—within it. One of the aims of the Ecomuseum is to preserve the logging heritage of the valleys via such exhibits as the murals at Chemainus and the Forest Museum in Duncan. Find brochures outlining driving tours through the Ecomuseum at the Duncan Travel Infocentre at 381 Trans-Canada Highway, 746-4421, or at the Ecomuseum Office, 160 Jubilee Street, Duncan, 746-1611.

Chemainus River ❖ Rockhounders are reminded that the riverbed of the Chemainus River is the source of an unusual soapstone and the rare flowerstone. The latter is a stone with flower-shaped quartz crystals in it—the older the rock, the bigger the flower. Best spot for hunting for these unique souvenirs of your trip is just off Highway 1 by the double bridge, immediately north of the Mount Sicker intersection. Watch for the Esso gas station about seven miles north of Duncan.

Golf ❖ Golfers! The Cowichan Gold and Country Club, right on the Trans-Canada highway, welcomes visitors.

Kerry Park ❖ Here's a short walk for short little legs needing to climb out of the back seat for some exercise: a scenic jogging trail starts from the north-east corner of the parking lot beside the Kerry Park Recreation Centre (west of the village of Mill Bay). It follows Shawnigan Creek, and locals tell us it's especially nice in the fall when the leaves have changed colour.

99

Spectacle Lake Provincial Park ❖ We like our provincial parks left in natural condition, unmarked by blacktopped roads, concrete washrooms, and other evidence of society's need to impose order on an unruly universe. Hence, we prefer Spectacle Lake to nearby *Bamberton Park* (a prime example of the aforementioned "Let's-Tidy-Up-Nature" thinking). Spectacle Lake lies serene and peaceful, awaiting the trout fisherman or the swimmer. Walkers can ramble along the trails circling the lake and enjoy a restful nature break. Look for the signs on Highway 1 leading west to the park, just north of Shawnigan Lake Road.

Summer Chamber Music School ❖ Shawnigan Lake School is the setting for a world class chamber music school each summer. Students stage public concerts every week. Call the school— 1975 Renfrew Road in Shawnigan Lake—at 743-5516 for information on when and how much.

Where to Eat

Arbutus Cafe ❖ One of us finally made it. Before the first edition of Island Treasures we had tried—repeatedly—to eat at the Arbutus Cafe because the locals raved about it. We were always unsuccessful and eventually put it in anyway, on the theory that a place this popular *had* to be good. Since then, the tiny cafe has expanded and Carolyn got lucky on one visit to Duncan and secured a table, outside on the raised balcony. We are happy to report all those hundreds of Duncan residents were right—the Arbutus Cafe is great. Try it. 195 Kenneth Street, 746-5443.

The Galley Coffee Shop ❖ Located at the Shawnigan Lake Marina, the Galley Coffee Shop offers an outdoor patio area overlooking the water, or indoor seating in an old fashioned diner, complete with a short counter and stools, or long booths. You'll find small children lined up for ice cream cones, home baking, and country music playing on the countertop radio. The Galley's menu can only be described as "down home"—where else have you seen an entire section devoted to Canned Favourites like port and beans? We recommend this (*not* for the pork and beans) as a pleasant water view stop for coffee and the famous butter tarts. Follow the signs just south of the village to Shawnigan Lake Marina.

Gibson's Thrifty Foods ❖ When you're trekking past the village of Mill Bay, and you feel the need for a little something, turn east off the Trans-Canada at Deloume Road and into the parking lot of this supermarket. The in-store bakery contains a delightfully homey sitting area with a big bay window, pretty wallcoverings, and colonial-style tables and chairs. Buy a muffin or sweet from the display case, help yourself to coffee from the pot, and enjoy at well deserved sit-down. Although the giant cookies were recommended as the locals' favourites, we loved the currant and almond loaf even more – delicious!

Alternatively, head next door to **The Creamery** if you want a real meal. Nachos, made-to-order sandwiches, giant burgers on cheese buns, homemade soup, warm muffins, and fresh salads are the order of the day here. In the summer, sit outside at an umbrella-topped table and soak up some rays; in colder weather, warm up inside with a hot frothy apple juice with cinnamon. This is pressed from the fruit of a locally famous grower named Bezzola. You'll never taste anything closer to the taste of a real apple than Bezzola's juice, hot or cold. Friendly service and a pretty green and cream decor make this spot a winner.

Oak and Carriage ❖ Proving once again that pub food does not necessarily mean pickled eggs and melton mowbray pies, the Oak and Carriage offers an every-changing selection of daily specials on the chalkboard, including excellent homemade soups like the thick beefy goulash. Go for the schnitzel (highly recommended by locals) if it happens to be on the board when you visit. The interior is suitably oak beamed and Tudor-ish with obligatory fireplace and dart boards. Although the upholstery looks a bit tired, we're happy to report that the bathrooms are spotlessly clean – always an important sign, we think. Very popular with Valley residents. Just off the beaten track at 3287 Cowichan Road. (Follow Trunk Road west from downtown Duncan. It becomes Government Street – briefly – and then becomes Cowichan Lake Road) Phone: 746-4144.

The Red Rooster ❖ This is your classic roadside diner – a non-descript red and white building beside the Trans-Canada Highway, about seven miles north of Duncan. This is *not*, however, the classic roadside diner made famous in the 1970 film *Five Easy Pieces*. (Everyone had told us this myth; a Victoria resident who had worked on the film set us straight after the first edition of Island Treasures appeared.) Jack Nicholson should have eaten here though – the staff is cheerful and friendly, and the decor is still, thank heavens, untrendily Early Diner with arborite tables, vinyl padded booths, a counter with stools and paper napkins in chrome boxes. The food is wonderful, from the fresh baked pies to the homemade soup. On one visit, the couple at the next booth had driven south from Nanaimo to meet another couple who had headed north from Victoria – just for breakfast! This is one of our favourite spots for a delicious, home-cooked, inexpensive meal. Closed Monday and Tuesday; on other days look for the traffic lights by the gas station at Mount Sicker Road, 8432 Trans-Canada Highway, 246-9342.

Pioneer House Restaurant ❖ A magnificent bar dominates this roadside restaurant, transplanted from a Montana saloon of the Wild West era. While you're enjoying a delicious breakfast, a burger served on a fresh Kaiser bun, or one of the legendary homemade cinnamon buns, you can imagine the days of cowboys, boots planted on the bar rail, sliding mugs of beer along the length of the bar. An open fireplace, authentic log construction and a rustic Western ambiance (including washrooms marked "Bucks" and "Does") complete the illusion. Whippletree Junction, 4675 Trans-Canada Highway, two miles south of Duncan, 746-5848.

Lisette's ❖ Tucked away in the back of the Canada building is the charming, family-run Lisette's. The menu, which changes seasonally, is broadly continental and offers such European specialties as schnitzel with mushroom sauce. Everything is homemade, starting with the bran muffins to go with your morning coffee. Inside the building at 225 Canada Avenue, 746-8286.

Salsa's ❖ The many variations wrought upon the humble tortilla in Mexican cuisine are the specialty in the engaging Salsa's. It's cheap, it's good and we liked the way the handsome host danced between the tables. It's also very tiny so go early or late or make reservations for lunch or dinner. Closed Sunday and Monday. Upstairs, off a little lane at 119 Kenneth Street, 746-4302.

Here are a few spots for that special occasion—when you don't mind spending a bit more on fine dining, plush decor, and exceptional service.

Bluenose Restaurant ❖ The Bluenose serves "the best Dungeness crab in Canada," according to one of our Duncan friends. Who are we to argue? Messy but good, the crab is just one of the shellfish options in this steak and seafood house perched on the edge of Cowichan Bay. Prime ribs, barbecued ribs, and chicken are available for non-fish lovers. Dinner only; the adjoining coffee shop takes care of quick snacks. At 1765 Cowichan Bay Road, 748-2841.

The Inner Passage Dining Room ❖ This well-known restaurant is at the Inn at the Water Resort (see *Where to Stay*), and is another favourite spot for loyal regulars as well as visiting tourists. Breakfast, lunch, afternoon tea, and dinner are served overlooking beautiful Cowichan Bay. Dinner specials included a varied selection of crêpes – stuffed with shrimp, crab, scallops, and such—or beef and seafood choices. It's at 1681 Botwood Lane in Cowichan Bay—look for the signs pointing you to the Inn. Dinner reservations recommended, 748-6222.

Mai Tai Dining Lounge ❖ Perched up on the bank overlooking Maple Bay, east of Duncan, is the exotic Mai Tai, a wood-and-glass structure which looks like it should be located under South Sea Island palms rather than among the evergreens of coastal BC. If you walk through the wooden tunnel entrance, past ivy-rimmed pools, and into the high-ceilinged dining room, you will find a creditable seafood-plus restaurant and a stunning water view that equals any foreign shore. Long a favourite of local residents, especially for the Sunday Brunch smorgasbord. Follow the Maple and Genoa Bay signs from Duncan to 6161 Genoa Bay Road, 746-7796.

The Masthead ❖ Sporting a nautical decor appropriate to its bayside location in the Valley's oldest building, the Masthead offers seafood dinners, plus a Sunday seafood buffet brunch, both highly recommended by our resident sources. At 1705 Cowichan Bay Road in the village of Cowichan Bay, 748-3714.

Where to Shop

Brenda's Favorites ❖ We mention this Duncan shop because it is another source for the wickedly caloric Harlan's Chocolates, handmade on Saltspring Island. You can also get ice cream on a hot day, or stock up on coffee beans with unusual names like "Tanzania Peaberry." You might even find a nice little gift among the pottery and china selection. In the Village Green Mall, 180 Central, behind the Duncan Plaza on Trunk Road, 746-4088.

Cobble Hill Herb Farm ❖ If, like us, you are interested in gardening and cooking, a stop at the family-run Cobble Hill Herb Farm is a must. Wander along the brick paths of the traditionally laid-out gardens, absorbing all the sights and scents of familiar and not-so-familiar plants. Then pop into the showroom to see dried herbs (with the current crop hanging from the ceiling), homemade herb vinegars and jellies, dried flowers, wreaths, and potpourris. Bees from a neighbour's hive buzz around the herb garden – their honey is sold in the shop as well. Easy to locate; turn west off the Trans-Canada Highway onto Cobble Hill Road at the first set of lights north of Mill Bay. The farm is just 200 yards along, at #3025, 743-3094.

Hill's Indian Crafts ❖ You're in deepest Cowichan sweater territory here, the home base of these hand-knitted pullovers and zip front cardigans. Outdoors types love them because the raw wool sheds water and keeps the wearer toasty warm while fishing, hiking or walking the dog. Hill's Indian Crafts have top quality sweaters, plus toques, mitts, and socks if your budget can't handle a sweater. 5206 Trans-Canada Highway, 746-6731. Incidentally, if your're interested in native crafts, take a look at Arts of the Swaqwun Gallery. It specializes in Coast

Salish art, carving, silkscreens, jewelry and rockwork. Next to the Saan store at 80 Trunk Road, 746-5000.

Cowichan Opportunity Centre ❖ In our eternal quest for the perfect butter tart, we set out to explore the *Cowichan Opportunity Centre*'s bakery. A listener who heard us interviewed on Duncan's CKAY radio station tipped us off to this sheltered workshop and we're glad she did. The staff turn out an amazing variety of goods in the kitchen here, ranging from the sweet (cinnamon buns, giant cookies) to the savoury (pork pies, lasagna). A number of local restaurants and pubs serve the kitchen's homestyle fare; if we lived in Duncan, we'd be steady customers for party hors d'oevres like sausage rolls and baby quiches. This is a commercial kitchen, not a neighbourhood bakery, so be prepared to buy goods packaged by the dozen or, in the case of squares like Nanaimo bars, brownies, and toffee shortbread, by the panful. Trust us, this is no hardship. It is only through extreme self-control that we manage to avoid devouring their gorgeous butter tarts a dozen at a time. To find this out-of-the-way gem, turn west off the Trans-Canada Highway onto James Street. (Easy to see - just look for the world's largest hockey stick, formerly at home at Expo 86 in Vancouver and now permanently set up at the Cowichan Community Centre.) Turn right onto Clements Street just past the paint store, and you'll see the Opportunity Centre at 35856. Phone 746-7411.

Rainbow Gallery ❖ Fans of Robert Bateman like this gallery's emphasis on Bateman and other wildlife artists. The gallery offers professional framing, and the owner is both knowledgeable and friendly. 127 Station Street, 748-2339.

Sages ❖ What may pass as just a framing shop deserves a second look even if you're not having anything professionally framed. Sages adjoining gift gallery is dominated by a handsome antique display case, containing attractive hand-crafted jewelry. Both of us have picked up some terrific stuff here for gift-giving: authentic fossils, carved wooden decoy ducks, and nifty fishing accessories like the zippered sheepskin-lined case Jill picked up for her brother-in-law's fishing flies. At 24 Station Street, 748-0888.

Sins ❖ Virginal nighties compete with the brothel look at *Sins*. There is white here, but it's silk, sheer, and slit up to the waist and down to the navel. The widows are very merry and adorned with black lace, and there are also sensual silk shortie nighties in jewel tones with matching kimonos. Exquisite! It's all for the bedroom but not necessarily for sleeping. The shop is tucked away at the back of a retail complex at 281 Canada Avenue; 748-7467.

While here, check out the other little shops that carry everything from Esprit designer fashions to greeting cards to terrific shopping bags. We're not kidding—these are sturdy-handled bags with great graphics. (You'll need a bag to cart all your souvenirs around in so you might as well have a chic one.)

Kenneth Street

Our favourite area for Cowichan Valley shopping is Kenneth Street in Duncan. We think you'll enjoy the variety and selection offered by the merchants along this attractive row.

The Tulip ❖ Starting at the intersection of Canada Avenue, find a smaller version of Jill's favourite Dutch deli in Victoria. The Tulip is jam-packed full of Dutch meats, cheeses, chocolate, candies, and traditional cookies. Savoury spices and flavouring mixes for Indonesian specialties, as well as the famous Delft blue kitchenware and Dutch language books are also stocked. At 21 Kenneth Street, 748-0144.

Pots and Paraphernalia ❖ There are kitchen stores in bigger centres that could take a lesson in display from Pots and Paraphernalia's owner. Stock is colour-grouped to create an eyecatching look, and shadow box shelving enables you to appreciate every attractive coffee mug. Even the neatly-folded dishcloths are arranged according to colour in baskets! The front of the store contains cooking gear and fresh coffee beans; in the back are bathroom and bedroom needs, including fragrant Crabtree and Evelyn toiletries. This place makes buying a humble potato peeler a delight. At #115, 748-4614.

Fabrications ❖ Fabrications no longer stocks the decorative sewing supplies and children's wear we originally admired. They have, however, expanded their range of women's clothing, accessories, and jewelry. We love their earring selection which includes some unusual knock-em-dead designs. Last time we were in, we also drooled over white cotton nightdresses (those of the vestal virgin variety) and the terrific sweat tops with appliqued features. Prices are still ridiculously reasonable. 125 Kenneth Street; 746-4751.

Volume One Bookstore ❖ If your next project is to write a romance novel, you'll love the romance writer's phrasebook that we discovered at Volume One Bookstore (pick one phrase from each chapter...) We also found a good selection of cooking, gardening, homebuilding, and remodelling titles, and our kids approved of the children's section. Posters, cards, and prints round out the inventory in this engaging book shop. At #149, 748-1533. Second location at #19-2720 Mill Bay Road in Cobble Hill.

The Red Balloon ❖ This is the kind of toy store that parents and grandparents love. Handmade felt mobiles, creative European puzzles and wooden toys, and co-operative family games are crammed in here – and not a battery-operated toy to be seen! If you're after unique, non-commercial toys, selection here is good. At #145, 748-5545.

Westphalia Bakery ❖ Warning! Do not enter the Westphalia Bakery is you are remotely concerned about keeping your daily calorie count below 5000. We had heard about this Duncan landmark from several sources in the area before we set foot inside, so we were prepared for the famous rye and multigrain bread baked here. This is bread the way bread should look and taste: dark, heavy, and wonderful! Jill's favourite sweets include the poppy seed strudel, apple fritters, and cinnamon donuts. Carolyn likes their pizza buns – a quick, not-too-big lunch on the run. Duncan locals recommend the Black Forest Cake as "the best in town," but we were too stuffed to sample so we're taking their word for it. Another delightful discovery, at #187, 746-4622.

Mill Bay Salvation Army Family Thrift Store ❖ We have to admit it. When someone first recommended the Thrift Store to us, we both lifted our eyebrows are said, "Oh, really?" But it kept coming up, from various sources, so we finally decided to take a look. What we found was a clean bright store, with merchandise nicely displayed, clothes on hangers arranged by colour—even the odd dishes and vases were lined up according to colour on their respective shelves! We also found bargains: brand new Tabi pants for $1.75, and lined, pure wool pants from Mr. Jax for $3.80. We have both hit the jackpot every time we visit here—admittedly, we do have to search through a lot of dross to find the gold, but that's half the fun of this shop. Turn west off the Trans-Canada Highway at the Shawnigan-Mill Bay Road, and look for the small complex at #855, 743-2123.

Whippletree Junction ❖ Pull off the main highway about 3 1/2 miles south of Duncan to spend a little while wandering around this jumble of shops. Second-hand goods, from militaria to office furniture, abound. You can find Christmas decorations year round at *Christmas House*, crafts and supplies at *The Loom*, plus jewelry, leather goods, wicker, and ice cream cones. Chris Hill of *Wagon Wheel Antiques* carries the best supply of obsolete ammunition north of Warshal's in Seattle. The buildings date from the turn of the century and were moved to this site, where they resemble an old-fashioned village lining a square paved with old brick.

Where to Stay

The Valley is dotted with campsites, family cottages, and modern motels. One of our favourites is this hotel, which offers a water view from its airy dining room, The Inner Passage, and nearby lounge, as well as from each of its fifty-seven one-bedroom suites (kitchenettes are available at extra cost). These are some of the most spacious units we've every stayed in—more like full apartments than hotel rooms. There's an indoor pool, sauna, and whirlpool; friendly staff can arrange fishing, sailing, diving, golfing, or tennis on the island's only grass courts. Rates start at $55 double. We like this location for quick getaway weekends from Victoria, and as a convenient jumping-off spot for exploring the Cowichan Valley. It's at 1681 Botwood Lane, Cowichan Bay, 748-6222. Look for the Cowichan Bay sign east of the Trans-Canada Highway.

Fairburn Farm ❖ And for something completely different—how about a farm vacation at Fairburn Farm? This is a 130-acre working farm. All you homesick prairie types can pitch in and help with the chores. There are six guest bedrooms in the 19th century farmhouse, and the wholesome meals incorporate all the bounty from the land—look for homebaked bread and pies, and even fresh butter and cheese. Guests can join in seasonal activities like maple syrup gathering, lambing, haymaking, or harvesting—or just hike along the rural trails and relax. Your kids will love sleigh rides in the winter, and buggy rides in the summer. Even if you're not staying overnight, you can enjoy the hearty farmhouse fare; lunch, dinner, or afternoon tea are served to the public by reservation only—forty-eight hours advance notice is required. Rates range from $60 to $115, with family rates available. Reservations are compulsory—contact owners Darrel and Anthea Archer at R.R. #7, Duncan, V9L 4W4 or 746-4637. The farm is located 1½ miles along Jackson Road, off Koksilah Road which runs west of the Trans-Canada, or off Allenby Road in Duncan.

Grove Hall Estate ❖ Take a 1912 Samuel Maclure–designed mansion, fill it with museum-quality antiques, set it amid 17 acres adjoining Quamichan Lake, and you have sumptuous Grove Hall. This is B & B with swank. Amenities include a tennis court, billiard room (with antique table), and three spacious guest rooms each decorated to a unique theme (Singapore, Indonesian, and Siamese—the latter with, of course, *twin* beds).

The interior is breathtakingly filled with exquisite antiques and magnificent carpets collected by owners Frank and Judy Oliver during their travels to the Orient. Doubles start at under $100 and include a hearty farm-style breakfast. No children, pets, or smoking please. 6159 Lakes Road (east of the Trans-Canada Highway, off Trunk Road in Duncan) 746-6152.

Heron Hill Bed & Breakfast ❖ Unlike many B & B establishments which tend towards adults only, Vicki and Gordon Simpson of Heron Hill welcome families. There are three guest bedrooms on the ground floor of Heron Hill; the largest has twin beds plus a set of bunk beds. Guests share an attractive bath and a cozy sitting room (with fireplace, TV, a private patio and a kitchenette). Vicki teaches preschool so the place is well-supplied with toys, books, and games. The house is modern, set high on a hill with terrific sea views. The Simpsons also operate Heron Hill as a small farm—another bonus for visitors with children, who will be enchanted by the baby lambs in the spring. We like staying here very much. We especially like the warm and hospitable Simpsons. Reasonable rates start at $30 single, doubles at $40, and a family of four at $55. At 3745 Granfield Place (ten minutes south of Duncan, take Fisher east off the Trans-Canada, right on Cheeke, right on Telegraph, left on Aros to Granfield), Cobble Hill, V0R 1L0, 743-3855.

Sahtlam Lodge ❖ One of our sources spent a very satisfactory naughty weekend here, in one of the little cottages dotted about the expansive riverside grounds. She rather liked the rustic appeal of log walls chinked with moss, but if you'd prefer something more polished, try one of the charming bedrooms in the main lodge.

The Cowichan River, famous for fly fishing, flows past the lodge. Left your hip waders back home? Just sit on the big veranda that wraps around most of the building and watch (and listen to) the river. Locals claim this river as a great "tubing" venue; climb aboard your inner tube upstream and float lazily (and sometimes crazily!) towards town. Indoors, the great fireplace in the living room invites feet up on the padded foot rail while you read your trashy novel. The food is good; we recommend an outdoor veranda table in the summer. BYOB as there is no liquor licence. Campers take note: owners Val and Dave Hignell have added a sleeping platform with tented sides to the property for slightly upscale campouts. At the end of a very pleasant scenic drive – 5720 Riverbottom Road, R.R. #2, Duncan, V9L 1N9, 748-7738.

For details of Bed and Breakfast accommodation in the Cowichan Valley, contact the Duncan-Cowichan Travel Infocentre at 381 Trans-Canada Highway, Duncan, V9L 3R5, 746-4421.

Cowichan Lake

On your way north or south, you might want to plan a mini-trip west, on Highway 18, to see the communities lining Cowichan Lake. The turn-off is just a few minutes north of Duncan, and the road leads through the Cowichan Valley Demonstration Forest. Signs indicate scenic lookouts and explanations of what you're looking at in this forest management project.

Cowichan is the largest fresh-water lake on Vancouver Island and, yes, the fishing's great here. Some claim that the Cowichan River makes this area the "Fly-Fishing Capital of the World." As if to confirm that boast, within two minutes of unpacking our picnic lunch during our last visit at the **Kinsmen Duck Pond Park**, we watched a very small boy land a very large trout from the foot bridge. The park, at the corner of Park and River Roads in the village of Lake Cowichan, has a children's playground and a river swimming hold, complete with floating dock, diving board, and slide.

We also like the picnic park across South Shore Road from the Riverside Inn, which has tables, an unusual fountain, and restrooms on the banks of the Cowichan River.

There are many ideal spots along the river and around the lakeshore for picnics. Make a quick visit to the Co-op if you forgot to load up the picnic basket before you left home.

Before or after your picnic, we recommend a stop at the **Kaatza Station Museum**. Housed in an old E & N railway station, this community museum does a very creditable job of preserving and interpreting the logging, lumbering, mining and railroading heritage of the Cowichan Lake area. A series of tableaux, à la the Royal BC Museum, graphically display pioneer domestic life, the claustrophobic enclosure of a copper mine, and the retail charms of an old-fashioned general store. The museum's excellent collection of old photographs enhances the displays. Open 12–4 Thursday to Monday from Victoria Day to Labour Day; 1–4 Friday,

Saturday and Sunday the rest of the year. At Saywell Park, South Shore Road, 749-6142.

Complement a visit to the museum during the summer season with a free tour of the nearby forests and mills.

Forest Tours ❖ Demonstration forest, July and August only, Saturdays at 11 a.m. North Cowichan Municipal Forest, July and August, Sundays at 11 a.m. Woods tour, May 1 to September 27th, Monday, Wednesday and Friday 10 a.m. to 3 p.m. and Tuesday from 2 to 4 p.m. Leave from Fletcher Challenge Tour Centre at Lake Cowichan.

Mill Tours ❖ From May 4th to September 28th, Fletcher Challenge Heritage Mill at Youbou, Fridays 1 and 3 p.m. Meet the guide at the mill entrance. MacMillan Bloedel Mill at Chemainus, Tuesdays at 1 p.m. Catch the bus at BC Forest Museum, Duncan. Canadian Pacific Forest Products Mill at Ladysmith, Tuesdays July 31st, August 7th and 14th only. Catch the bus at the BC Forest Museum, Duncan. For reservations for any of the tours, call 746-1611.

You can drive all around the perimeter of the twenty-mile long lake. Only part of the circle is paved, however; the rest is public access logging road. Allow at least two hours if you decide to do the circuit. Along the way you will pass the logging communities of **Mesachie Lake** and **Honeymoon Bay**. In spite of its almost irresistibly romantic name, this village is an industrial forest community, site of log booms and company housing. The bay was named by a Mr. March who brought his new bride to homestead here on the lakeshore.

The nine-hole **March Meadows Golf Club and Driving Range**, just west of the townsite of Honeymoon Bay, is open to visitors.

Almost next door you'll see the sign marking the **Honeymoon Bay Wildflower Reserve**, which is a woodland delight during the months of April, May, and June. An illustrative board in the parking lot describes the wildflowers (including enchanters' nightshade, trillium, and cow parsnip) you'll find here.

Also nearby is **Gordon Bay Provincial Park**, known among Islanders as one of the few provincial campsites with *hot showers*. Boat launching ramps and a pebbly swimming beach are here too, but watch out for the steep drop-off not far from shore.

The North Shore Road from the village of Lake Cowichan takes you, not surprisingly, along the north shore of the lake, to the village of **Youbou** (pronounced "you-boe"), home of a major lumber mill. This route passes the *Teleglobe Canada Satellite Earth Station,* where you can take a free weekday tour during the summer months (a must for the scientifically minded), and historic *Meade Creek,* where modern-day goldpanners still like to try their luck.

Hiking, kayaking, and canoeing are other popular pastimes here. Stop at the Lake Cowichan Travel Infocentre at the junction of Highway 18 and Lake Cowichan Road for more information about this pleasant and scenic valley, or phone 749-4141.

Chemainus

Just north of Duncan is Chemainus, "The Little Town That Did." Did what? Instead of rolling over and dying when the MacBlo sawmill shut down in the summer of 1983, Chemainiacs turned to the walls of their public buildings and covered them with beautiful, larger-than-life murals, creating an instant tourist attraction. Is it worth detouring off the main highway to view these award-winning works of art? You betcha!

To get here by car, turn east off Highway 1 onto Henry Road (green highway signs warn you it's coming up). Turn left just past the Mount Brenton public golf course and follow the Chemainus Road into the centre of town. If you're coming here from points north, a pleasant alternate route is to turn left just south of Ladysmith and travel through the pretty seaside community of Saltair. The E & N train will also deposit you right by a mural.

What to See and Do

The murals, of course. Virtually every public building has some aspect of the town's history depicted on its walls; the overall effect is quite awesome. New murals are added yearly, so if you're visiting during the summer months you're likely to see an artist at work."

Tours ❖ There are various ways to tour the murals. The simplest and cheapest is to follow the yellow footsteps painted on the sidewalk and let them lead you around.

For a mere $1, you can pick up a map for a self-guided walking tour with a bit of explanation of what you're looking at. Maps are available at the Pharmasave on Willow Street and in most gift stores in Chemainus.

If you're interested in more details about the murals, look for the Book of Murals. It costs $12.95 and makes a nice memento of your visit. The book has a map in the back and is sold in most shops in Chemainus.

Group travellers can contact the Festival of Murals Society to arrange for a volunteer guide. Cost is $2 per person and you get to hear some interesting tales of Chemainus's history from a local. Call 246-4701.

New in the summer of 1990 is a novel way to tour the murals: via a mini-motorized train! Tours take approximately an hour and the train operates daily all summer season and on weekends and holidays during the winter.

Waterwheel Park ❖ When you start to feel hot and bothered after all this mural gazing, grab an ice cream and retreat to shady Waterwheel Park, across from the Fire Hall and RCMP Station, at Willow Street and Waterwheel Crescent. The wheel in the park is a smaller replica of the one which powered the first Chemainus sawmill in June 1862.

The park has been spruced up of late; a wide path leads through it to a lane which takes you to Old Town.

Old Town is centred in lower Chemainus, near the ferry to Thetis Island. More spectacular murals cover the walls of shops and restaurants here. As an extra bonus, you can admire neat cottages and pretty gardens as Old Town is more residential than the Willow Street commercial area. Incidentally, MacBlo has re-opened a smaller, more efficient mill in Chemainus and you can often see ships loading lumber in the harbour.

Kin Park ❖ Kids who are getting antsy should bring their parents along Willow Street to Esplanade Street where they'll see Kin Park. Swings, slides, picnic tables, and a bit of a beach to play on will restore their equanimity.

Where to Eat

You won't starve in Chemainus. Willow Street has various take-out outlets but our favourite remains *Billy's Delight Ice Cream Parlour*. Waffle cones, featuring 28 flavours of ice cream are the specialty here. The sweet aroma which wafts out to the sidewalk will entice you inside to sample Belgian waffles and muffins as well. 9752 Willow Street, 246-4131.

For a sit-down meals, try one of these:

Upstairs Downstairs Cafe ❖ Take a pretty pink and grey interior, plus a second floor balcony for outside dining, add an interesting, varied menu and you've got the Upstairs Downstairs Cafe. A number of vegetarian dishes are offered—although the kitchen also turns out a terrific hamburger. The fries are the best on the Island. Everything is freshly made and attractively presented, and prices are reasonable. 9745 Willow Street, 246-2135.

Tea Leaves & Coffee Beans ❖ This cappuccino bar is a handy spot for a quick pick-me-up. The kitchen turns out very creditable sandwiches and salads, and the coffee and tea, of course, are excellent. An extra plus are diet exchange notes on the menu, an unexpected but thoughtful touch for diabetics and others on restricted diets. 9747 Willow Street, 246-3711.

Where to Shop

"All of Chemainus" replied one of our correspondents to our questionnaire request for Great Gift Ideas.

Yep, serious spenders can shop 'til they drop in Chemainus. Although there are stores stocking everything from books to kitchenware, the main emphasis is on antiques and handcrafts.

Antiques ❖ If you like poking through shelves laden with treasures from yesteryear in search of a pair of silver sugar tongs just like Grandma had, you'll be in collector's nirvana in Chemainus. There are three major centres where over 75 antique dealers have set up shop. Each centre is divided into a series of little rooms where you can browse to your wallet's content. While there is some furniture, the emphasis is more on small collec-tables: silver, jewelry, books, toys, kitchenware, linens, dish-es...(you'll be sorry you gave Grandma's old Fiesta china to charity when you see what it's worth these days.) Collectors of mid-century nostalgia will find odd items such as eight packs of Coca Cola. Prices are surprisingly reasonable. Willow Anti-que Mall is at 9756 Willow Street, 246-4333. Stevenson's Antique Mall, 9877 Maple Street, 246-9908 and Old Town Antiques, 9867 Maple Street, 246-4832 are both in lower Old Town, near the Thetis Island ferry dock.

Handcrafts ❖ It's impossible to tour Chemainus without bumping into a craft store of some sort. Original paintings, limited edition prints, pottery, fabric art, woodwork, jewelry, stained glass...if it's handcrafted, Chemainus has it.

Great West Art ❖ Great West Art remains one of our favourites, both for display and content. The two-level formal gallery holds original art, much of it by mural artists; terra cotta, wood and stone sculpture; and large, raku pottery show pieces. A wood and glass showcase displays precious gemstones, intricately handcut by a master gem-cutter.

The original Willow Street gallery, across from the post office, continues to offer handcrafts, paintings, and pottery; a recently added third gallery, a few steps away, concentrates on limited edition prints and framing. Find these two galleries at 9780A Willow Street and 9764 Willow Street; the fine art gallery entrance is around the corner on Legion Street. Phone 246-2041.

The Showcase Gallery ❖ We liked the original tiny gallery, but like the expanded version even better since there's more room for the pottery, the glasswork, the fabric art and the paintings. 9739 Willow Street, 246-9414.

Heatherfields ❖ We're suckers for shops like this. Offer us potpourri-filled embroidered pillows, baskets of dried flowers and books on English country style and we'll have our chequebooks open. All this and an adjoining Ralph Lauren boutique too. Tucked away on the Willow Street boardwalk, 9752 Willow Street, 246-3281.

The Chemainiac Shop ❖ If you like to show off your travel background by means of your T-shirt, you can add to your collection with an "I'm A Chemainiac" T-shirt from the Chemainiac Shop. Put a pin on your hometown on the wall map which shows where all the thousands of visitors to Chemainus come from. 9752 Willow Street, 246-4621.

Ladysmith

"Ladysmith's major claim to fame is its geographic location: it straddles the 49th parallel", we wrote in the last edition of this book. We went on to dismiss the business section of town as "the usual number of unremarkable shops, cafes and gas stations" and recommended a stop to visit the Arboretum.

That was 1986. This year, we want you to turn west off the highway and go up the hill to the business section. A revitalization/heritage project has restored and smartened Ladysmith's commercial streets, winning the Western Canada Award of Excellence in the process. If you're interested in the evolution of twentieth century business architecture, you'll be delighted by Ladysmith's storefronts. Walking tour maps are available in the Travel Information Centre; signs in shop windows provide building histories and before-and-after photos.

A store we like a lot is *La Piquanticity Gift Shoppe*, for appealing handcrafts and fresh coffee. 440 First Avenue, 245-3411.

What to See and Do

The Arboretum ❖ One thing hasn't changed from our first edition of *Island Treasures*. We *still* recommend a stop at the *Arboretum* on the east side of the highway. Over 25 different specimen trees are planted on this beautiful site (perfect for picnics). Botany buffs can pick up an identification guide at the Travel Information Centre in the Black Nugget Museum. One of the rare species, for instance, is the Dawn Redwood, the "living fossil tree" - thought to be extinct until 1945 when it was discovered in central China. There are logging artifacts here too, such as the 1924 Steam Yarding Donkey, but the old locomotives our children enjoyed climbing on years ago have been relocated to the nearby Railway Museum on the Heritage Harbour Site.

Black Nugget Museum ❖ We like this privately owned museum, a former hotel moved to its current site in 1906. The restored bar room looks like something out of an old western; the owner's impressive collection of antiques and memorabilia in the rest of the hotel is set up as a series of tableaux a la the Royal BC Museum in Victoria. Open noon to 4 p.m. daily; admission $2 adults, children 75 cents, under 7 free. 12 Gatacre Street, 245-4846.

Where to Eat

George's ❖ George's is plunked bare inches from the Trans-Canada Highway, hardly off the beaten track. Despite its proximity to the road, the sunny back veranda is quite quiet and offers a splendid view of the harbour. The fare is continental with lots of seafood. Stop in for lunch on your way up or down the Island, as the lunch selection is varied and interesting. We like it! 413 Esplanade, 245-2292.

The Crow and Gate ❖ About twelve miles north of Ladysmith is our other choice for a stop: the *Crow and Gate*. This is an

English-style country pub, set far back from the road. You can dine outside on the backyard patio overlooking the duck pond, or indoors near the cozy fireplace, under beamed ceilings. The lunch and dinner specials, which change daily, are mostly old standbys like steak and kidney pie, potato cakes, or "bangers and mash." (Hands up those who know what this British favourite is.) We highly recommend this comfortable, popular place, where you are sure to join in for the evening singalongs. It's on Yellow Point Road—watch for signs north of Ladysmith, phone 722-3731. P.S. Cash only please.

Where to Stay

There are a couple of hotels here that have been long time favourites of Victorians—including us—for getaway weekends not too far from home.

Yellow Point Lodge ❖ This is the only privately-owned hotel we know that's affiliated with a registered non-profit society. The Friends of Yellow Point (or FOYPs, as they are affectionately known) have been gathering for working weekends in the off-season for many years, to help fix up the Lodge. For $5 you too can become a FOYP and enjoy all-expense paid winter weekends, painting, clearing brush, or building new cabins. If you prefer to come in the summer as a regular guest, you'll find rustic cabins, a main Lodge building with a stunning view of the water, and a wonderful seclusion in the parkland setting. The staff and the FOYPs are like extended family, and you'll feel part of the family too, within minutes of your arrival. The homemade food is good, and there are snacks (including bed-time cocoa) served in the lounge throughout the day.

A disastrous fire in 1985 destroyed the original log lodge, which had been hand-built by Gerry Hill in the twenties. The Hill family started rebuilding almost as soon as the ashes cooled from the fire.

Leave the kiddies at home as no children under 16 are allowed. Two "must-dos" at Yellow Point: don't miss the sunset as seen from the hot tub outside on the beach rocks; and be sure to visit the little pottery studio nearby, where Ayn Maxham sells her unique bowls and plates, normally found only in pricey Big City shops. You can save some money and go home with a beautiful souvenir of your Yellow Point weekend. The modern cottages are $149 per couple, the more rustic ones are $84 to $114. Oceanview rooms in the main lodge are $149, non-view rooms are $139. All prices include three mountainous meals and endless snacks. R.R. #3, Ladysmith, V0R 2E0, 245-7422. Follow the signs off the highway.

Inn of the Sea ❖ Another popular weekend destination for harried Victorians is Inn of the Sea, only sixty miles north of the city, yet combining maritime wilderness with luxurious comfort. Sixty modern units, ranging from individual rooms to two bedroom suites with full kitchens, are stacked in several low-rise buildings along the waterfront property. Some buildings face their neighbours, so if you'd like a sea view, be sure to ask when you make your reservation. There's a heated outdoor pool, and a fine dining room overlooking the water. Double rates for rooms start at $75. Open year-round at 3600 Yellow Point Road, R.R. #3, Ladysmith, 245-2211.

Nanaimo

Nanaimo, with its population of over 50,000, is Vancouver Island's second largest city. It is also known as the **Hub City**, the **Bathtub Capital of the World**, and the source of that dieter's downfall: the Nanaimo bar. It started as a coal mining community in the last century, but today forestry, tourism, and fishing are its main industries. The Nanaimo waterfront is a major deep sea port, and the Departure Bay ferry terminal is the second largest centre for travellers arriving on, or leaving, the Island. We think Nanaimo has a lot to offer both the day tripper and the long-term tourist, and hope our guide will inspire you to do some exploring on your own here.

What to See and Do

Nanaimo Festival ❖ Over the last few years the Nanaimo Festival has evolved into an exciting and unique form of regional theatre. The Festival commissions plays from Canadian writ-ers, dealing with local subjects, people and legend. This is regional theatre at its best, re-interpreting an area's history for the residents, and giving visitors an insightful view below the surface. The Festival runs from late May to the end of July, and all performances take place in the Malaspina College Theatre. Phone 754-7587 for tickets and information on this year's plays.

And from the sublime to the ridiculous – summertime in Nanaimo is also the occasion for the annual *Bathtub Race*. Daredevil "tubbers," ensconced in their single-person crafts fitted on flat planing boards and powered by 7.5 hp motors, make their way across the thirty-four-mile course to Vancouver's Kitsilano Beach. Two decades after its beginnings as a light-hearted stunt, "tubbing" is now a serious sport, with its own summertime circuit, corporate sponsors, and (the ultimate accolade) television coverage. The Great Race takes place on the third weekend in July, with a week's worth of hoopla – including a parade and soapbox derby – preceding the event.

Malaspina College ❖ From its perch on the lower slopes of Mount Benson, the College commands a stunning view east over the city, harbour, and Strait of Georgia beyond. The 165-acre campus itself is pretty stunning – a prime example of West Coast cedar and beam architecture, blending perfectly into its wooded environment. The buildings are stepping up the hillside, and the grounds offer terraced walkways among wild roses and evergreens. *The Arboretum* has a bark trail winding through a tract of unspoiled natural forest. You will find a log cabin here, built as a class project. Also on campus is the small but lovely *Tamagawa Gardens*, a gift to the College on its tenth anniversary from its sister institution, Tamagawa University in Tokyo. Landscaped the simple, understated Oriental way, with evergreens, azaleas, and a tea house, the garden contains a pool filled with Japanese koi fish that have been raised by fisheries students. The *Madrona Exposition Centre* has two galleries, with touring displays from local and international artists.

To get to the College, go straight up Fifth Street past historic *Harewood Elementary* (where Jill attended school). The College is at 900 Fifth Street on the north side of the road, across from the Canadian Forces Base. Phone 753-3245.

P.S. Just a few minutes away, on the other side of the CF Base, is the *Morrell Wildlife Sanctuary*, located on Nanaimo Lakes Road. The preserve is leased by the College for research and educational programs; you can ramble through a stand of second-growth Douglas firs, or observe a variety of indigenous flora and fauna, plus beavers in the Beaver Pond.

Nanaimo Harbour ❖ Loyal Victorians that we are, we almost hate to say it, but we must reveal this Truth: Nanaimo's harbour is as beautiful as Victoria's. If may even be more interesting to walk along because it's a working harbour—you'll see tugs, fish boats, log booms, and sea planes here. Walk through the chain of charming parks that follow one upon the other along this waterside promenade, offering a wonderful close-up of a deep sea port in action.

Start at **Piper Park** (not to be confused with **Piper's Lagoon**, which we'll come to later), located behind Harbour Mall. The Tourist Bureau office is here as well—follow the signs. You'll also find a petroglyph, a restored turn-of-the-century miner's cottage, a steam locomotive, and a 360 degree view of the harbour and city centre. The **Centennial Museum** is located in this park, with displays of local history, including a coal mine, a blacksmith shop, and a general store.

Below the Museum, on Front Street, is **Log Trophy Park**, which contains (you guessed it) a giant log, donated as a symbol of friendship by Port McNeill citizens. Across Front Street you'll see **McGregor Park**, a handy spot from which to view the fishing fleet in the harbour.

Next comes **The Bastion**. This relic was built by the Hudson's Bay Company in 1853 and, although it has been abandoned for most of its history, is the oldest surviving structure of its kind in the west.

After that you'll walk past the brand new **Seaplane Terminal**, an enchanting building, based on classic Victorian lighthouse design. The next green spot on the walkway is

Georgia Park, one of the city's oldest. If offers an interesting juxtaposition of formal gardens next to a display of authentic Native Indian canoes and totem poles.

Swy-a-lana Lagoon Park, completed in August 1984, is the link between Georgia and Maffeo-Sutton parks. From the bridge you can view the unique manmade tide lagoon, complete with starfish and sea cucumbers. Native Indians operate a traditional carving shed here.

At neighbouring *Maffeo-Sutton Park* you'll find a putting green, tennis courts, a nautical theme adventure playground, picnic tables, and the civic arena. In the summer you can take a tiny passenger ferry to nearby *Newcastle Island*. It's a five-minute ride that the kids will love (especially when the boat hits the wake from passing ships.) The dock, and mooring buoys for visiting sailors are on the island's south side. From here you can hike or cycle around the grassy meadows and coastline, or explore the old Pavilion, once a popular site for weekend dances. Drinking water and picnic or camping facilities are available too. There are caves, tidal pools, birds, and wildlife (well, not too wild – deer, raccoons, and rabbits) on this 765-acre island. Swim in Kanaka Bay or the dock area, and let the children fish from the wharf. We recommend Newcastle Island as a fun day-outing for families.

Backtracking to Maffeo-Sutton Park again, you now climb a flight of stairs to Pearson Bridge in order to cross the Millstone River. On the other side, pick up the *Queen Elizabeth Promenade*, which takes you to *Newcastle Park*. Local residents favour the small sandy beach here; you'll also find picnic tables and a view from the grassy slopes of boats moored at the neighbouring Nanaimo Yacht Club.

PARKS, PARKS, AND MORE PARKS

Nanaimo really caters to nature lovers, with an astonishing 2,700 acres set aside in more than two dozen parks scattered around the city and environs. Here are our personal highlights:

Bowen Park ❖ We recommend this ninety-acre park, especially if you're travelling with children. The developed part of the park contains a recreation complex, outdoor swimming pools, tennis and squash courts, and a jogging circuit. We like the hiking trail which winds alongside the Millstone River and passes a fish ladder, waterfalls, and a Nature Centre with duck pond, barnyard, and totem poles. There's a rhododendron grove and plenty of other plant and wild life to enjoy. Located on Bowen Road at Wall Street.

Colliery Dam Park ❖ Way back when coal mining was Nanaimo's major industry, this dam was built to form two lakes, providing a source of fresh water for the colliery operation. These days the lakes are stocked with cut-throat trout—swimmers can enjoy the water too. Hiking trails circle the lakes, and there's plenty of local flora and fauna to observe in the forests, as well as some interesting natural caves dating back from the ice age. Two entrances: one at the corner of Wakesiah and Sixth Street, the other at Nanaimo Lakes Road.

Gabriola Island ❖ *Galiano Galleries* is not, as you might expect, an art studio on the Gulf Islands, but rather a twelve-foot-high rock formation resembling a tidal wave. It is found on scenic Gabriola Island, a twenty-minute ferry ride from downtown Nanaimo. Spanish explorer Captain Dionysio Galiano named the three-hundred-foot natural sandstone wonder after himself. Today you can explore the coastline, swim, dig for clams, and picnic at either *Gabriola Sands* or *Drumbeg Beach Provincial Park*. The ferry leaves from the dock adjacent to Harbour Park Shopping Centre.

Petrogyph Park ❖ The origins of petroglyphs are shrouded in mystery. Various experts have offered various theories explaining the existence of these prehistoric rock carvings on the Island. We like to go and gaze at the powerful primitive images in Petroglyph Park, which still has a "sacred grove" feeling despite its proximity to the highway. Information signs will tell you what is known about the figures represented. In the same area are replicas of the carvings for those who wish to do rubbings (the real petroglyphs are too fragile to be handled). Look for the sign on the Trans-Canada Highway immediately south of Nanaimo.

Piper's Lagoon Park ❖ One of the loveliest of Nanaimo's waterfront parks, this peaceful twenty-acre isthmus, once the site of a whaling station and Japanese fishing village, shelters the lagoon. You'll find hiking trails criss-crossing the rocky bluffs, wildflowers, a sandy beach, and beautiful water views—with the possibility of spotting sea lions or killer whales. Kids love this park because of the unlimited opportunities for climbing and exploring. It's on Place Drive, off Hammond Bay Road.

Planta Park ❖ Botanists will love this unique park, which features samples of almost every native plant in the region. Allow a good hour to wander through this unspoiled retreat. It's reached via trails from Planta and Stephenson Point roads, off Hammond Bay Road.

Sealand Park ❖ This is an isolated retreat to find so near the city! Hike along a deep ravine beside Molecey Creek, through dense woods that are habitat for deep. The trails eventually open out onto the shore. Access is via either a short trail from the north end of Shoreline Drive, or a large path from the east end of Waldbank Road, which runs parallel to Hammond Bay Road north of the city. (Take Rilla, Brickyard, or McGirr from Hammond Bay to connect with Waldbank.)

Sugar Loaf Mountain ❖ Early risers should climb to this spot at sunrise, when a splendid vista of Nanaimo's surrounding waters unfolds. Access is via a staircase that runs up the back of the mountain, off Sherwood Drive and Marion Way in the north Departure Bay area.

Westwood Lake ❖ The lake itself is man-made, all 153-acres of it, and stocked with cut-throat trout. Hikers can ramble through the rest of the parks 261 wilderness acres (allow two to three hours) and then enjoy a swim and a picnic. At the end of Westwood Road.

SPORTS

Diving ❖ Naturally, in a coastal city like Nanaimo, water sports rate highly. Diving opportunities range from easy, shallow, inshore dives for the novice to challenging, fast-water dives for experts. We suggest divers contact one of the dive shops such as Seafun, 300 S. Terminal Avenue, 754-4813, for gear, rentals, charters, and other information.

Fishing ❖ As you might expect, fishing is also big here. We hear that Nanaimo has the best angling success for any West Coast area.

Lest you think that's just a typical fisherman's tall tale, we should point out that it's confirmed by fisheries biologists who keep track of catches and fish concentrations. Salmon is king, but Nanaimo's many lakes and rivers offer opportunities for freshwater fishing, too. Try *Johnson's Hardware*, 39 Victoria Crescent, 753-2531 for information.

Sailboarding ❖ What water sport requires light, easily portable, cheap equipment? Sailboarding, also known by its trademarked name, Windsurfing. Nanaimo's many breezy bays are perfect for this increasingly popular recreation. *Kona Bud's Yacht Shop* offers gear, lessons, and rentals for enthusiasts (along with canoe, bicycle, and tennis equipment rentals) at 2855 Departure Bay Road, 758-2911.

Golf ❖ Golfers have a choice of the eighteen-hole *Nanaimo Golf and Country Club*, Highland Boulevard, Island Highway North, 758-6332, or either of two other courses: *Rutherford Acreage Golf Centre*, a par 3 12-hole course (plus mini-golf) at 4700 Rutherford Road, 758-6811. or *Gabriola Golf and Country Club*, a 9-hole course at South Road, Gabriola Island, 247-8822.

Hiking ❖ The *Green Mountain* area attracts serious hikers in the summer months, and enthusiastic skiers of all ages during the winter season. Information on trails, hours, and facilities is available at the Tourist Information Centre, 100 Cameron Road, 753-1191.

Tours ❖ Attention all history buffs! Enjoy a self-guided *Walking Tour of Old Nanaimo*. The charmingly illustrated brochure "In

Pioneer Footsteps"—it's free at the Tourism Info Center, 266 Bryden Street, 754-8474—leads you imaginatively through the history of the city, with plenty of opportunity to capture architectural details with your camera. Highly recommended for those who wish to catch the early spirit of Nanaimo.

The *Pacific Biological Station* is a fisheries research centre dedicated to preserving the marine resources of Canada's Pacific Coast. The staff of 170 conducts studies in eight different areas, and is often supplemented by scientists from other nations, attracted by the centre's pre-eminence in new fisheries research. Guided tours are available in the summer. Because of the hands-on approach, we particularly suggest this tour for budding biologists in your family. The station is located on Hammond Bay Road, and reservations are essential, as tours are limited to fifteen people. Phone the Public Information Officer at 756-7000.

Where to Eat

Bluenose Chowder House ❖ When we're catching a ferry to the mainland around mid-day, we make sure we have enough time to stop at the Bluenose Chowder House for a big bowl of seafood chowder, enjoyed outside on the deck in the summertime, where we can drink in the view as well as our wine. There is also a hearty serving of fish and chips on the menu. It's closed on Mondays. Find it at 1340 Stewart Avenue, 754-6611.

The Brown Bag Alternative ❖ Local residents put us on to two favourite eateries: The Brown Bag Alternative and The Little Lumber. The Brown Bag is exactly as it sounds: a cheerful daytime diner offering good, wholesome fare (soups, salads, sandwiches) for downtown lunchers on weekdays. It's at 299 Wallace, 754-5711.

Dot's ❖ Dot's is a little roadside diner. Once upon a time, there actually was a Dot who became famous for her pies. Although Dot no longer bakes them, these homemade pies must be seen to be believed. The lemon meringue version seems to defy gravity as it towers above the pie plate! You can order breakfast, lunch, or the daily Dot's Special here, but we'd advise you to skip the protein and go straight for that pie. For about $8 you can take one of these giants home with you. Look for the large sign beside the small trailer, on the west side of the Trans-Canada Highway a few miles north of Nanaimo. Phone 390-4020.

Gina's ❖ We are rectifying a major omission from the first edition of *Island Treasures* by including this Nanaimo favourite here. We hope you'll make an effort to seek out Gina's. It's cheap and cheerful, tacky but friendly, decorated with strings of lights that look like red and green chili peppers, and painted, in true Mexican style, in bright red, blue, and green. (That's the inside. The outside is blue and hot pink.) The kitchen does a mean tortilla – and tostados, chimichangas, burritos, fajitas, quesadillas – and does it cheaply and well. We like it. Perched alarmingly on the edge of a cliff behind the Courthouse at 47 Skinner Street, 753-5411.

The Grotto ❖ One of our long-time favourites is The Grotto. The mood here is relaxed and friendly – an eclectic assortment of plants, posters, fishing floats, and general memorabilia surrounds you as you enjoy the simple but tasty seafood, steaks, or that fine salad bar. Soups and sandwiches are just right for light eaters. Open for dinner only, Tuesday to Saturday, at 1511 Stewart Avenue, near the BC Ferries dock, 753-3303.

Katerina's Place ❖ We've also enjoyed Greek food and the inviting atmosphere downtown at Katerina's Place. Nibblers can combine several appetizers for a delicious light meal in the restaurant's lounge, and we hear that the Sunday Brunch here is a winner. It's a 15 Front Street, 754-1351.

Lighthouse Bistro and Lounge ❖ We were delighted to find that the Seaplane Terminal building on the waterfront contains the Lighthouse Bistro (downstairs) and Lounge (upstairs). Aromatic homemade soups, plump meaty burgers, pasta, and superlative desserts from the Malaspina Bakery are just a few highlights from an imaginative menu. Every table in the pink and pale grey interior offers a water view. Phone 754-3212.

The Little Lumber ❖ Tucked away in the industrial park area, not far from Beban Park, this restaurant sports Mediterranean decor, Greek specialties. It is popular for lunch, which you can get every day except Sundays, when they're open only for dinner. At 2231 McGarrigle, off Northfield, 758-1932.

Where to Shop

Nanaimo is known as The Shopping Centre Capital of North America. The city has more square feet of retail space per capita than any other on the continent. Most of this space is concentrated in the various malls north of town along the Trans-Canada Highway. If you like the utter reliability and consistency of the chain-store-filled malls, read no further. If, on the other hand, you prefer to shop in a store that is firmly marked by the owner's personal idiosyncrasies, read on.

The Artisan's Studio ❖ Right next door to the Book Store on Bastion, the Artisan's Studio is an excellent co-operative craft shop featuring the work of Vancouver Island artists. Quality is first-rate, and prices are reasonable. We particularly liked the variety in pottery, the pen and ink work, and the large stained glass creations. This is a good place to find unique gifts to take home! At 70 Bastion Street, 753-6151.

The Book Store on Bastion Street ❖ This is a must for book lovers. The selection is wide and well laid-out; the stairs leading to the second floor are lined with unusual calendars and cards; and the *whole* top floor is children's books (plus a good parenting section!) Chairs and cushions encourage browsing by little bookworms, and service is warm and friendly. At 76 Bastion Street, 753-3011.

Johnson's Hardware ❖ We don't know why Johnson's Hardware is called a hardware store. It looks more like sporting goods to us, but it is the sort of place that the male of the species goes crazy for. Fishing gear and various other odds and ends, irresistible to men, are jumbled together in a store that looks like it was there when Nanaimo was little more than a gleam in some realtor's eye. Fishing advice is freely dispensed by the know-ledgeable staff; they can also arrange fishing charters. Local sources tell us all the hardware is in the basement, and the staff is equally knowledgeable about it as well. At 39 Victoria Crescent, 753-2531.

My Favourite Things ❖ Right across the street from the Artisan's Studio, in the Coast Bastion Inn, is one of the most intriguing hotel gift stores we've been in. Rather than the usual tourist bric-a-brac, My Favourite Things contains a carefully chosen assortment of local pottery and other crafts, fragrant Crabtree and Evelyn toiletries, pretty stationery, books, and novelties. It's on the right, off the lobby, as you enter the Coast Bastion Inn, at 11 Bastion Street, 753-4144.

Where to Stay

Coast Bastion Inn ❖ Nanaimo is well set up with the usual chain hotels, all of which provide the usual amenities. Newest and swankiest of these is the highrise Coast Bastion Inn. The main advantages are its central downtown location, and the view of Nanaimo Harbour and the city centre. At 11 Bastion Street, 753-6601.

Haven-By-The-Sea ❖ If you want to be out of the bustle of the city, try the attractive Haven-By-The-Sea resort on Gabriola Island, only twenty minutes from Nanaimo by ferry. Doubles average $53. On Davis Road, phone 247-9211.

Schooner Cove Resort ❖ Alternatively, Schooner Cover, north of Nanaimo near Nanoose Bay, boasts first-class accommodation with sea views, and facilities like a pool, sauna, and tennis courts in wooded seclusion. Double rates start at $75. At Dolphin and Outrigger Roads, 468-7691.

Tally Ho Town and Country Inn ❖ We like the convenient location of the Tally Ho. Besides a decent dining room and lounge, it also has a heated outdoor pool in a central courtyard. Rates start at $58 double. At 1 Terminal Avenue, 753-2241.

Parksville ❖ *Qualicum*

We like this popular resort/retirement destination because it's a convenient base for exploring the many parks and attractions nearby. At the same time, the area provides a picture-postcard setting for visitors who don't want to move a muscle on their beach blankets.

Parksville, with a population just over 6,000, has every tourist amenity—in fact, your first view of Parksville from the south is an eight-block strip of gas stations, restaurants, car dealerships, and garish signs.

Qualicum Beach, six miles north, is a quieter beach community of 3600. (Monarchists, take note: Charles and Di flew up here to visit at a private home when they were in BC for the opening of Expo.) The actual downtown section, high on a hill west of the main highway, is a picturesque little shopping area in which to browse away a summer afternoon.

This is usually the turn-off point for visitors heading to Pacific Rim National Park at Long Beach. Stop for last-minute supplies and snacks or, better yet, settle in for a pleasant beach vacation, even if it's only for a day.

What to See and Do

There's plenty of scope for the outdoorsy visitor in this scenic area.

Beaches! ❖ At low tide the sand stretches out for over three hundred feet, great for beachcombing, suntanning, and clamdigging. At *Parksville Beach*, below the Information Centre in the middle of town, you can watch—or enter!— the *Annual BC Open Sandcastle Competition* every July, or enjoy *Theatre in the Park* on Sunday afternoons.

Fishing ❖ Fishing here is, of course, terrific for both salmon and trout. The Englishman River is rated among the top five steelhead rivers on the Island, so stop at the Tourist Information Centre, at the junction of Highways 4 and 19, for charter, moorage, and marina information.

Golf ❖ Find nine-hole golf courses at *Eaglecrest*, open to the public every day except Tuesday and Thursday mornings, and at *Qualicum Beach Memorial*, just a three-iron hook from downtown.

A short drive away is a wealth of natural beauty; here are some of our favourite outings.

Big Qualicum River Fish Hatchery ❖ You don't get to be famous for great salmon and steelhead trout fishing without a lot of work and planning. That's what you'll learn about at this development project, which operates through the Salmonid Enhancement Program to increase the population of these fish. Best time to see spawning salmon leaping up the fish ladders is October and November, while April is a good month to watch steelhead. Big Qualicum was the first modern enhancement project undertaken in BC, and visitors are invited to tour its trails, maps, tanks, and river-level viewing room year round. Watch for the signs half a mile north of the Horne Lake turnoff on Highway 19, sixteen miles north of Parksville.

Cathedral Grove ❖ This grove of Super Trees is more correctly called *MacMillan Provincial Park*, but we've never heard anybody, anywhere, call it that. It was officially named after the founder of the logging company which donated this 300-acre tract of woodland to the province in 1944. The largest trees in this grove are members of the *Pseudotsuga menziesii* family, which you will no doubt immediately recognize as Douglas firs. Some of them are 800 years old, survivors of a forest fire that raged here about 300 years ago. These firs are second only to the redwoods as the tallest of all North American trees. Circular trails through the grove take ten to twenty minutes to stroll, and we insist that you stretch you legs and savour the humbling sensation of being dwarfed by nature's giants. Cathedral Grove is a compulsory stop on your way to Long Beach. Look for the sign on the south side of Highway 4, about twenty miles west of Parksville.

Englishman River Falls ❖ Originally called "Rio De Grullas" – River of Cranes – by eighteenth-century Spanish explorers, this river was renamed a hundred years later in memory of an early English immigrant who had the dubious distinction of drowning here. Today, it's the site of a 240-acre provincial park, which includes campsites, picnic areas, hiking trails (allow thirty minutes for a riverside round trip), swimming and fishing holes, waterfalls, bridges, and wildflowers, cedars, and dogwood trees (these are BC's provincial tree; they blossom in May and June). Follow the signs off Highway 4, about eight miles west of Parksville.

Hamilton Swamp ❖ "Sounds awful," wrote one of our Parksville contacts, "but for nature lovers is very interesting." He was describing this bird sanctuary, not far from the village of Coombs, where you can circle a natural woodland swamp on a well-marked, thirty-minute trail. Turn of Highway 4 onto Coombs Road (first on your right past the Old Country Market), then left onto Highway 4A, where you will see the parking lot about three miles down the road.

Horne Lake Caves ❖ Are you a budding spelunker? You might want to detour off Highway 19, about twenty minutes north of Qualicum Beach Information Centre, to visit the beautiful Horne Lake Caves. Visitors are encouraged to wear helmets and bring flashlights. A word of advice here: don't shine your light on the roof of the cave or you'll have the entire spider population in mad descent. Turn west onto Kenmuir Road at the PetroCan gas station on Highway 19 – you'll see the Horne Lake Store and Cafe sign – and continue along the winding road, over the tracks, to the fork for *Spider Lake*. There is a provincial picnic area along the lake, but if you're heading for the caves take the right fork. After ten miles of dirt road you will cross the Qualicum River, park your car, and then hike three miles to the caves. Horne Lake, by the way, is famous for good fishing. May to October is rainbow, Kamloops, and cutthroat trout time; from July to October you'll find the best black bass fishing on the Island.

Little Mountain Lookout ❖ Here's the place to find a panoramic view over Englishman River and the community of Errington, west of Parksville. Look for Little Mountain Road, off Bellevue Road, which is off Highway 4 on your way from Parksville west towards Coombs. Follow Little Mountain Road right to the top, where you'll find a small parking area. Don't forget your camera!

Little Qualicum Falls ❖ Four miles north of Englishman River, on Highway 4, you'll see the turnoff for Little Qualicum, said by some to be the most magnificent provincial park on the Island. Here the Little Qualicum River drops several hundred feet down the slopes of Mount Arrowsmith in a series of foaming waterfalls that have carved a number of narrow gorges through the rock. We like the view from the bridge over the lower falls at the halfway mark of the lookout trail. You can camp and picnic here too. The picnic area is surrounded by native arbutus trees, sprawling giants identified by their red limbs, shedding colourful curls of bark year round.

Mount Arrowsmith ❖ This is one of the Island's newest ski areas, providing both downhill and cross-country challenges, and, in the off season, several scenic hiking trails among alpine flowers. Even the novice hiker can probably climb Arrowsmith's main trails, originally marked out in 1908 by railway crews. Although the six to nine hour trek winds to the 6000-foot summit, its gradual grade and well-maintained condition make it a manageable walk. There are four other routes leading up Arrowsmith, but all require logging road transit. We recommend the main trail, which starts at the Cameron Lake picnic site, just east of Cathedral Grove.

Rathtrevor Provincial Park ❖ Every local resident will tell you that this is *the* beach to head for on a hot summer day. The park area was at one time the Rath family farm. You can still see evidence of the barn and farmhouse. It overlooks one of our favourite stretches of sandy beach—Jill still gets nostalgic about childhood sandcastles created here. Campsites, a picnic area, change rooms, cooking shelters, nature trails, and a visitor centre are all provided. On summer evenings you can stroll over to the outdoor amphitheatre, east of the campground entrance, for free nature talks, slide show, or films from the park naturalist. You might spot the Canadian Coast Guard search-and-rescue hovercraft as it flies above the water surface on its way to answer emergency calls along the coast. Rathtrevor is two miles south of Parksville on Highway 19.

Rhododendron Lake ❖ Wild pink "rhodos" bloom in incredible profusion beside this woodland lake in late May and early June. If you're a sucker for these beautiful native shrubs—as we are!— you'll try to time your visit for the springtime show at this ecological reserve. Follow the signs a few miles south of Parks-ville that take you off Highway 19 and put you on the North-west Bay logging division road west of Nanoose. Remember: this gravel route is a working logging road, so obey posted restriction signs.

Where to Eat

You'll see many restaurants and coffee shops—from cheap to pricey—in these beach communities and surrounding area. These are some of the places we think you'll enjoy.

In Qualicum Beach, for breakfast, quick sandwich lunches or just coffee and a freshly baked muffin, we like two pretty cafes in the 100-block of 2nd Avenue: *The Gourmet Cafe*, 752-2113 and *Trisha's Restaurant*, 752-2224.

The Judge's Manor ❖ When we feel like dressing up and heading for someplace expensive, it's a toss-up between the Judge's Manor and Ma Maison. The former is a charming place filled with English antiques, where the adventurous can enjoy unusual continental entrées like locally-raised squab, seasoned with coriander from the garden and napped with a pear cider sauce. Located across from the Town Office, at 193 W. Memorial Avenue, 248-2544.

Ma Maison ❖ On the other hand, Ma Maison is French French French. We like the lamb with spicy mustard sauce, but haven't worked up the appetite yet for "les cuisses de grenouilles," better known to Anglophones are frogs' legs. The decor is countrified coziness itself, set on a lovely treed acreage, with gardens, creek, and waterfalls, 393 Island Highway, 248-5859.

JD's Dining Room ❖ Our pick for a night on the town is the "Old Boys" Dining Room at the Qualicum College Inn. Loyal regulars rave about the good food and superb view at this former private school. 427 College Road, just north of the crowded beach strip along Highway 19, 752-9262.

Rocking Horse Ranch Pub ❖ Another out-of-town winner, this time south of Parksville in Nanoose, is the Rocking Horse Ranch. It serves hearty fare, like ranch burgers and seafood chowder, in a picturesque setting surrounded by corrals, a rodeo arena, and arbutus groves. Summer weekends usually mean outdoors barbecues, delicious home-cooked dinner specials, and bluegrass entertainment. To get there, turn east at the Nanoose traffic lights by the Gulf Station, onto Northwest Bay Road. Turn left onto Sanders Road. Phone 468-7631.

Spinnaker Seafood House ❖ Farther south, in Parksville, we're happy to recommend Spinnaker Seafood House, an unassuming diner that serves up burgers, fish and chips, and a bit of everything else, at reasonable prices. One customer wrote to us all the way from Ste. Anne de Bellevue, Quebec to tell us why this is a favourite part of her annual BC holiday! It's just south of downtown Parksville, on the east side of Highway 19, 248-5532.

Tudor Tea Rooms ❖ For a substantial sit-down meal that is still within your budget, try lunch, afternoon tea, or a light dinner at the Tudor Tea Rooms. You will enjoy their own garden-grown fruits and veggies, served on Royal Albert bone china. 3336 West Island Highway, opposite Buller Road, 752-6053.

Trees ❖ One Victoria fan wrote: "If you like a terrific hamburger, try the small restaurant called Trees at the junction of Church Road and the Alberni Highway. In good weather the delightful owner serves you at rustic tables right outside the cafe, and everything is homemade and delicious." It's our kind of place! Phone 248-9776.

Kalvas Restaurant ❖ "Good food!" wrote one of our readers, thus filling our first criterion for a restaurant entry. We and our source agree on the kitchen's sure had with seafood. We also approve of the restaurant's cleanliness, classical music selection and non-smoking area. 180 N. Moilliet, Parksville, 248-6933.

Where to Shop

Camera Arts Gallery ❖ Take your holiday film here for developing and then spend some time enjoying the pottery, the unusual glass screens decorated with intriguing sandblasted designs, and the side room displaying country crafts. 671 Memorial Avenue, Qualicum Beach, 752-9970.

Cottage Gift Boutique ❖ There may be a square inch of space in here without something gorgeous filling it, but we couldn't see it. Compulsive shoppers will be in nirvana browsing from housewares to linens to scented bath goods. Unique is an overworked word but you really *will* find some unique gifts in this shop, ranging from scented sachets to pop into the clothes dryer to stuffed fabric ducks which double as doorstops. Right on the corner of Memorial and 2nd Avenue in Qualicum Beach, 752-9321.

Coombs ❖ A disastrous fire in August 1987 destroyed a large part of picturesque Coombs Emporium. Within a month, thanks to the equivalent of a barn-building bee, the Coombs market was on the road to reconstruction. We are happy to report all is thriving again, including the goats on the roof. Stop in for anything from ice cream to fresh produce to handcrafts on your way to Long Beach via Highway 4.

Just west of Coombs, two-and-a-half miles past the Market, you will find the turnoff for Hilliers. Take an interesting side trip to Eva Feursenger's *Water Gardens*. Water lilies, flowering rush, water hyacinths, tropical and hardy pond blossoms make up the most impressive and colourful collection we've ever seen—a must for owners of fish ponds. At the end of Howard Road you will see a sign on the left; follow the gravel road until another sign appears, marking the Feursenger farm.

One last stop is the summer roadside stand where you can buy homemade tarts, pies, bread, garlic pickles, jams, and, best of all, real Ukrainian perogies, "made by Mother herself." The couple who own this farm decided on a food stand rather than a fruit stand, and now folks from California to Quebec make this ethnic delight a regular stop on summer vacations. We can see—and taste—why. Just off Highway 4 on 4A, on the way to Qualicum Beach.

Errington Community Farmer's Market ❖ We received a very nice letter from Gerry Shaw, the driving force behind this market for over twelve years. She had read of our book in the local paper and was excited about sharing word of a Saturday "institution" in her community. Farmers, gardeners, and artists gather here from 10 a.m. to 1 p.m. each Saturday during July and August to sell farm produce, fresh eggs, home baking, and handicrafts. About 6000 customers visit the market every summer; the inside scoop says to get here early since it's so popular with local folks. Also on the Market property is *Errington Cottage*, which houses the work of several local artists and craftspeople. It's open Tuesday through Saturday from 11 a.m. to 4 p.m. To get there, follow the signs on Highway 4 west of Parksville. Take Errington Road to Grafton Road. You'll spot the Market on the corner.

Larry Aguilar Pottery Studio ❖ Having long-admired Larry Aguilar's work at the Gallery Shop in Victoria, we were delighted to learn of his home studio. Both functional and purely decorative pottery, porcelain, and raku pieces are sold here. It's worth a visit just to see the lovely Bonsai display and the Japanese Koi pond outside. Closed Sundays. Find the studio by going north of Qualicum Beach, just past the Little Qualicum River. Turn left onto Texada Road, two blocks up to Ganske Road. Watch for signs. Phone 752-9332.

Mulberry Bush Book Store ❖ Here's a Qualicum Beach book store we like, this time for new paperbacks and hardcovers. You'll find Qualicum locals browsing through a good selection of all sorts of books—or picking up greeting cards, prints, the weekly paper, and developed film (one day service). 130 Second Avenue, 752-9722.

Where to Stay

This region is one of the most popular beach vacation spots on the Island, so expect to find a large number of motel, hotel, and cabin accommodations. The seaside at Qualicum Beach, for example, is lined elbow-to-elbow with waterfront or water view units. It's a bit *too* crammed for our liking, but obviously just right for thousands of perennial visitors. Here are a handful of our personal picks for this area.

Just south of beautiful Rathtrevor Provincial Park, and sharing the very same gorgeous sand, are a small number of older cottage resorts which have recently been updated. Some, like *Tigh-Na-Mara* (248-2072) and *Graycrest on the Sea* (248-6513), are situated on a bluff overlooking the water, with paths leading down the hill to the beach.

Bayside Inn ❖ If you're looking for newer-than-new luxury accommodation, the Bayside Inn, a resort hotel opened in 1985, has 100 beautifully appointed mountain or ocean view rooms. Double rates start at $84. Amenities include indoor pool, jacuzzi, saunas, tennis, racquetball, and squash courts. It's just a few minutes north of Parksville at 240 Dogwood Drive; phone 248-8333 for reservations and rate information.

Beach Acres ❖ Extensive renovations have turned this long-time Parksville seaside favourite into an upscale resort. Two bedroom modern cottages and oceanview condo suites have replaced the rustic summer cabins, and a recreation complex offers such amenities as an indoor pool and sauna. The wonderful sandy beach still remains the same, however. Double rates start at $100, including a fully equipped kitchen. 1015 East Island Highway, 248-3424.

The George Inn ❖ Jill, who prefers the quieter Brit ambience of Qualicum, likes the Olde English aspects of the George. A Tudor half-timbered exterior, ivy clad walls, and covered verandas make this a visual winner. We like the staff, too, and the noticeable personal touch here. There's a pool and sauna, but what we really like is the Sunset Dining Room, which, contrary to what you might expect from hotel restaurants, offers imaginative and first-rate fare. The room is nicely appointed in dark blue and red with fireplace and two banks of windows offering a view of the golf course and the sea beyond. Room rates drop dramatically in the off season; in summer doubles start at $65. 532 Memorial Avenue, 752-9236.

Island Hall Resort Hotel, Sea Edge Motel ❖ Further north, in "downtown" Parksville, is the famous Island Hall Resort Hotel. This is nice enough, a modern sort of motel (indoor pool, spa, tennis courts) that is popular with meeting and convention groups. 181 West Island Highway, 248-3225. We enjoyed our stay here, but prefer their next-door neighbour, Sea Edge Motel, 248-8377, which is about one-third the size and less expensive to boot. Both share exactly the same lovely beach and are convenient to town for shopping. Ask for a one or two bedroom unit on the ground floor. Rates start at $68 double, with special seniors' discounts in the off season. We suggest staying here, but eat the occasional meal—especially the renowned Sunday buffet—at Island Hall's Dining Room next door.

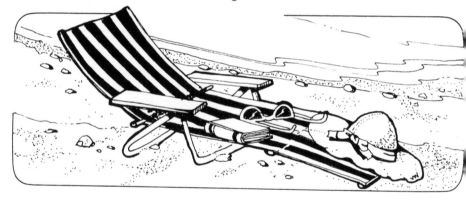

Old Dutch Inn ❖ "We had originally planned to stay at the Old Dutch Inn for two days, but found the hospitality of Mr. and Mrs. Teijgemann, the owners, plus the fine dining to be such that we extended our stay to two and a half weeks." So wrote a San Francisco reader after the first edition of this book came out, and we couldn't have said it better ourselves. The motel has clean and comfy rooms (across the road from the famous beach), indoor pool, sauna and spa, and best of all really outstanding meals from award-winning Chef Teijgemann, who, incidentally, was personally invited to cook for Queen Elizabeth, no less. Room rates start at $64 double. 110 Island Highway, 752-6914.

The Willow ❖ Locals told us about a different sort of overnight place in Qualicum Beach. It's called The Willow, a Tudor-style home with only four rooms (with shared or private baths) and a charming guest parlour. Nightly rates, averaging $44 double, include full English breakfast. The Willow is within walking distance of the beach and the golf course. Phone 752-5851 for reservations.

Port Alberni

This thriving community of 20,000 sits thirty miles inland from the west coast of Vancouver Island. It is a major deep sea port on the long Alberni Inlet, often referred to as the Gateway to the Pacific. Alberni also shares the title "Salmon Fishing Capital of the World" with Campbell River, Nanaimo, Port Hardy...

"It's a great place to live it you love the outdoors," writes Port Alberni resident Julie McCaig, "so much to see and do! Because of our large tax base, we have many more recreational services and facilities than one would normally expect in a city our size. It's all close, all accessible, and easy to find. Fantastic for children!" As well, "there are a lot of arts and crafts people in the Valley, and taking the time to find them can be very rewarding."

Although its fishing, skiing, and hiking attractions draw tourists to the Alberni Valley, the forest industry has been the lifeblood of the area since the turn of the century. There are several mills here, processing lumber, plywood, pulp, and newsprint; you can smell evidence of their presence

if the wind blows the right (or wrong!) way as you approach town. But don't let that put you off. Plan a visit to this scenic valley on your way to Long Beach.

What to See and Do

Alberni Valley Museum ❖ This museum houses its displays in drawers that can be opened for a peek at their contents – a system called "Visible Storage." You can also start up a full-scale steam engine, work the controls used to cut lumber, and even tap out a message on the famous Bamfield lifesaving telegraph line. West Coast native exhibits, including a fine collection of Noot-ka woven basketry, relics of the area's pioneer forest industry, and even artifacts from a nearby archaeological dig that dates its first inhabitants from 2000 B.C. are part of the fascinating display here. It's all at 4255 Wallace Street, in the Echo Community Centre, 723-2181.

Echo Community Centre & Pool ❖ While you're at the Museum, take a look at the whole Echo Centre complex. It's the perfect place for rainy days – and we wish every town was lucky enough to have a centre like this! Here are not one, but three swimming pools (no charge on summer afternoons), sauna, whirlpool, a jogging track, concert hall, and even a public library where visiting borrowers are welcomed. 4255 Wallace St, 723-2181.

Hiking Trails

The Alberni Valley has hikes for the slowest toddlers or the most experienced trekker. Two for the toddlers, recommended by Julie and Gary McCaig, are the Roger Creek Trail and Polly's Point.

Polly's Point Trail ❖ This is a pleasant, easy hike with good views overlooking the Alberni Inlet. Access is from Hunter's Marina, on the waterfront, one mile south of downtown.

Roger Creek Trail ❖ The Roger Creek Trail is about three miles each way, through nicely shaded forest. The round trip will take three hours at a relaxed pace. You'll pass bridges, creeks, a swimming/fishing hole, and lovely scenic views over a slate canyon. The entrance is off Highway 4, just east of the Tourist Information Centre. Look for the small parking lot and the "Nature Trail" sign.

Della Falls ❖ Much more arduous is the trail to the highest waterfall in North America, spectacular Della Falls. The 1443-foot cataract is one of several in Drinkwater Canyon at the head of Great Central Lake. The canyon can be reached by canoe, power boat, or chartered plane, and then a difficult eleven-mile trail – blocked by snow until mid-June – leads the super fit hiker to the falls. Allow three or four days, preferably in August, for this adventure. Take Highway 14, off Highway 4, to the lake, or ask at Tourist Information for a trail guide.

Mount Arrowsmith ❖ The regional park, in Port Alberni's back yard, provides breathtaking views across Georgia Strait to the Coastal Mountains. Arrowsmith is an all-year attraction for residents and visitors who come during the winter ski season to enjoy intermediate downhill or cross-country skiing, or during the summer to wander the miles of well-marked hiking and climbing trails. This 1500-acre park is reached via a thirteen-mile gravel logging road. Look for the turnoff five miles east of Port Alberni on Highway 4.

West Coast Trail ❖ For those of sturdy limb, Port Alberni is the jumping-off point for the northern section of the West Coast Trail. A cruise down the Inlet on the M.V. *Lady Rose* will take you to Bamfield and the start of the Trail (see the Pacific Rim section for more details on this hike).

Lady Rose ❖ Imagine a day cruise on a stout little packet freighter. You'll travel with about a hundred other adventurers, some geared up for a canoe or kayak trip through the Broken Group Islands; some ready for the week-long trek on the world-famous West Coast Trail; and others, like you, who just want to relax while watching stunning marine scenery, abundant wildlife and seabirds. The M.V. *Lady Rose* leaves Port Alberni from the Argyle Street Dock at Harbour Quay every morning, makes a handful of stops to deliver mail, cargo, and passengers at Kildonan, Bamfield, Gibraltar Island, and Ucluelet, and is back home by late afternoon. Cost varies from $20 to $30 return (depending on how far west you want to sail), and children from eight to fifteen pay half fare. For reservations or informa-tion call 723-8313.

Mill Tours ❖ During the summer, visitors are invited to take free guided tours through pulp, paper, and saw mills. Children must be twelve or older. Call for tour schedules: Alberni Pacific Division, 724-6511, or Alberni Pulp and Paper Mill, 723-2161.

Robertson Creek Hatchery ❖ The prize winner at the Salmon Fes-tival may have had its start in life here, where nine million young chinook salmon—not to mention a million or so coho youngsters and a few hundred thousand steelhead trout—are produced each year. Visitors are invited to tour the hatchery, its concrete raceways, rearing channels and ponds, and incuba-tion boxes. If this is all Greek to you, make a stop here, near picturesque Great Central Lake, on Highway 14 off Highway 4, about ten miles northwest of town, 723-3837. A super time to visit is September and October, but the lovely walking trails are a big hit any time of the year.

Sports

Fishing ❖ The annual *Salmon Festival*, held each Labour Day week-end, promises a whopping $10,000 first prize for the largest salmon caught during the three-day festival. Even if you're not in the running for prize money, you're invited to stop at the Information Centre at the Port Alberni-Ucluelet junction, right behind the big carved Welcome sign, for local tips on the current hot spots for fishing.

Golf ❖ The *Alberni Golf Club* is a nine-hole, par thirty-five course with a driving range and full clubhouse facilities. It welcomes visitors seven days a week, on Cherry Creek Road, off High-way 4 past the Alberni Mall, 723-5422. The *Pleasant Valley Gold Course* is a par three course of Highway 4 in North Port Alberni, 724-5333.

Racquet Sports ❖ Tennis players will find plenty of courts around town, including those at the High School, 4000 Burde Street; A.W. Neil School, 5055 Compton Road; E.J. Dunn School, 3500 Argyle Street; Stirling Arm Field at the Alberni Athletic Hall; and the Sproat Lake Community Centre, near the Water

Bomber Base. You can play racquetball or squash at the **Court House Racquet Club**, 3123 Third Avenue (call 723-5922 to book a court).

Sproat Lake Provincial Park ❖ This is the locals' pick for a day of hot weather swimming. There's good warm bathing water here, as well as a boat launch, picnic sites, excellent fishing, and campsites. Just left of the beach you can see ancient petroglyphs on the shoreline cliffs by the wharf.

While you're visiting Sproat Lake, follow the signs to visit the world's largest forest fire water bombers. The **Martin Mars Water Bombers** are operated by Forest Industries Flying Tankers, a collective formed by five major BC forestry companies. The bombers play a crucial role each year when the fire hazard is dangerously high because of our long, dry summers. During a forest fire crisis, these huge planes load an incredible thirty tons of water within twenty-two seconds, by skimming along a lake surface a seventy miles an hour. This load is thickened, in the tanks, to a gelatinous consistency that will hold together when it is dumped, and can cover three or four acres of burning forest. Tours are arranged during the off season – meaning anytime except dry summer months.

Stamp Falls Provincial Park ❖ This provincial park not only offers a picturesque setting, but is also the best place around town to see the annual fall salmon spawning phenomenon. Brilliant red salmon return to the streams from which they set out as eager youngsters several years before, coming back to lay their eggs and die. Anytime after mid-October is the best time to watch.

Take Beaver Creek Road off Highway 4 towards Tofino, and follow the Stamp Falls signs.

Where to Eat

For a quick bit on the run, or an affordable no-frills meal, we like any of the following.

Bakeries and Delis ❖ The *Mountain View Bakery and Delicatessen* owned by a charming Dutch couple who offer Dutch specialties and authentic cheeses, has fresh cream-filled baked goods that are especially yummy for dessert. 3727 Tenth Avenue. *Yvette's Deli & Coffee House*: Homemade goodies like gargantuan lemon meringue tarts, muffins which are a whole meal in themselves, and divine soups make Yvette's a local winner—especially good if you'd like to elbow up to the local RCMP constabulary who eat here all the time. 4926 Argyle, 723-8622. Another hot spot for local snackers is the *Donut Shop* at Harbour Quay, for irresistible fresh donuts and coffee, 723-2213.

Paradise Cafe ❖ "Wonderful soup" reported one of our sources, a regular luncher in this very attractive restaurant. The rest of the continental menu rates raves as well, and they're open for lunch and dinner at 4505 Gertrude Street, 724-5050.

Canal Restaurant ❖ Near the Clutesi Marina is the Canal Restaurant, where Greek specialties are served in the patio, bistro, or restaurant overlooking the Alberni Canal. 5093 Johnson Street, 724-6555.

Chinese Food ❖ For plain-Jane oriental fare, try the *Pine Cafe*, 2940 Third Avenue, 724-0011. *The Chopstick House*, at the corner of Beaver Creek Road and River Road, has more exotic cuisine. Phone 724-5042. We like the *Dollar House* for slightly improved decor, quick service and no MSG added if requested. 3981 10th Avenue, 724-1124.

Little Bavaria ❖ If you are hankering for fine German cooking, you will enjoy a visit to Little Bavaria. Lunch and dinner are served in candlelit comfort at 3035 Fourth Avenue, 724-4242.

Four Winds Restaurant ❖ When we asked locals about their favourite place for a night out, we heard about several of the
restaurants already mentioned – take your pick! – as well as the
new Four Winds Restaurant, the only waterfront eatery in
town, which serves fresh seafood. Located at the Harbour
Quay, 723-2333.

Courtyard Restaurant ❖ The restaurant at the Timberlodge Motor
Inn was frequently cited by residents as being "consistently
good" for breakfast, lunch, and steak, seafood, or prime rib
dinners. We haven't tried it yet, but are happy to take the locals'
word for it. Port Alberni Highway, five minutes east of town,
723-9415.

The Stork ❖ Here's an older home converted to a charming restau-
rant, perfect for impressing your sweetie at dinner or lunch.
Pricey by Port Alberni standards, but worth it. 4356 Gertrude
Street, 724-1122.

Where to Shop

Rollin Art Centre ❖ A visit to the Rollin Art Centre is a good start
for those interested in getting a feel for the work of Alberni
Valley artisans. The Centre is the permanent home of the
Community Arts Council and its twenty-plus member groups:
from pottery to painting, live theatre to dance. Upstairs at the
Centre is a fine gallery that features local artists' work, and a
variety of touring exhibitions. They also offer afternoon tea and
theatre sports entertainment in the summer months. Admission is free. The Centre is at the corner of Eighth Avenue and
Argyle Street, 724-3412.

Crafts and Gifts ❖ Another worthwhile source of crafts and gifts is
the *Windfish Gallery* (5069 Johnson, 723-7131) for locally
produced artwork and handicrafts.

Alberni Harbour Quay ❖ Another must for collectors of local crafts
is a visit to Alberni Harbour Quay, overlooking the busy deep
sea harbour. Several shops and market stalls offer browsers a
wide selection of artwork, and also of fresh fish and produce.
This is a great place to stroll, enjoy live entertainment, have a
waterfront picnic, or watch the fishing fleet at work. Climb the

Clock Tower for a terrific view of Alberni Inlet and Mount Arrowsmith beyond. Forestry giant MacMillan Bloedel has a Forestry Visitor's Information Centre here that is a must for kids. They can explore the hollow tree and fascinating displays, or take advantage of the tours of nearby forests. All 724-7888 for information. The Harbour Quay is at the foot of Argyle Street.

Whiskey Creek Store ❖ Everybody coming to Port Alberni stops at Whiskey Creek Store, halfway between Parksville and Port Alberni for an ice cream. Gary McCaig, our resident goldmine of insiders' tips, reports: "The small size cone is huge; I once actually saw someone eat the medium size; I have never known anyone with enough courage to order a large!" How can you resist? Look for the Esso gas station sign on Highway 4, east of Port Alberni.

Fresh Produce ❖ Want to pick up farm fresh fruit and veggies? Try either *Rage's Farm*, on McKenzie Road off Beaver Creek Road on the way to Stamp Falls Provincial Park, or *Naesgaard's Farm Market*, on River Road on the way to Long Beach.

Parker's Hobby Corner ❖ Amazingly, this seems to be one of the busiest stores in town! It's popular with travelling families who can pick up innovative, pre-packaged back seat toys and games. The staff is friendly and helpful. 4908 Argyle Street, 723-6832.

Clock Tower Gallery ❖ Handily situated in the waterfront Quay, the Clock Tower Gallery offers an excellent selection of native and wildlife art, local pottery, and sculpture by Babe Gunn. Well worth a look at 5440 Argyle Street, 724-5999.

The Flour Shop ❖ This entry should actually be under a category of Where to Shop and Eat. Not only do the bakers produce different specialty breads every day, they also provide a little eating area with daily lunch specials such as sandwiches made with their croissants and buns. They also make the world's best peanut butter Nanaimo bars. On Johnson in the Adelaide Shopping Mall, 723-1105.

Where to Stay

Hospitality Inn ❖ The Hospitality Inn offers rooms reserved for non-smokers. Attractive package deals for guided fishing/whale watching fans include dinner, a night's accomodation, continental breakfast, a box lunch and late check-out all for $180 per person, double. They'll even clean, wrap and freeze your catch for you—all you have to provide in this very inclusive deal is your fishing license. Rooms only start at $70. 3835 Reford Street, 723-8111.

The Barclay ❖ Built recently to replace the old hotel claimed by fire, this centrally located hotel offers such amenities as an outdoor pool, plus a whirlpool and sauna. Rates start at $60 double. Right downtown at 4277 Stamp Avenue, 724-7171.

The Maples ❖ West of town, on beautiful Sproat Lake, you might prefer the rustic cottage resort called The Maples. It features a sandy beach, perfect for swimming or tanning. There are also boat, sailboard, and hobie cat rentals, and facilities for lake activities like water-skiing and fishing. We like this location because it's only minutes from town services, yet is out in the clean, fresh-air countryside. It's on Lakeshore Road, write R.R. #3, Port Alberni, 723-7533.

Pacific Rim ❖ *Tofino, Ucluelet, Bamfield*

The Pacific Rim area experiences more rain annually than any other place in Canada—it wasn't until our third or fourth visit that we were treated to a sunny day that made the Pacific look like a postcard picture—but who cares? Not the thousands of tourists for whom this west coast strip of Vancouver Island is a mecca. It is second only to Victoria as the Island's prime vacation attraction.

At either end of **Pacific Rim National Park** (which includes the twelve-mile stretch of **Long Beach**) are the small communities of **Tofino** at the north, and **Ucluelet** at the south. The resident population of just over 2,500 is mainly involved in the logging, fishing, and tourism industries.

Tofino, on a peninsula surrounded on three sides by ocean, is one of the oldest white settlements on the coast, dating back to the 1880s. Today it retains its maritime charm, with spectacular scenic views in every direction. Just offshore is historic **Meares Island**, site of recent bitter political battles between Indians, environmentalists, and logging companies with development plans.

Ucluelet is a village with a tongue twister of a name (it means "safe

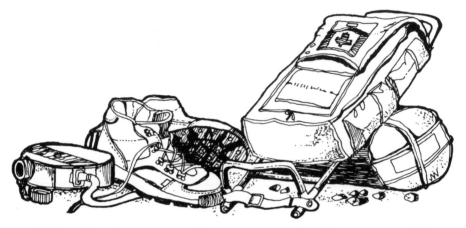

harbour") and a more sprawling appearance than its compact neighbour Tofino. Most of Ucluelet's first settlers came here because of the rumours of incredible gold finds in nearby Wreck Bay. Vicious coastal storms, however, destroyed early good workings as fast as prospectors could set up new sluiceboxes. Most eventually switched over to fishing and logging for a more reliable livelihood.

Further south, on the other side of Barkley Sound, lies the tiny (population 208) fishing village of **Bamfield**, the northern terminus of the rugged West Coast Trail, and the site of a Marine Station. The Bamfield Marine Station is operated by four western universities as a marine biology research and teaching facility. Field trips for interested adults and families are often offered from September to April through such institutions as local community colleges, the Vancouver Acquarium, the Royal BC Museum, the BC Federation of Naturalists and Elderhostel.

A unique feature of Bamfield is the boardwalk which hugs the shoreline of Bamfield Inlet. It is maintained by the Department of Highways because it *is* the highway. Access to Bamfield is either via the *Lady Rose* from Port Alberni, or by car on gravel roads from Port Alberni or Youbou. Warning: these roads eat trailer hitches, as Jill's friends found out. If you're towing a boat, make sure all your connections are nice and snug before you set off.

Whether you're drawn to this area for whale watching, beachcombing, or hiking seaside trails above giant Pacific breakers, we wish you a long, relaxing stay – and sunny weather! Pull on a sturdy pair of walking shoes, grab your bathing suit, and get ready for some of the most stunning scenery you'll ever lay eyes on.

What to See and Do

Pacific Rim National Park ❖ This, the first National Marine Park established in Canada, includes three quite separate areas: the world famous *Long Beach* region, the *Broken Group Islands*, and the *West Coast Trail*.

Hiking the beaches and trails is the best way to enjoy beautiful Long Beach, but remember that rising tides can trap hikers in low-lying areas. Well-marked trails intersect the Park. The *Willowbrae*, for example, was part of a twenty-five mile overland route between Tofino and Ucluelet, and was once wide enough to accommodate horse-drawn vehicles! Lots of free interpretive programmes are offered by Park naturalists all summer; stop at the Information Centre for details. Also make a stop at the *Wickaninnish Centre* for several photographic displays, a natural history museum, and a twenty-five minute film called "Great Ocean" – plus a coffee shop!

Swimmers who don't mind the icy challenge of crashing waves will love the water along here. Keep in mind those fast riptides, and never use inflatable floats that could carry you far from shore and safety. This is good surfing water; regional Surfing Championships, sponsored by a Nanaimo Kayak club, are held at Long Beach every October. Expert sea kayakers and open water canoeists have reported sixteen-foot waves along nearby Cox Bay. Park at Wickaninnish Centre as far west as you can, and walk west up the beach straight into the bush to explore the awesome sand dunes along this stretch, some towering like apartment buildings around your head. You can practise jumping off sand cliffs, but watch your bare feet in the summer – the sand is blistering hot, even when it's windy.

Beachcombers looking for something *really* different to add to their shell-and-driftwood collections will find that the beaches in the Park sometimes yield a rare treasure: Japanese fishing floats. Hundreds of these delicate glass balls, ranging in diameter from a few inches to a gigantic five feet across, have survived the trans-Pacific voyage from Japan (or Korea, China, and Russia) over the past seventy-five years. If you're very luck–and very patient–you might manage to nab one.

The Broken Group Islands are a haven for canoeists, boaters, and wilderness campers, who think the hundred small islands at the mouth of Barkley Sound are the ultimate in getting away from it all. Access, by boat only, is across open water which can be treacherous at times, although conditions in inner waterways are good. Marine charts and navigational equipment are a must, or hire a charter boat to bring you from Port Alberni, Ucluelet, or Bamfield. Because these islands are part of a national park, you'll even find a park warden–on a floating cabin off Nettle Island!

The forty-five-mile West Coast Trail runs from the tiny fishing village of Bamfield in the north, to Port Renfrew in the south. This is definitely *not* a trek for the lazy stroller. We have heard of a group that *runs* this trail every year. Count on five or six days of steep, often slippery grades, deep gullies, and lots of wet weather along the way. In spite of the rigours involved on this difficult trail, over 5000 visitors a year hike the route along what is known as the "Graveyard of the Pacific" because of the number of ships destroyed by the west coast's heavy seas. The trail itself developed from the Life Saving Trail hacked out after the 1906 wreck of the S.S. *Valencia* and the deaths of 126 passengers. Most hikers make this a one-way trip, so arrangements must be made in advance–either leave a vehicle at each end of the trail, or have somebody pick you up on a given date.

If you'd like to impress your friends by saying that you have "done the West Coast Trail," without actually conquering the entire rugged course, join day hikers on the first four or five miles of the north trail, going as far as Pachena Lighthouse, south of Bamfield. It's a pleasant and easy trail, starting from Ross Bible Camp at the eastern end of the Ohiaht Indian Band campground at Pachena Beach.

The Parks Office has a wealth of necessary information, available at no charge, for people interested in this hike. Write the Pacific Rim National Park Superintendent, Box 280, Ucluelet, BC, V0R 3A0.

P.S. If you find the though of this hike too daunting, we should point out that Jill's son, Stephen, did the trail, full backpack and all, when he was just a lad of ten.

Having exhausted every square inch of the Pacific Rim National Park, let's move on to investigate some of the other delights of this area.

Bamfield ❖ A twenty-minute walk west of Bamfield brings you to *Brady's Beach*, a picturesque picnic spot. Seashell collectors will discover lots of prize specimens, and the water is safe for swimming

Hot Springs Cove ❖ An hour from Tofino by private boat charter, or considerably less time if you can afford the thrill of a chartered plane trip, and you'll be relaxing in *Maquinna Marine Park*'s hot springs. A series of four basins catch very hot spring water as it cascades twenty feet over rock cliffs. Depending on which basin you choose, you can soak in progressively cooler water until you reach the cold ocean. From the boat or plane moorage, a thirty-minute hike brings you to the hot springs. To get here, ask about boat or plane trips at the information centres listed under whale watching.

Imperial Eagle Channel ❖ All the islands in Imperial Eagle Channel offer a bonanza of beaches and caves to explore. Many of the caves contain spectacular stalagmites and stalactites, and, occasionally, human remains. Access to the islands is by boat, ask at the wharf for information on seaborne tours or fishing charters.

Sea Kayaking ❖ How about an ocean adventure in a sea kayak? The Tofino Sea Kayaking Company provides both guided one-day paddling tours (no experience necessary—instruction provided), and single or double kayak rentals, complete with life jackets, paddles, flares, and anything else you might need to enjoy your time on the water safely. Find them at 320 Main Street, Tofino, 725-4222.

Tofino Airlines ❖ One of the most spectacular views of the Pacific Rim area is from the air. A 20-minute scenic flight on Tofino Airlines is a breath-taking thrill from take-off to landing. View coastal scenery which includes magnificent whales, the never-ending surf of Long Beach, and a whole island covered with fat brown sea lions basking in the sun. Tofino Airlines can also fly you to a secluded island beach, yours alone for an afternoon picnic or overnight camp, and pick you up when you want to return to civilization. Fly to Hot Springs Cove, or farther up the coast to Nootka Beach, for other fantasy getaways. Highly recommended. Located at the foot of First Street, Tofino, 725-4454.

Toquart Bay ❖ On your way west towards Long Beach, you'll pass a sharp left turn off Highway 4, well known to locals as the route to Toquart Bay. It's a bit off the beaten track, but you'd never know it by the number of campers, clam and oyster diggers, and fishermen that line the sandy beach here. We have seen photographs of this bay showing miles of idyllic ocean shoreline with not a soul to be seen, but these pictures must have been taken on a quiet day in the middle of winter. Things are certainly crowded here in the summer. We mention Toquart because of the spectacular view of Barkley Sound and nearby mountains and islands. Plan on a forty-five minute drive from the Highway 4 junction (where the road forks towards either Tofino or Ucluelet) to reach the bay. Ten miles west along Highway 4 towards Port Alberni, you will find the sharp turnoff south, and then an immediate left turn up a steep hill. Take this three-mile stretch of logging road until another fork appears, then bear left. You'll pass **Maggie Lake** on your right, famous among residents for its trout fishing. Look for the Toquart Bay sign on your right, a short distance along this road. There are free, primitive camping sites along this beach, plus a boat launch.

West Coast Maritime Museum ❖ This privately run showcase is housed in a building that, over the years, has been a mission, a World War II army barracks, and a United Church. Today you'll see memorabilia of local shipwrecks; mining, fishing, and logging displays; and an exhibit of native Nootka history—including a replica of Chief Maquinna's distinctive bowl-shaped hat. (Maquinna was the ruler of over 50,000 Nootkas.) The museum is open daily during the summer months, at the corner of Third Street and Campbell Avenue in Tofino. Admission $1.

Whale Watching ❖ Every February, like clockwork, thousands of Pacific grey whales begin their journey from southern California waters to feeding grounds off our Island coast, ending a fasting period started in autumn of the previous year. By March, little charter boats full of excited whale watchers fill the bays and shoreline here to catch a glimpse of these gentle giants. In December we see the greys again, on their return trip from summer vacation spots in the Arctic. Some days you'll see lots and other days, nary a one! There are several whale watching charter boat outfits in the Pacific Rim area, but we recommend Ocean Pacific Whale Charters. Owner Jamie Bray has been offering excellent two and three hour cruises on the *Lady Selkirk* since 1982. Even if you don't spot a whale (Carolyn's sailing lucked out last tour and followed a beautiful grey for hours), you'll enjoy Jamie's informative narration of just about every scenic or historical landmark you pass along the coast. Phone 725-3919 for rates and departure times. From March until June, the peak of the annual migration period, landlubbers *might* be able to spot whales from shore. Ask at the National Park Office for tips.

Odds 'n' Sods ❖ From golf at the nine-hole course at the Grice Bay Road turnoff (next to the Long Beach Airport), to diving, especially exploring local waters for more than 600 shipwrecks, to salmon fishing and nature cruises, the Pacific Rim is a recreational paradise. The information centres – the Tofino Information Bureau at Campbell and Third streets, and the Ucluelet Tourist Information Centre at Pat's Camera Shop in the Davison Plaza – have recommendations and information on these and many other sporting activities.

At the risk of sounding like nags, we must stress that the whole of this area is ecologically fragile. Please, please, please, treat Mother Nature's beauty with respect so that it is still unspoiled for succeeding generations to enjoy.

Where to Eat

Besides run-of-the-mill fare you'll discover in motel coffee shops along the coast, you will also find these local favourites.

The Common Loaf Bake Shop & Cafe ❖ Not only is this a very good bakery, but it is *the* meeting place for the politically conscious environmentalists who thrive in Tofino and surrounding areas. There's an outdoor patio overlooking the ocean where you can enjoy your still-warm baked goods and think political thoughts in the warm weather. Next to the L.A. Grocery at 131 1st Street, Tofino, 725-3915.

The Crab Bar ❖ What a find! All you order at this gift shop-turned tearoom-turned crab bar – is crab, beer and bread. The crab is so fresh you can literally watch the afternoon's catch being hauled up from the crab dock down the hill and unloaded through the open window into holding tanks beneath. Choose a whole or a half crab meal, which includes sourdough bread, plenty of melted butter, an interesting daily side salad ranging from broccoli and mandarin oranges to marinated raw veggies. You'll think you've died and gone to crab heaven. Ask the friendly staff for tips on crab cracking if you're a novice. Open for lunch and dinner in the summer; dinner only during most of the off season. It's at 601 Campbell Street, Tofino, 725-3733.

Jolyn's Bake Shoppe ❖ If you don't have plans to go to Ucluelet for any other reason, you *must* make a stop at Jolyn's for an apple cinnamon fritter. These are incredible dinner plate sized dough-nuts of heroic proportions, probably enough to feed a family of five. You'll also find Nanaimo bars, cinnamon buns, cookies and bread, plus little tables for eat-in coffee breaks, but don't leave without the fritters. At the Davison Plaza in Ucluelet, 726-7041.

The Loft ❖ "Mandarin peach cheesecake – made by the manager – ex-quisite!", raved one of our sources. "Chocolate mousse cake – delicious!" she added. Add in some hearty breakfasts, home cooking, attractive presentation, friendly service and an appeal-ing West Coast decor and you've got The Loft, well worth visiting while in Tofino. You can eat outdoors in the summer, on the very pretty patio. Check the interesting interior display of beaded crafts and native art. (Roy Henry Vickers' work is featured; his Eagle Aerie Gallery is across the road.) 346 Campbell Street, Tofino, 725-4241.

Peninsula Cafe ❖ This Ucluelet restaurant comes recommended by our Tofino friends, Harvey and Karen Henderson. "It's a typical Chinese-American menu," says Harvey, "with things like pork chops, egg sandwiches, terrific Chinese food, and great sea-food." It's at the Peninsula Motor Inn, 1648 Peninsula Road, Ucluelet, 726-7751.

Pot Belly ❖ For a reasonably-priced breakfast, lunch, or dinner, look for the Pot Belly restaurant. Delicious homestyle food – like their Pennant Sandwich (shrimp, asparagus, ham, and Swiss cheese on rye)—is a big hit with residents and visitors alike. The friendly, courteous service is great too. It's at 1566 Peninsula Road, near the Co-op store in Ucluelet, 726-7441.

Schooner Restaurant ❖ A longtime Tofino landmark, this attractive restaurant is the place to hit if you feel like getting dressed up and going out to celebrate something special. (Remember though, this is the West Coast, so dressing up still looks pretty casual.) Try the famous clam chowder (it's a twenty-year-old recipe) or the Vancouver Island oysters in a tangy sauce. Renowned for its seafood, the Schooner's kitchen also turns out homemade desserts and homebaked dinner rolls. Childrens' menus are available, and the daily specials are a good bet. 331 Main, Tofino, call for reservations at 725-3444.

Smiley's ❖ Breakfast in the bowling alley? Yes, sir, this is Ucluelet's most popular diner, jammed with locals rather than tourists. Desserts are baked fresh daily—try the pies!—homemade soups are delicious, and the fish and chip specials feature locally caught fish every day. Zero decor, but we like it. While you're here you can play video games or bowl a few frames. On Peninsula Road, on the way into town, across the street a bit from the Canadian Princess, 726-4213.

Three Crabs Deli-Cafe ❖ Stop at the Three Crabs for some take-out picnic fare on your way to the beach. The staff will whip up a picnic lunch in a basket for you, complete with wine glasses, smoked salmon, lovely salads and more. Try the "Egg McDeli" too. 637 Campbell Street, Tofino, 725-3715.

The Whale's Tale ❖ Try the Whale's Tale restaurant in Ucluelet. This is your basic steak and seafood place, but nicely fancied up in a pleasant sea view location. Next to the Thornton Motel, at 1861 Peninsula Road, 726-4621.

Where to Shop

The traveller will find sources for food, lodgings, gas, and the odd ice cream cone in the Long Beach area, but for a good selection of local art and handcrafts we recommend the following:

Du-Quah Gallery ❖ The Du-Quah Gallery is in a traditional longhouse-style building that houses native artwork like Nootka masks, moccasins, beadwork, and basketry (including that famous Maquinna hat!) 1971 Peninsula Road, Ucluelet, 726-7223.

Sandpiper Arts Centre ❖ The Sandpiper Arts Centre, a local artists' co-operative, has a fine collection of paintings, photographs, pottery, and native Indian work. 278 Main Street, Ucluelet, 726-7331.

Image West ❖ This little Ucluelet craft shop is worth a stop if only to admire the innovative decor and display, including the resident sea lion, basking for eternity on an indoor seascape. Beach-combed artifacts, whale bones, shark's teeth, some really fine pottery and local crafts, books, and high quality T-shirts are just some of the features here. 1754 Peninsula Road, Ucluelet, 726-4487.

Eagle Aerie Gallery ❖ "This building," we said to artist Roy Henry Vickers, "is a work of art!"

He laughed, agreeing with our assessment of his Tofino gallery. "You're right," he replied. "My brother Art helped me build it."

Vickers is a West Coast native Indian artist (a grad of Victoria's Oak Bay High), who has attracted world-wide fame. Inspired by the lines of the traditional West Coast Indian longhouse, this gallery is a must-see. The stunning lighting effect, haunting music, hand-carved totems supporting giant cedar beams, and Vickers' lyrical paintings have drawn international acclaim since 1986. During the average summer, over 150,000 people tour this spectacular museum. If you pale at the price tag of an original Vickers, head for the back where a selection of books, art cards and lithographs are reasonably priced souvenirs of this fine gallery. 350 Campbell Street, Tofino, 725-3235.

Where to Stay

Green Point Campsite ❖ Campers planning a summertime stay at the National Park's Green Point site must expect a long wait — and we're talking *days* in some cases. First come, first served is the rule here, with long vehicle line-ups forming in the early morning hours. By 11 a.m., when the number of daily vacancies is confirmed, the same number of waiting vehicles is allowed past the gate. The overflow is left to find a night's lodging elsewhere. Those who brave the long wait tell us that this is the best campsite anywhere, just a seashell's throw from the magnificent surf of Long Beach.

Schooner Trail Campsite ❖ A more primitive walk-in campsite is available at the north end of Long Beach, at the end of a thirty minute walk on the Schooner Trail. Some private cottage resorts near Tofino offer campground facilities as well.

Poett's Nook ❖ In Bamfield, Poett's Nook, about four miles east of the village, is the favoured spot for campers. There is a boat-launching site here as well.

Ocean Village Beach Resort ❖ Just north of Long Beach, on the way to Tofino, you'll pass a strip of oceanfront cottage resorts on the west side of Highway 4. Our favourite here is Ocean Village Beach Resort, two miles south of Tofino. All of the comfy and rustic Gothic Arch cottages face beautiful McKenzie Beach. (Beachcombers like the tiny offshore island that is reached via a sandbar at low tide.) This is a regular winter destination for Victoria families, who say that the best time to see the Pacific is during the fierce storms which re-arrange the shoreline by the hour. You can float in the heated indoor pool while you watch. Double rates start at $72. Write Box 490, Hellesen Drive, Tofino, V0R 2Z0, or phone 725-3755.

Canadian Princess ❖ Lodgings in the Ucluelet area are generally "in town," with some views overlooking the Ucluelet boat basin. One hotel, the Canadian Princess, is actually an old west coast steamship moored permanently in the harbour. Single and multiple berth staterooms with shared bath are available. Remember that these are very small cabins compared to your average motel room (you *are* on a ship!). There are also some full facility rooms in the main lodge building, plus a dining room and lounge. The Princess' big draw is the variety of fishing and whale-watching charter packages offered. Double rates start at $48. Off Peninsula Road, write Box 939, Ucluelet, V0R 3A0, or phone 726-7771.

West Coast Motel ❖ Close by is the West Coast Motel, with a number of rooms, one or two bedroom suites, and some welcome features like a racquetball court, sauna, indoor pool, and even some in-room whirlpool baths. A super recommendation comes from friends who stayed at the West Coast Motel. The owners, Marc and Marcelle Noel, took the time to mail a child's toy, forgotten in the suite, back to our friends in Victoria. People who go out of their way like that deserve a pat on the back and our patronage. Double rates here start at $50. 247 Hemlock, Ucluelet; write Box 275, V0R 3A0, or phone 726-7732.

Burley's ❖ Our third pick for Ucluelet is Burley's, a waterfront home on the inlet south of town, which offers scenic views from every window. They'll even let you take out their rowboat if you ask nicely. A continental breakfast—served anytime—is included in the room rate, that starts at about $35 double. 1078 Helen Road, 726-4444.

Bamfield Trails Motel ❖ We have enjoyed our Bamfield stays in a housekeeping unit at the clean and modern Bamfield Trails Motel. It is convenient to everything (mind you, it's hard not to be convenient to everything in a place as tiny as Bamfield). Double rates start at $55. Write Box 7, Bamfield, V0R 1B0, or phone 728-3231.

Pacific Sands Beach Resort ❖ The Cox Bay site of Pacific Sands Resort will appeal to travellers yearning for wild, crashing breakers just outside the bedroom window. All units at Pacific Sands—cedar housekeeping cottages, fireplace suites, or rooms in the main lodge—are just a few steps away from the bay's scenic shoreline. It's pure West Coast! Watch for the sign at 4120 Pacific Rim Highway, about halfway between Tofino and the National Park. Call the Pettingers for rate info at 725-3322.

Bed & Breakfast ❖ An increasingly large number of private homes, ranging from modest village bungalows to spectacular seaside digs, offer B & B in the Pacific Rim area. One such place worth a visit is Joan Dublanko's B & B at Chesterman's Beach, just south of Tofino. You'll find three separate units, including a private cottage, on this awesome one-mile stretch of sandy beach. Rates average $100 a night with a breakfast of homemade muffins, breads and fruit. 1345 Chesterman's Beach Road, Tofino, 725-3726.

Comox Valley

If, by some cruel accident of fate, we had to move away from our beautiful Victoria, we hope this would be our new destination. The three major communities in this valley – *Comox*, *Courtenay*, and *Cumberland* – share one of the prettiest parts of the Island, nestled between snow-capped mountains on the west and the Strait of Georgia on the east. Europeans are known to call this area "little Switzerland" because of the spectacular mountain scenery.

Each community, though geographically close, retains a separate and unique style. Comox, like many other Vancouver Island towns, has its historical roots in the Hudson's Bay Company, which sent the original settlers here to farm in 1862. The native Indians called this area "Komuck-way," meaning "abundance" or "plenty." This was later shortened to "Komoux," and finally "Comox." Today this town is the fastest growing in the valley, due in part to the presence of a Canadian Forces Base which

is the Valley's single largest employer. Over 1,800 people are on direct payroll here, with an estimated 8,000 military personnel, civilians, and dependents directly associated with the base. The BC ferries' dock in Comox is served by daily sailings to the mainland via Powell River. We recommend this trip to visitors who want a scenic circle tour, which includes the Sunshine Coast area, en route to Vancouver.

Courtenay is the largest community in the Valley, with a population of 9,647. Besides supporting farming, fishing, and logging, Courtenay is the district's cultural and commercial centre.

Here you'll find cosmopolitan restaurants and a charming shopping district with cobbled streets, brick planters, and Courtenay's famous "Mile of Flowers."

Cumberland has a long history of coal mining dating back over a century; back in 1887, in fact, this tiny community was a full-fledged city and boasted the largest Chinatown north of San Francisco.

Most tourist spots toot their horns about being a "year-round vacation-land." Although it's a tired phrase, it really is true for the Comox Valley. Twenty miles from valley towns are the major ski areas of Forbidden Plateau and Mount Washington; the all-year mild climate allows fishing, golfing, and outdoor sports, and the rural beauty of the valley (including the largest potato farm in British Columbia) is a scenic delight any time of the year. If we're starting to sound like a glossy tourist brochure, it's because we are hooked on this place. Read on...

What to See and Do

ACTIVITIES

Golf ❖ Sporty types looking for golf, fishing, water sports, and such have come to the right place. There are four golf course in the district: **Pacific Playgrounds** at Saratoga Beach, about thirty minutes north of Courtenay on Highway 19; **Sunnydale Golf Club**, an eighteen-hole course a few minutes north off Highway 19; **Comox Golf Club**, and **Longlands Par 3**, both in Comox. Stop at the Tourist Information Centre, 2040 Cliffe Avenue in Courtenay, for information and directions.

Fishing ❖ While you're at the Information Centre, you can contact one of the Valley's fifty licensed fishing guides. These folks have their own special fishing spots, but they'll share their secrets for a fee. Rates start at $20 per hour for a party of four, and include rods, tackle, lure, bait, and light snacks.

Jogging ❖ There are lots of joggers' routes throughout the Valley, and a cinder running track at *Comox Valley Sports Centre*, off Howard Road, off Highway 19, just north of Lewis Park.

Water Sports ❖ Water sports fans are invited to sailboard in Comox Harbour, off Goose Spit, or at Comox Lake, near Cumberland. We're in SCUBA diving paradise here, and the Comox Valley's sheltered waters support marine life surpassing that of tropical waters. *T.D. Sports*, at 2885 Cliffe Avenue in Courtenay, organizes local dive charters.

If you're not into diving, maybe "Tubing" is for you. "Tubers" are people who float down the Puntledge River on giant inner tubes. A *Tubers' Trail* has been constructed near the entrance driveway to the Lower Puntledge Hatchery (see Hatchery entry for directions). The steep, marked trail, bordered by handrails, leads you to the riverbank. Spectators can watch this splashy spectacle anywhere along the Puntledge, or at Courtenay's *Puntledge Park*, off Fifth Street.

Courtenay Youth Music Centre ❖ For almost twenty years, the Courtenay Youth Music Centre's summer festival has been a hit with tourists and townspeople alike. Nearly every night during the five-week run of this unique music school and festival, you can attend events ranging from dinner theatre at local restaurants to jazz concerts, children's opera, or free music in the park. Admission tickets can be purchased separately (festival schedules are posted everywhere around town), or as part of a Season's Pass or Mini Pass. Phone the Festival Office at 338-7463 for this summer's information.

Filberg Lodge and Park ❖ The late Bob and Florence Filberg raised their family in this Art Deco classic overlooking Comox Harbour. Although Mr. Filberg spent his last years in Hawaii, the house was beautifully maintained and after his death, the nine-acre estate was left for the public to enjoy. We aren't sure whether to classify this place as a park, a museum, or an art gallery; it's a show place for local artists and craftspeople, and every summer is the site of the *Filberg Festival of Arts and Crafts*. Your children will enjoy the hands-on animal farm and petting zoo on the lovely grounds. Admission is absolutely free, but donations are invited. The Lodge is at the corner of Comox Avenue (the main commercial street in Comox) and Filberg Road.

Forbidden Plateau ❖ Native Indians used to call this ski resort area "Hi-Yu Cultus Illahe," meaning "plenty bad place." Lest this scare you off, the legend goes that the Comox Indian men, fearing attack from nearby Cowichan warriors, sent their women and children up into these mountainous highlands for safety, but after battling the enemy, the Comox could not find a trace of their families. They feared that horrible hairy giants had thrown them over the cliffs of what is now Cruikshank Canyon. Because of this, the Plateau became Forbidden. You'd never know its unwelcoming history today, judging from the popularity of these slopes during ski season. Even in summer the chairlift operates on weekends and holiday Mondays from 11 a.m. to 3 p.m. The view over the Strait of Georgia is breathtaking, and you can pop into the coffee shop or Kandahar Lounge for refreshment. Summer rates for chairlift tickets are $3 per person. Under the ski-tow right-of-way are wild blueberry bushes, loaded in late August and September. To get here from Courtenay, travel west on First Street, turn right on Condensory Road, and left out to Piercy Road. From there, twenty minutes will bring you to the base.

Goose Spit ❖ Just half a mile from downtown Comox, this long sandy peninsula juts into Comox Harbour and is the site of colourful sailboarding regattas each Saturday. The Spit if also a training area for Sea Cadets from all parts of Canada—you might hear shots ringing across the Harbour. Located at the foot of Hawkins Road.

Kye Bay ❖ This is the locals' favourite beach for picnicking and swimming – and certainly one of our favourites too. Public access and limited toilet facilities are at Elks Park. The water depth can stay constant for hundreds of yards, which makes for warm swimming. This sand castle paradise is perfect for young children, who will be thrilled every time an air force jet roars overhead from CFB Comox at the top of the hill. (See our *Where to Stay* section for information on cottages along this beach, and for directions.)

Lewis Park ❖ You'll see this picturesque riverside park as you travel north along Highway 19, just over the old bridge past downtown Courtenay. Even if you're not planning a stay in the Comox Valley, you should take time for a short break at Courtenay's oldest park on your way to points north. It's a pleasant place for a stroll along the river, a picnic under tall shade trees, or even a summertime dip in the outdoor swimming pool. Tennis courts, lawn bowling, and a recreation centre are also here.

Mount Washington ❖ Another popular ski resort area, Mount Washington has been in operation since 1979, luring skiers to its challenging steep runs, easy beginners' slopes at Handle Tow, and cross-country triple-track-set trails. (By the way, the Nordic Lodge here bakes cinnamon sticky buns that are the equal of the famous ones fondly remembered by UBC alumni.) Mount Washington is also a good starting point for day hikes in the summer months. Backpackers looking for a five to six hour return trip can drive up to the ski area, then follow well-marked trails across *Paradise Meadows* to beautiful, high-level *Moat Lake*, or to *Circlet Lake*, reached after an even easier hike. Both trails are in good condition, very gradual, and the trout in both lakes are apparently just begging to be caught.

A more strenuous hike – serious hiking boots are best – is the Battleship Lake, Lady Lake, and Croteau Lake route. Fast hikers can reach Croteau Lake in 90 minutes; allow two and a half hours for a more relaxed pace to enjoy the wild rhododendrons, fishing and swimming water, and panoramic views. Follow directions to Mount Washington Ski Resort Road and drive to the Cross-Country Ski Lodge. Trail starts on the downside of the parking area about halfway along. The Battleship Lake trail is across the meadows.

Museums ❖ When you have an uncontrollable urge to learn more about the history of the Comox Valley, two area museums will enlighten you. The *Courtenay & District Museum* bills itself as the largest log cabin in the world. It occupies the main floor of the Canadian Native Sons building, built in 1928 entirely of vertical logs. Here you'll find a replica of a Comox Indian longhouse, antique logging and agricultural equipment, Indian masks, carving and weaving, and the Kath Kirk doll collection. 360 Cliffe Avenue, 334-3611.

A short drive from here is the *Cumberland Museum*, which offers displays of the coal mining history of the area, models of the former Chinatown and "Japtown" (their term, not ours), and a pictorial history of the disastrous fire that burned entire city blocks of this once-bustling coal town.

At the corner of First and Dunsmuir, in the village of Cumberland. Phone 336-2445.

Puntledge Hatchery ❖ Displays of a different sort can be found at the Puntledge Hatchery, constructed by the federal and provincial governments to restore the chinook and coho salmon populations after the damming of the Puntledge River effectively destroyed their runs. Visitors can see both the upper hatchery, just off Piercy Road (on the way to the ski areas), and the lower site, at the end of Powerhouse Road, off Lake Trail Road.

Tribune Bay Provincial Park ❖ Although its *not* in the Comox Valley (actually, it's not even on Vancouver Island), we can't resist recommending this *Hornby Island* landmark. For years, Victorians have make the long trek up-island to spend part of the summer at what has been called the finest sand beach in the Strait of Georgia. This lovely day-trip destination is *the* place for beachcombers and shell-collectors. Pack a picnic lunch, hop on the hourly ferry at Buckley Bay (twenty minutes south of Courtenay on Highway 19) to *Denman Island*. Follow the road across that island to the ferry terminal at Gravely Bay, where you catch the ferry over to Hornby Island. Tribune Bay is about five miles from the ferry landing, just a skip north of the Co-op crossroads. (The bulletin board at the Co-op store, incidentally, is a calendar of the small island's activities.)

Hornby Island Festival ❖ Every year, in early August, Hornby Island is the site of an 11 day festival of visual and performing arts. Past players have included such widely diverse well-knowns as the Purcell String Quartet and that goofy Newfie theatre troop, CODCO. Don't miss it if you're in the area. Phone the Festival Society at 335-2734 for information on this year's events.

Walks ❖ Pick up a copy of the *Blue Heron Book of Trails and Walks in the Comox Valley*, a mere $3.95 in most bookstores around town. This little booklet gives an extensive listing of the many scenic hikes available in the valley, complete with maps and directions.

Where to Eat

The Old House ❖ We hardly need to mention The Old House. Whenever the subject of food came up in relation to the Valley, the name of this restaurant was first on everyone's lips. Situated in a lovingly preserved 1938 rustic home, built originally for the Kirk family (Mrs. Kirk's doll collection is on display at the Courtenay Museum downtown), the Old House has been setting culinary trends since opening in 1973. Specialties range from medallions of reindeer to Grandpa Horvath's Fish Pot. We especially liked the Sunday brunch menu, and recommend the baked potato stuffed with eggs, bacon, spinach, and cheese, and topped with Hollandaise sauce. All the baked goods—croissants, French brioches, fresh fruit muffins, delightful bread—are prepared in the kitchen here. You can dine more casually in the pub-style restaurant downstairs, or outdoors on the latticed deck overlooking the river. Reservations are compulsory upstairs; sometimes it's so packed that service becomes more lax than the stiff prices would have you expect. Still, we think the rustic charm and good food merit a visit. At 1760 Riverside Lane—watch for the sign on the right side of Highway 19 as you turn onto the new bridge towards Campbell River. Phone 338-5406 for those all-important reservations.

La Cremaillere ❖ Another elegant riverside restaurant, also in Courtenay, is La Cremaillere (pronounced La Crem-aye-air). This lovely Tudor-style building is a picturesque setting for fine French cuisine, professionally and artistically presented. Incurably romantic types can reserve a private dining room for two. 975 Comox Road, 338-8131.

Dutch Deli Sandwich Shop ❖ For a quick, reasonably-priced daytime spot, we like the Dutch Deli Sandwich Shop, at the corner of Fourth Street and Duncan in downtown Courtenay. Here you can custom order great looking designer sandwiches on a wide choice of breads, bagels, and buns, bulging with things like Montreal smoked beef, shrimp, eggs, or sprouts. Fresh salads — from fruit to Greek — and homemade soups are available too. You can even have a glass of wine or beer with your lunch.

Courtenay Bakery ❖ Skip the Dutch Deli's dessert (everything except the butter tarts comes from the nearby SuperValu grocery store) and walk around the corner to Fifth Street and the Courtenay Bakery, the only real bakery-style bakery in Courtenay. Coffee and tea are sold here too, so you can sit at one of the little tables inside while you indulge your sweet tooth.

Leung's ❖ One day Carolyn walked into Leung's, expecting to buy a couple of cans of juice for her thirsty children. She found not only a jam-packed grocery store, but also a long counter with stools, the kind you used to find in the "luncheonettes" of old dime stores. Nothing fancy here, but the stools were all taken by people happily enjoying basic burgers, grilled cheese sandwiches and real milkshakes in metal containers. Rock-bottom lunch or snack prices, and a nostalgic trip back in time! 456 Fifth Street in Courtenay, phone 334-3824.

McSwiggins ❖ Highly recommended by locals was the deep dish sour cream apple pie at McSwiggins, so we nobly threw our jaws into action and our waistlines into oblivion. This is apple pie to die for. McSwiggins serves what might just be the Best Coffee on the Island. Besides the pie, there are fresh muffins and cinnamon buns, excellent homemade soups, made-to-order sandwiches and hearty breakfasts for early risers. Open 7:30 a.m. to 5 p.m. at 2270 Cliffe Avenue (still the Island Highway here) at the corner of Mansfield, across from the gas station. (This is a Farmer's Market complex with an art store, a bakery, a place to get Ukrainian foods and fudge, and a secondhand store with wonderful bridal gowns in case you happen to be eloping and using this book as your travel guide.) McSwiggins telephone: 334-2231.

Where to Shop

Edible Island Whole Foods ❖ Whether you're stocking your beach cabin with a week's worth of groceries, or just want fruit and snacks for another long stretch in the car, you'll find a number of commercial chain grocers around the Valley towns and roadside fruit stands lining Highway 19 in the summer months. One of our Valley favourites is the Edible Island Whole Foods Market. This worker's co-operative is one of the largest natural foods distributors on the Island. Besides a really fine display of seasonal fruits and veggies – organic of course – Edible Island sells bulk baking supplies, herbal teas, natural cosmetics, delicious juices and sodas, and great hand-packaged trail mix blends for the hungry snackers in your back seat. (We recommend their own "Merville Mix.") 479 4th Street, Courtenay, 334-3116.

Black Creek General Store ❖ If you pass Nurmi road on your way to the North Island, and discover that you've forgotten to load up on groceries in Courtenay, you could pull over when you see the Black Creek Country Market on the right side. This place is a combination general store/grocery/liquor store/coffee shop/ice cream stand/gas station/souvenir shop, all crammed into one ordinary little building.

Arts Alliance ❖ The tiny storefront on Fourth Street hardly hints of the extensive delights found at Arts Alliance. The front of the shop showcases handcrafts created by local artists. Every piece is juried and the strict standards show in the high quality of the work attractively displayed.

Go down the stairs at the back of the shop and find a surprisingly spacious art gallery. Fourteen shows a year are scheduled; subjects range from local experimental work to community shows (like student work from North Island College).

The Alliance is also active in promoting the performing arts in the Comox Valley, so drop in to find out what the latest offering is. Open 10 a.m. to 4 p.m. at 367 Fourth Street, 338-6211.

Dower Cottage ❖ Another good bet for a memento of your Comox Valley vacation is Dower Cottage, one of those places almost too cute to be true. Everything in this storybook cottage of a gift shop is tastefully displayed. It's on the grounds of the Old House restaurant, between apple trees and the strawberry patch. (See our **Where to Eat** section for directions.) 1730 Riverside Lane, 338-7151.

Country Charm ❖ This Courtenay furniture and gift shop has some unusual home-oriented crafts for sale. On Duncan Avenue between Fourth and Fifth Streets, 442D Duncan. Phone 338-9513.

Robert A ❖ A store where you can look for trendy togs by two of our favourite designers, Ralph Lauren and Simon Change, is the chic boutique called Robert A. At 475 Cliffe Avenue, Courtenay, 338-7333.

Blue Heron Books ❖ Over in Comox, near the Lorne Hotel (said to be BC's oldest licensed hotel), bookworms will find Blue Heron Books, an interesting store with a good selection of marine and nautical titles, plus a well-stocked juvenile section. 1803 Comox Avenue, 339-6111.

Laughing Oyster Books ❖ A Courtenay bookstore which caught our eye was Laughing Oyster Bookshop. We think you'll enjoy the warm, cozy, woodlined atmosphere here. It's a nice place to browse on a rainy afternoon. 250 Sixth Street, phone 334-2511. Also check out the **Book Shell** in the Driftwood Mall, 338-5943.

ABC Books and Second Page Used Books ❖ We're lumping together these two secondhand bookstores for bargain hunters. They're conveniently located around the corner from each other in Courtenay but the stock is quite different. *ABC* is a mecca for comic collectors; they also have tapes, records, and quite a decent selection of secondhand books in clearly marked sections.

Second Page, run by an ex-librarian and her partner, is higher brow with shelves full of hardcover classics and better quality paperbacks. It's a good place to find some out-of-print gems.

ABC is at 324 Fifth Street, 334-4888, and Second Page is around the corner at 546 Duncan Avenue, 338-1144.

Clarion Books & Music ❖ Clarion Books carries a remarkably eclectic selection of books which ranges through food, gardening, metaphysics, philosophy, travel, fiction of all kinds, and an excellent children's section. This range would be appealing enough for an average bookstore, but is amazingly so here because half the store space is given over to classical music records, cassettes, and compact discs. We think this says a lot for the owner's unerring taste in both music and literature. We think you'll agree that Clarion is a real find. It's at 480B Sixth Street, Courtenay, 338-7722.

The Needle Loft Studio ❖ Elizabeth Dyck reminded us that travellers who take their needlework and crafts projects with them on holidays might enjoy a visit to the Needle Loft Studio. Well, we did just that, and it is wonderful! The Studio is housed on the second floor of a barn-shaped garage, part of a pretty hobby farm that resembles a children's story book illustration. Books and patterns line one wall of the Studio, and examples of various kinds of needlework are displayed on tables, walls, chests—every inch of space seems to have some gorgeous handcrafted something on it. This shop carries a complete line of embroidery floss, cross stitch charts, specialty needlework books, fabrics, accessories like clocks, mirrors, unique frames, silver and porcelain boxes, and related products. If you're a needleworker, we can guarantee you'll go nuts in here. The Studio is open weekdays 9 to 5; and on the second and fourth Saturdays of the month from 10 to 2. Look for the red barn at the top of Mission Hill, two miles north of Courtenay at 4914 Island Highway, 334-2361.

Blue Chicken Antiques ❖ This might sound like a strange name for an antique shop until you arrive and note that there are actually blue chickens (the decorative variety) outside the door. Inside, the tiny premises are jammed to the rafters with glorious stuff. The rafters are included because there are bisque doll heads stuck on pegs along the roof beams (not as grisly as it sounds, really), plus assorted jugs, bits of horse harness, and kerosene lanterns. Every square inch of shelf space is filled, and there is another room at the other end of the building where furniture is displayed. Prices are very reasonable, and no collector should miss this gem. Open daily at the corner of Wentworth Road and the Island Highway, two miles north of Courtenay, 334-2853.

Where to Stay

Many of the hotels and larger motels in the area offer attractively priced room, ski, and transport-to-the-slopes deals in winter. Some slide right into the fishing season during the summer months, with tackle-and-boat charter packages. You'll find a large number of full-service hotels and budget motels, totalling 750 rooms in all, plus over 400 woodsy campsites.

Kye Bay ❖ Our summer recommendation is to stay out by the water where you can relax at the beach all day and still be close to town. Two areas we like, both out of town, are Kye Bay and Merville. Kye Bay is lined—cheek-by-jowl, we must admit—with tiny housekeeping cottages, but the beach here is so gorgeous we think it is a super place to bed down for a week. Our favourite place is ***Kye Bay Guest Lodge and Cottages*** at 590 Winslow, 339-6112. Weekly rate for a one-bedroom cottage is $350, for a two-bedroom it's $390. Find it by going north on Lazo Road in Comox, taking a sharp right past the air base down a steep road to the beach.

The Alders ❖ In Merville, which is a pleasant twenty-minute drive north of Courtenay, you'll want to watch for the sign on the east side of Highway 19 that says The Alders. We warn you that this resort of seventeen rustic waterfront cabins is so popular that you might have trouble booking a week (or even a weekend), but do give it a try. There is a quiet, *private* beach, some rock outcroppings for tidepool explorations, and blue-green water for fishing and swimming. Rates start at $400 weekly. Write P.O. Box 2, Merville, V0R 2M0, or phone 337-5322. It's at the end of a terrible gravel road (about ten minutes drive for Carolyn's VW Rabbit); watch for the Stardust Drive-In on Highway 19 for the turnoff sign.

North Island

Campbell River

Campbell River, 165 miles north of Victoria, is fishing crazy. The coffee shops open at 5 a.m. or before, to accommodate early risers; every deli or meat market offers smoking and canning services for the big ones that *don't* get away; and you can buy fishing licences from local shopping-centre kiosks. Inside the lobbies of most hotels you will find huge chalkboards announcing the "Catch of the Day." The *Anchor Inn*, a modern seaside hotel, has an electronic chalkboard that sends the day's results to each guest room's television screen via a cable feed from their computer.

With over 200 licensed fishing guides to take you casting, mooching, or trolling, Campbell River proudly claims to be the "Salmon Fishing Capital of the World." (A word of warning here, however: *every* community north of Nanaimo will welcome you, with giant billboards, to the best salmon fishing in the world.) Campbell River does seem to have historical backing to its claim, though. Local Indian guides recall early days when it was rumoured you could cross the Passage on foot atop the teeming salmon. And BIG? Year after year the largest chinook salmon—fifty-five to sixty-five pounds—in the World Salmon Fishing Championships are caught in Campbell River waters. The *Tyee Club* was formed here in 1925. To qualify for membership, catch a tyee (a chinook weighing over thirty pounds) with the regulation tackle you will use if you are with a registered guide (as you should be).

We would like to state right now that we are only interested in fish when it appears on our dinner plates, suitably stuffed or sauced, for our gastronomic enjoyment. The mechanics of how it gets from the water to the dining room interest us not at all. Check out any of the excellent local fishing books for the nitty-gritty details of how to catch the little beggars. Call us when they're cooked.

Campbell River began almost by accident, as a smaller cousin to the thriving community on Quadra Island, across Discovery Passage. In 1900, only five settlers lived in what is now Campbell River. The Thulin family built a small hotel here to accommodate loggers and sportsmen, drawn here even then by the famous fishing. A second, and then a third hotel became necessary to separate the rowdy loggers from the more genteel fishermen from the city. Soon after came a trading post, a wharf, and a dance hall. When the giant Elk Falls hydro project was built in 1948, the quiet fishing and logging community began growing to its current population of 18,000.

Campbell River makes a good base from which to explore the North Island. It has all the shopping, hotel, and restaurant facilities you would expect in a regional centre, and even if, like us, you're not keen on fishing, it offers travellers a wide variety of interesting day trips.

What to See & Do

The Campbell River Chamber of Commerce puts out one of the most complete and varied tourist brochures we've seen. It's called "Things to Do in Campbell River," and lists no less than twenty-eight sightseeing outings of interest to visitors. Here's a sampling of our favourites.

Campbell River BMX Club ❖ Do you have a small bike strapped onto the back of your Winnebago? If so, you *must* visit the new 1600-foot BMX Supertrack. According to local officials, this is the "best track in BC." It has a fourteen-foot-high starting hill, an electronic starting gate, and a shorter, alternate route for beginners. Two Vancouver BMX experts visited this Super-track and admitted that it surpassed both of theirs. So there, you Big City bikers! Next door to the ice rink/swimming pool complex, at 565 Pinecrest.

Campbell River Museum ❖ Want to take a boat trip to Maud Island? A caving trip to Gold River? A bog walk around Strathcona Park Lodge? If you have only a few days here, and you want to catch the highlights in a short period of time, you can't do better than to stop at the Campbell River Museum. Not only does this little building house displays of early Campbell River (and remember, this is a town that started to grow during the forties), but it also offers Museum Tours: an impressive array of trips, scheduled several times a week, to almost anywhere you'd want to go. Qualified leaders take small groups out at a very reasonable cost. Just pack your camera, a snack, and sturdy shoes. Stop at the Museum for a detailed, three moth schedule of tours. Tyee Plaza, 1235 Island Highway, 287-3103.

Discovery Pier ❖ Since its opening in July 1987, Canada's first salt-water fishing pier has been a year-round hit. Amenities along the 600 foot long pier include glassed-in shelters that allow the angler to fish in comfort during bad weather; four fish-cleaning stations; an inclined fishing rail with holes in it for rod holders; and bait cutting boards. Although there is a small fee for adults, seniors and children fish for free, and seasons' passes are also available. Rent gear, pick up tips, and buy treats from the concession stand run by Barb and George Bryant. Look for good fishing beyond the Government Wharf, across the road from Pier House Bed & Breakfast. Phone 286-6199 for more info.

Diving ❖ You can rent SCUBA equipment and get inside information on the best diving spots at *Beaver Aquatics*, located near the Quadra Ferry dock in the Discovery Inn Marina, 975 Tyee Plaza, 287-7652.

NATURE WALKS

You don't need to be a mountaineer to enjoy some of the scenic hikes around Campbell River. Easy trails, a boon to car-cramped legs, criss-cross the countryside around here.

Elk Falls Provincial Park ❖ A ten-minute drive north of town toward Gold River brings you to lovely, wooded Elk Falls Park. This park features a waterfall over a deep gorge. The fall is most impressive in early spring when the river is high. Later on, especially during a hot, dry summer, it can shrink to a medium sized trickle. There's a picnic spot and walking trails, plus easy hiking past a virgin stand of Douglas fir trees.

Haig-Brown Kingfisher Creek Project ❖ The name is a mouthful, but don't miss this interesting series of trails and boardwalks through overgrown fields, down to the Campbell River. Guided tours are offered during the summer months. Take Campbell River Road to the blue gate opposite the Catholic Church. Tours start from the booth.

Miracle Beach Provincial Park ❖ Follow the signs south of Campbell River to Miracle Beach, where you will find campsites, day facilities, and a beach. There are guided nature hikes, speakers, and outdoor slide shows in the summer months.

Nunns Creek Park ❖ Located right in town, this is a preserved wooded area with a wide path accessible by wheelchair. The entrance is behind the Ironwood Mall, off Sixteenth Ave.

Quinsam River ❖ The trails along the Quinsam River, north of town, also follow the Campbell River downstream, from where it hooks up with the Quinsam, to the *Quinsam Salmon Hatchery*. Try a mid-morning visit to the Hatchery; a fascinating, self-guided tour tells you more than you ever wanted to know about our coastal salmon. Follow the tour with a brisk nature walk and a picnic lunch at the tables along the Quinsam River. The hatchery is on the Campbell River Road to Gold River, about five minutes from town.

Ripple Rock Trail ❖ The famous Ripple Rock Trail is an intermediate hiking path through the woods to seaside lookouts that offer impressive views of Seymour Narrows and Maud Island, especially at changing tide. Ripple Rock was the scene of the world's largest man-made, non-nuclear explosion when the rock—a navigational menace, six feet below the water surface at low tide—was blasted to bits in 1958. (True, there's not much of a thrill in staring at water which used to cover a giant rock, but this is a nice hike.) Allow one and a half hours to get to the lookout. The trail starts on the right-hand side of Highway 19, about ten miles north of town on the road to Sayward.

Willow Creek Trail ❖ When you're in the airport neighbourhood, you might try Willow Creek Trail. This is even easier than Ripple Rock, and takes an hour to complete. Here you will see forest primeval, cut by Willow Creek, crossed by many bridges, and very peaceful. The turnoff is on the left on Erickson Road

(Airport Road), past Fairmile Road and opposite the last two houses.

Quadra Island ❖ Quadra, one of the Discovery Island group, is the closest to Campbell River. The ferry dock is just north of downtown on the Island Highway, and signs directing you to Quadra Island are everywhere. Ferry service is frequent, every half hour in the summer, and inexpensive. The trip takes only fifty minutes.

Once over on scenic Quadra, you will be in the tiny village of *Quathiaski Cove*. A minute's walk up the hill brings you to a very pleasant neighbourhood pub, *The Landing*, complete with stained glass windows, homey atmosphere, and a pizza/burgers/seafood menu. Phone 285-3713. Other stops near the village include the *Q-Cove Plaza*, on the road to Rebecca Spit, where you can buy groceries in the only store we've ever seen which accurately calls the junk food aisle, "Junk Food." You can also explore a handful of craft, curio, and book shops.

The turnoff towards *Cape Mudge Lighthouse* leads you to this famous landmark, visible from every park of the Campbell River waterfront.

The *Kwagiulth Museum and Cultural Centre*, also in the village of Cape Mudge, has a display of world-famous potlatch regalia, tribal masks, and costumes. Its unique architecture was inspired by the shape of a sea snail. Across the street is a tiny park with ancient stone petroglyphs, part of the largest collection of such rock carvings on the Northwest coast.

We liked *Rebecca Spit Provincial Park*, about twenty minutes from Quathiaski Cove, but were disappointed that the beach surrounding this long finger of land is very rocky—if there's any sand here, we couldn't find it! Still, it's a picturesque

picnic spot. Swimmers might do well to drive over to *Village Bay Lake*, on the north end, for a sandy beach and warmer swimming.

Salmon Festival ❖ You're in for a treat if you can time your visit during the first weekend in July. The annual Salmon Festival attracts huge crowds to the parade, salmon barbecue, arts and crafts displays, Indian dancing, and other outdoor stage shows and water sports. Call the Salmon Festival office at 287-2044, or drop in at the Tourist Bureau for a schedule of events.

Strathcona Provincial Park ❖

The oldest provincial park in British Columbia is located about one-and-a-half hour's drive southwest of Campbell River. Two areas of the park, *Buttle Lake* and *Forbidden Plateau*, have some visitor oriented developments, but most of the 500,000-acre park is undeveloped and appeals primarily to travellers looking for Real Wilderness. Three large chunks of the park are designated as Nature Conservancy Areas, where no internal combustion engines are allowed. These areas preserve outstanding examples of scenery and natural history, undisturbed, so far, by the progress of modern civilization. Backpackers only, please.

Strathcona Park Lodge ❖ The part of the park we like – and certainly the most accessible to visitors from Campbell River – starts with the scenic drive along Campbell and Buttle lakes. The road hugs the lakeshores almost all the way, and passes Strathcona Park Lodge just outside the park boundary. This lodge, on Campbell Lake, is both a place to stay and an Outdoor Education Centre. It provides modern lakefront accommodation and meals, in several packages ranging from one to seven days. Double rates range from $50 to $99 per day. An extensive repertoire of programmes and wilderness skills training is offered: rock climbing, kayaking, cross-country skiing for experts, senior citizens' hiking weeks, and workshops on photography, quilting, or yoga, are just a few examples. Write for complete details of the season's offerings: Box 2160, Campbell River, BC, V9W 5C9. Radio phone number N693546; reservations only at 286-3122.

Westmin Resources Mine ❖ Once inside the park (with stops for swimming in good weather at the *Buttle Lake* or *Ralph River*

campgrounds) follow the road all the way to Westmin Resources Mine at the southern end of Buttle Lake. You can thank
Westmin for the excellent road along Buttle Lake through
Strathcona Park. Unlike most provincial parks, Strathcona has
allowed mining and logging since Day One, and the paved road
past waterfalls, creeks, nature trails, and mountaineering hikes
is mainly a transit rout for miners. (Be prepared for an attack
of Ecological Shock when you arrive at the wasteland that is
the mine.) During the summer months you can get a free tour
of the mine, at 10 a.m. and 1:30 p.m. on weekdays. The tour
takes about an hour, and would-be miners, suitably hard-
hatted, are led inside the mill where the ore minerals—zinc,
copper, and lead—are concentrated. You'll see the giant crush-
ing, grinding, and filtration machines, all wonderfully noisy and
smelly. Children love this adventure.

Where to Eat

Like most tourist destinations, Campbell River has more than its share of
fast-food chain outlets. For "adventures in dining," try one of the following.

Gourmet By The Sea ❖ This waterfront favourite is nine miles south
of Campbell River, on the main highway. Fine seafood, prepared in beguiling Continental style (from pickled salmon to
prawns in cognac sauce), and fresh—never frozen salmon is
served. Though we haven't sampled it yet, the herbed rack of
lamb is "out of this world," according to locals and regular
summer visitors. Note that twenty-four hours notice is required for this dish on weekdays. Try the bistro for light casual
dining. Theatre buffs will be interested to learn that actress/
singer Joelle Rabu, who scored an overwhelming success on
stage as Piaf in the musical production of the same name, is the
daughter of Gourmet By The Sea owners. The restaurant is
located beside Bennett's Point at Oyster Bay, 4378 S. Island
Highway. Phone 923-5234 for reservations, or to order the
lamb or any other specialty menu item.

Grape Vine Bistro ❖ This bistro has moved since the first edition of
Island Treasures, but we're pleased to report that in its new
home, attractively done up in burgundy and cream, the cuisine
is still stuff worth writing about. You'll find homemade soups,

lots of salads and appetizers, terrific stuffed potatoes, and entrees leaning towards chicken and fish selections. Cheese-cake and other caloric temptations are displayed near the front door, right at drooling level. It's a clever management ploy to make sure you leave room for dessert. It works! At 859a 12th Avenue, in the 12th Avenue Plaza, behind Overwaitea. Phone 287-2831.

Shagpoke's ❖ Every table in this tasteful, off-white and wicker room affords the best view in town. The caesar salad was highly recommended by residents, but we found it a mite salty for our palates (still, if you like anchovies...) An appetizer we did like was the deep-fried camembert, served with bearnaise sauce – delicious! Fresh seafood is the thing to order here. In fact, if you crane your neck you can probably see the wharf below, where today's catch is being cleaned. Homemade desserts are a nice change for a hotel restaurant; the Thomas children rank the Mud Pie as "the best!" Expensive, but worth it. In the Anchor Inn, 261 Island Highway, 286-1131.

Burger Joint ❖ A local hangout, with typical hangout decor (meaning none whatsoever), which is popular with residents and a nice change from the Golden Arches is *Del's Drive-In & Diner*. Find the quintessential "burgersfriesandshakes" menu, car hop service and lots of local colour. 1423 Island Highway, 287-3661.

Cold Tip ❖ Locals recommend "Jug Night" at *Painter's Lodge*, when $2.95 won't break your budget on the day before payday, but will satisfy your beer needs in the pub downstairs.

Where to Shop

With sincere apologies to the merchants of Campbell River, we can't come up with a lengthy list of highly-recommended places in which to squander your money. This may have something to do with the fact that there is an unusually large number of mall and chain store outlets here – useful if you discover that you forgot to pack your beach thongs or your child's bathing suit, but hardly a secret to out-of-town shoppers. Having said that, we should point out that we did like the following stores.

Fancy That ❖ Some people think that Campbell River, being the "Salmon Fishing Capital of the World," must have a fashion

reputation reflecting a population that goes around in rubber
hip-waders half the day. Not so—this women's clothing store
was recommended by long-time local residents who, we hasten
to add, are *extremely* well-dressed. The clothes in Fancy That
are stylish and attractively displayed, and the prices are competitive with those in big city stores. Across from Tyee Plaza
in Shoppers' Row, 287-9711.

Innovations Gift Gallery ❖ "Our shop is unique to the area," says
owner Raelene Johnston, "dut to the fact that we are the only
store in town that sells strictly quality Canadian made hand-
crafted gift products."

In our opinion, Innovations is one of the top craft stores on
the Island, scoring highly for the range of products, the impeccable workmanship, and the very reasonable prices. Although
it's hard to single out anything in a store of this high calibre,
the jewelry is outstanding and the woodwork, particularly the
innovative children's toys, is first-rate. Raelene's husband,
Stuart Arseneault, made the attractive cedar display units
which show the work to great advantage. The shop is a bit
tricky to find, but is a must-see. Head for the 13th Avenue
square, on 13th Avenue between the Overwaitea Plaza and
Ironwood Mall. Go to the back of the Square to find Innovations. Phone 286-9986.

Museum Gift Shop ❖ As a general rule, we patronize gift shops adjacent to museums because a) the selection tends to represent
Canadian rather than Hong Kong artists, and b) the money goes
to a good cause, namely, to support the museum. At the
Campbell River Museum, Tyee Plaza, 287-3103.

Page 11 Books ❖ We love bookstores like this: light and airy, full of
wicker chairs and leafy plants, with lots of room for browsing.
A friend of ours, Diane Hutton, used to drive here all the way
from Kelsey Bay to special order children's books. (The owner
is a former primary teacher with a soft spot for KidLit.)
Opposite the community hall at 410 Eleventh Avenue, 286-
6476.

Second Time Around ❖ Jill fell with cries of joy upon a classic,
long-spouted English watering can (long coveted in pricier
gardening boutiques further south, but finally affordable in this
second-hand shop housed in an old church). The stock here is

gardening boutiques further south, but finally affordable in this second-hand shop housed in an old church). The stock here is eclectic. Kites hang from the ceiling, antique bureaus hold assorted glassware, folk art adorns the walls. There is olde junque and new stuff, too. It's the ideal spot for those of us addicted to poking around flea markets and the like. 1409 Island Highway, 287-9577.

Where to Stay

Painter's Lodge ❖ When we were working on the first edition of this book, we inadvertently developed what we called the "Island Treasures Curse." As soon as we typed up a new entry, the place had a disturbing habit of burning down or going bankrupt. Painter's Lodge, the most famous fishing resort in BC, was one of our "victims," destroyed by a furnace fire on Christmas Eve 1985. The Lodge, operated by the Painter family since 1929, played host to famous fishing parties including Bob Hope, Bing Crosby, and John Wayne.

With some trepidation, then, we report that the all-new Painter's Lodge re-opened in 1988. The rebuilt lodge, on the shore of Discovery Passage, and adjacent cottages now total 63 units with double rates starting at $48. There's a pub, lounge, restaurant, heated pool, dock, fishing packages....Look for the Lodge sign north of town, off Highway 19, at 1625 MacDonald Road. Phone 286-1102 or toll free for reservations 1-800-663-7090.

Campbell River Lodge ❖ On the banks of the river, on the town side opposite Painter's, is the Campbell River Lodge, another older resort catering to fishing guests. Think rustic—these places are not like your typical city motel. The dining room, for instance, has been decorated by a carver gone berserk. Hand-carved wooden beams form the walls, stair railings, doorways, and even the ceilings; fish and King Neptune and mermaids stare down at you. Tacky but terrific. One morning we shared a continental breakfast – muffins, fresh fruit, and yogurt – while eight bald eagles soared over the river just outside our window. Fishing guides and charter boats are available, plus sauna, whirlpool, and racquet court. Rates average $60 double. Two minutes north of town at 1760 N. Island Highway, V9W 2E7, 287-7446.

April Point Lodge ❖ Another fishing lodge we like is a ferry ride away, on Quadra Island. April Point Lodge is a short drive from Quathiaski Cove on the island. It offers 200-acre seclusion, fine waterfront dining (homebaked pies, breads, and Mrs. Peterson's sticky buns), a saltwater pool, marina, and fishing packages. Accommodation is in simple lodge rooms, guest houses with fireplaces, or the deluxe three to five bedroom guest lodges, with double rates from $130 to $295 per day. Serious fishing fans and tired tourists come here to unwind and relax from mid-April to mid-October. Follow the signs at the Quathiaski harbour. For reservations write Box One, Campbell River, BC, V9W 4Z9, phone 285-2222.

Pier House Bed and Breakfast ❖ While Campbell River offers several B & B establishments, Pier House has the edge for several reasons, in our opinion. First, delightful owners Patricia Young and Peter Dwillies have the right touch to make you feel immediately at home. Second, the house itself has an interesting West Coast history. It was built in the early 1920s as a home and headquarters for Campbell River's first provincial policeman. Later, the house served as the town's courthouse. Renowned author, conservationist and judge Roderick Haig-Brown dispensed justice from the parlour.

Third, Patricia and Peter have restored their heritage home with unerring good taste and an eye to period authenticity. Antiques and decorative pieces fill the house; wallpaper and draperies reflect the 1920s elegance. Located directly across the street from Campbell River's new fishing pier, all rooms feature harbour views. Downright reasonable rates start at $33 (single) and $43 (double). Breakfast, served on fine bone china, with coffee poured from an antique server, will get you off to a good start. Pier House is smoke-free, bathrooms are shared, and although Patricia and Peter love children, their B & B is adult-oriented. 670 Island Highway; reservations 287-2943.

Coast Discovery Inn ❖ Dominating Campbell River's waterfront is this highrise resort hotel, part of the Coast chain of fine hotels. This is a popular facility with fishing types – the hotel will do everything from sending you out with an experience local guide to arranging for your catch to be smoked. The downtown location, deluxe view rooms, whirlpool and weight room make it popular with non-fishing guests, too. Rates start at $110 double. 975 Tyee Plaza; phone 287-7155.

Nasty arguments often arise between otherwise happily married couples, when one spouse's view of a perfect vacation is to lie on the beach while the other is eager to get into a battle of wits with a fish. Compromise by staying south of town at either *Miracle* or *Saratoga Beach*. A twenty-minute drive will put the fisherperson into Campbell River; meanwhile back on the sandy beach, the suntanner can have his/her fill of ultraviolet rays. Campers will like Miracle Beach, a provincial park with public beach access and day facilities. Saratoga Beach, one mile north of Miracle, offers a long strip of cottages and camping resorts lining a beautiful sandy beach.

Oyster River Resort ❖ Our very favourite place is the Oyster River Resort. The bright yellow cottages are tucked away from the other commercial resorts on the quiet, residential end of the beach. The Oyster River, a fifteen-mile long stream, is popular with fly fishermen seeking rainbow and cutthroat trout. As well, the new nature trail along the river is worth a visit to see nesting bald eagles. Look for the sign just west of the pub near the Oyster River bridge at Saratoga. For reservations at the resort write to R.R. #1, Campbell River, BC, V9W 3S4, or phone 337-5170. To find it, follow the sign east for Saratoga Beach on Highway 19. Visitors staying here are midway between Courtenay/Comox and Campbell River. You can enjoy the beach all day and still be within easy distance of the towns for dining out or sightseeing.

Stop in at the Campbell River Chamber of Commerce Travel Infocentre, 1235 Island Highway (in the stretch known as Shopper's Row), 286-0764, for a list of *Bed and Breakfast* homes, most with water views, or a complete registry of the thirty-plus modern motels and resorts in the area.

Gold River

This small logging community, population approximately 2,300, is located about sixty miles southwest of Campbell River on Highway 28. The drive alone is worth the trip because you pass through the northern tip of beautiful **Strathcona Park** after hugging the shores of Upper Campbell Lake.

Kayaking ❖ For serious nature lovers, Gold River holds a different appeal. First, the elite in the world of kayaking know Gold River because of its famous **Big Drop** a couple of miles down the river from town. This is what kayakers and white-water rafters call "big water" – a large volume of turbulent water with exciting parts like whirlpools and waterfalls. Even if you're not interested in taking your life in your hands on the river, you can watch those brave enough to try the Big Drop from the **Big Bend Park** picnic area (on Highway 28, just past the dump). Don't be put off by these directions. The park does offer a lovely sanding beach, shade tree, picnic tables, pit toilets, and fireplaces. Speaking of the dump, incidentally, it's a popular spot for viewing bears. STAY IN YOUR CAR! Look for the dump near the townsite, on Muchalat Drive.

Caving ❖ The caves near Gold River are another attraction. The **Quatsino Cave** is the deepest vertical cave in North America.

You can take tours of the **Upana Caves,** just north of town, or venture in by yourself. Both are open to the public. Stop at the Gold River Travel Infocentre, Village Square Plaza, for information, or write them at Box 39, Gold River, BC, V0P 1G0, 283-7123.

Cruises ❖ The other major reason to head for Gold River is to take a cruise on the *Uchuck III.* Every Thursday, year-round, the *Uchuck III* leaves Gold River at 9 a.m. to carry its cargo of supplies, mail, and passengers past the cliffs of Muchalat Inlet and up the Tahsis Inlet to Tahsis. The scenery is spectacular and the crew friendly and knowledgeable. The Uchuck III stops for an hour or so in Tahsis, allowing visitors times for a brief exploration of the the town, and arrives back in Gold River about 6 p.m. During July and August on Tuesdays and Wednesdays, the Uchuck III offers afternoon cruises through historic and beautiful Nootka Sound. There are brief stops at Resolution Cove (Captain Cook's first known landing place on the west coast) and Friendly Cove (where Captain Cook met the native chief Maquinna). The boat leaves Gold River at noon and arrives back at 6 p.m. Phone 283-2325 for schedules and information.

Coast Gold River Chalet ❖ After your cruise on this coastal freighter, you might want to stay overnight in Gold River at the Coast Gold River Chalet, right on the river. It has a heated pool, dining room and coffee shop, and rates start at $107 double occupancy. Phone 283-2244 for information and reservations.

Sayward Valley

The highway north from Campbell River to the end of the road at Port Hardy, is actually the route of old logging trails. The three-hour drive takes you through second-growth and newly-harvested logging areas—not a pretty sight, so give your camera a rest for this trip. But do stop at the lovely Sayward Valley, about an hour's drive north of Campbell River.

Sayward is a small logging and farming community (there has been a logging company here since 1905). We were lucky enough to hit Sayward during their July **Logger Sports Day.** This is a fascinating and thrilling display of chopping, climbing, log rolling, and other feats of derring-do peculiar to the logger's trade. The *Salmon River*, which flows past town, is famous for its trout population, and this, in part, accounts for Sayward's longtime popularity with sportsmen looking for an out-of-the-way yet accessible retreat.

Nearby is the tiny community of *Kelsey Bay*, another logging site which used to be the ferry terminus for the boat to Prince Rupert. Most of the timber leases in the valley today are owned by forestry giant MacMillan Bloedel, and most residents are MacBlo employees.

Telegraph Cove ❖ *Beaver Cove*

If Telegraph Cove were *not* at the end of a rough road, we suspect that it would be flooded with busloads of visitors, all oohing and aahing over its picturesque charm. As it is, the number of visitors has increased to the point where the handful of homes perched on stilts over the cove has been augmented by a spanking new building that houses a store, an ice-cream stand, a little coffee bar. The office of the *Bauza Cove Campground* (928-3131) is also located here. Bauza Cove, rumoured to be "the best campground in the North Island," is a very shady wooded campground; site 105 is the only one with any sun. Be sure to pick up a free copy of the *Bauza Cove Bugle* at the office.

Robson Bight ❖ A company called *Stubbs Island Charters* (928-3185) has made this village a household word among whale watchers: its boat, the *Gikumi*, makes daily trips out to Robson Bight for killer whale watching. We can't resist offering a little natural history lesson. In June 1982, Robson Bight was established as an ecological reserve, to protect what might be a regular calving ground for these whales. A "pod" of killer whales usually has five to twenty males, females, and youngsters. About thirty pods, totalling about three hundred whales, live along the BC and Washington State coastlines. An incredible nineteen of these pods are found near Robson Bight, just a skip away from Telegraph Cove. The day we first visited the Cove, the *Gikumi* had been chartered by a boatload of Seattle visitors; the following day it was booked by the University of British Columbia in Vancouver. Best to call ahead to reserve a whale-watching adventure.

Whales are not the only attraction here. The village has that neat-as-a-pin maritime feel to it, usually considered to be the exclusive property of eastern fishing villages, a la Peggy's Cove. In Telegraph Cove you can walk along the wooden boardwalk that rims the steep cove (only residents' cars are allowed on the walk). The town is owned by one man, who leases out the little houses lining the boardwalk. Residents are mostly fishermen or employees of the Telegraph Cove sawmill. Their tiny, wooden homes sport geranium-filled window boxes, and where the boardwalk hugs the shore, several ambitious gardeners have dug out immaculate rock gardens, with rhododendrons and ferns climbing the slope. The cove is famous as a SCUBA diver paradise. Highly recommended – bring your camera.

Beaver Cove ❖ You'll pass right through Beaver Cove on your way to Telegraph Cove. This is worth a camera stop when you catch sight of the picturesque bay. Beaver Cove is a dryland sorting and booming ground – as in "log booms." From here, the booms are floated out across the Georgia Strait to the mainland.

Alert Bay

The tiny fishing village of Alert Bay, on Cormorant Island, is the oldest established community on the North Island. A saltery for preserving salmon was built here in 1870. One of its major attractions today is the world's largest totem pole.

Although many other west coast totem poles lay claim to this record, the local folk are quick to point out to visitors that the Alert Bay pole is not only 173-feet high (compare *that* with your average fifteen-storey highrise!), but is also carved its full length. Other claimants, apparently, are all height and paint, but little actual carving. The totem pole in Victoria's Beacon Hill Park, incidentally, is the world's tallest *freestanding* pole. The Alert Bay pole was completed in the spring of 1971 by a team of local Native carvers. The team was led by seventy-three-year-old Jimmy Dick, who directed the carving of twenty-two figures: beavers, salmon, people, eagles, and a sun at the very top. You won't be able to see this sun with the naked eye, however, so don't forget to bring your binoculars to appreciate the intricate masterpieces way up at the top. The pole is located on the northwest tip of Cormorant Island, about a mile from the ferry dock.

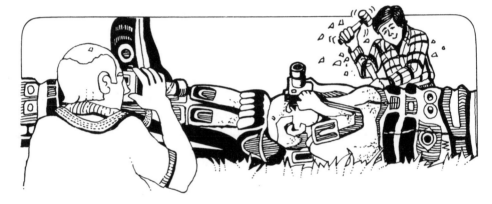

Museums, Galleries, and History ❖ We think the building on Fir Street that houses the *Library, Museum, and Archives* also deserves a stop. The tiny museum displays the story and culture of the native inhabitants of these northern rainforests.

The Namgis (Nimpkish) tribes were drawn here from their village homes at the mouth of the Nimpkish River over a hundred years ago, when the Church Mission was built on the island. The *U'mista Cultural Centre* on Front Street also serves as a museum, housing a permanent collection of traditional potlatch artifacts.

The heirloom masks, costumes, coppers, and priceless religious items were confiscated in 1922 by the white government officials who were upholding an 1800s ban on these traditional giving-away parties. The artifacts were kept for years in the Museum of Man in Ottawa and the Royal Ontario Museum in Toronto. Now back home where they belong (half of the collection is in the Kwakiutl Museum in Cape Mudge), the rare exhibit makes this centre one of the finest Native museums on the continent. Phone: 974-5403.

Alert Bay resident Krista Williams reminds visitors to stop at local historical sites, like the first Anglican Church, erected in 1879, where Sunday services are still conducted in the language of the Kwakiutl. You'll also see the Native cemetery, dotted with totem poles, by historic St. George's miniature chapel at Birch and Fir. The Tourist Information centre, across from the RCMP office, 974-5213, will provide you with a walking tour map of the village, that includes the church and other historical sites.

If you decide you want some Native art of your own after viewing the museums, drop into *The Art Class* on Fir Street. This sister shop to The Gallery in Port McNeill carries art and handicrafts with an emphasis on Indian art.

Gator Gardens ❖ Just north of the downtown strip is an Ecological Reserve featuring a bizarre variety of swamp flora stunted trees, and towering evergreens. A planked boardwalk crosses this interesting and quite different park.

Restaurants ❖ When you've worked up an appetite, try the family restaurants at the Orca or Bayside Inns, both on Fir Street.

Getting There ❖ Although Alert Bay has several campsites and three hotels, most visitors come over on the Inter-Islands ferry from Port McNeill for a day-trip only. This ferry carries 27 vehicles and up to 293 foot passengers. If you don't want to take your car, remember that a bus meets the Sunday noon ferry for Alert Bay tours. The pleasant cruise—you might be treated to the sight of a pod of passing killer whales—takes about fifty minutes and costs $2 per person. If you're in a big hurry to catch the world's largest totem, you can fly over in ten minutes from the Port Hardy airport.

We pass on to you two bits of trivia about Alert Bay:

1. Alert Bay has eleven miles of road and boasts more taxis per mile than any city in the world.

2. The current population of 1200 doubles every time a luxury cruise ship docks here in the summer, en route to Alaska.

Sointula

This little fishing village on Malcolm Island is worth a look. The same ferry that services Alert Bay also stops at Sointula, although not quite as frequently. (Runs are increased in the summer.) Check the ferry schedule for the 20-minute crossing, posted at the Port McNeill dock if you're planning a day trip to both spots.

Sointula, which means "harmony," was established at the turn of the century by Finns who wanted to create a Utopian community. There is certainly still a peaceful feeling to Sointula; if you want to soak it up for longer than a few hours you can stay at the *Malcolm Island Inn*, whose licensed dining room overlooks Johnstone Strait.

For something a bit more down-scale, head west to the *Rough Bay Ritz* for an A-1 hamburger. Incidentally, we're still deep in salmon country here. Try the Malcolm Island Inn for fishing charters, 973-6366.

To feed the spirit, visit *Jackie's Art Gallery*, right by the ferry dock, or *Shamans* in the Inn. Malcolm Island, like all of the offshore islands dotting the length of Vancouver Island, is home to a number of talented artists, and you'll find their work at Jackie's. Closed Sundays and Mondays; phone 973-6433. Shamans specialty is new and used books, particularly out of print volumes on BC and the north. As a reminder of the island's beginnings, the shop carries Finnish glassware; local crafts are also stocked. If you're visiting in November, the artistic community puts on a craft fair, complete with musical entertainment. Phone 973-6366.

For a taste of history, call the number posted on the door of the *Sointula Museum* on First Street and the person in charge will come and open it up for you so you can browse through fascinating artifacts and old photos of this community.

Sointula is the kind of place where you beachcomb, watch fishboats, look for eagles at the Rough Bay mud flats, and stroll along the fishing floats fence at Second Street and 15th Avenue. All this, and tennis courts too – next to the museum building.

Port McNeil

This northern community of 3,000 residents boasts, as its principal tourist attraction, the *World's Largest Burl*. If you don't know what a burl is, you must not frequent shops that make those dreadful high-gloss coffee tables from a giant slice of abnormal tree trunk. If you want to see what the largest deformed tree trunk in the world looks like, you will find it near the MacMillan Bloedel divisional office, two miles north of Port McNeill junction.

We think that there are many other attractive features in this area that deserve at least as much attention as a 22½-ton burl. For instance, the town itself is surprisingly modern, with lovely West Coast cedar homes lining pleasantly-treed streets, modern townhouse and condominium developments, and a small shopping and service area. Our biggest surprise was the discovery of one of the best restaurants on the island.

The Cookhouse ❖ It had been recommended to us when we were on an open-line radio program. Snobbishly superior, as we city-types tend to be, we had pictured a greasy spoon with stools and maybe a few leatherette booths, no doubt filled by uncouth denizens of the north. Imagine the sudden impact of reality when Carolyn and her tired, hot, travel-weary troop arrive at the *Pioneer Mall* late one afternoon, to be greeted: "Do you have reservations?" They were subsequently ushered into a tasteful, dimly lit, spacious restaurant. The food at The Cookhouse leans towards continental fare with professional presentation. The kitchen is in the centre of the room—you pass it on your way from the deli at the front to the restaurant at the back—and everything is squeaky clean, with gleaming copper, shiny tiles, and not even a loose counter crumb to be seen. The fussiest Old Country Baba would approve of these standards.

This is not a place for tight budgets. Dinner entrees approach $20; lunches average $8, but the service and quality is first-class and you certainly get value for your dollar. The bistro section caters to those who prefer to nibble their way through soups, salads, appetizers and desserts (like the unbelievable Nanaimo Bars, of a size so gigantic you'll be forced to share with your table companions.) Everything we've sampled here has been imaginative and delicious. Closed Sundays; and Mondays except for July and August. In the Pioneer Mall on Campbell Way, the main road into town from Highway 19. Reservations at 956-4933.

Craft Corner ❖ A couple of doors down from The Cookhouse is Craft Corner where you can find not only locally-made crafts and souvenirs, but also a listing of Bed and Breakfast homes in town. Try these for overnight accommodation and northern hospitality. We think the best reason to visit is to talk to Helen, who knows everything there is to know about Port McNeil and is generous with her knowledge. In the Pioneer Mall, 956-4544.

The Gallery ❖ A welcome addition to the Port McNeill shopping scene is this spacious store offering a selection of local art in an affordable price range; a very well-chosen book section with emphasis on local history, guidebooks, and cookbooks; and many craft pieces including some unique locally-made jewelry. Around the corner from Pioneer Mall on Broughton, 956-4033.

Dalewood Inn ❖ Here's an insider's tip: locals hint that the weekend seafood smorgasbord at the Oakwood Inn is a winner. Phone 956-3304 for information and reservations.

What to See and Do

Local resident Kathleen Kinley was very helpful in steering us to some out-of-the-way places around Port McNeill. She recommended the picnic sites that locals like best. "Pack the kids, the barbecue, and the cooled beer in the car, and head for *Cheslakees Campsite* or *Marble River Park*, and enjoy the beauty for nothing." Cheslakees is off Highway 19, south of town. It is the site of an old Indian village which Captain Vancouver visited, on the banks of the beautiful Nimpkish River, and offers campsites, a boat launch, and picnic tables. It is also a popular fishing spot for locals. Marble River is off the road to Port Alice and has the same features, plus attractive, heavily-treed hiking trails to *Bear Falls*.

Activities ❖ Outdoorsy types will think they've died and gone to heaven after they arrive here. There's canoeing and waterskiing on *O'Conner Lake*, SCUBA diving off the coast, downhill and cross-country skiing at nearby Mount Cain, hunting, and all levels of hiking. Don't miss the *Demonstration Forest* next to the MacBlo divisional office, two miles north of Port McNeill junction. Then you can tackle the waterfront trail that starts in the *Broughton Boulevard Campsite*. This walk follows the shore, passing Bear Creek, a sandy beach, and the old part of town (once known as Shelly). Further on, remains of an old logging camp can be visited. If the tide is out you can hike on for another hour and a half to *Ledge Point*. You'll know when you've arrived because of the weird, lunar-landscape appearance of the rock outcropping. (The petrified wood at the Alert Bay

Museum came from Ledge Point.) Bring your own water along, and remember to pack out what you bring in.

Hanuse Beach ❖ Early risers should visit Hanuse Beach, south of town. When you walk along the beach to the waterfall, you will catch one of nature's light shows as the early morning sun plays on the rocks around the falls. Take the Beaver Cove turnoff from the Island Highway, and follow it for about 200 yards to the road on the left. From there it is only a short distance to the beach and the mouth of Thiemer Creek. By the way, that's the village of Alert Bay across the water.

Logging Roads ❖ Port McNeill is the hub of a network of logging roads that beg the visitor to explore them. Be careful: roads are narrow and twisty, and weekdays are working days for loggers. It is best to keep your off-road travels limited to the weekends. Ask at the Information Centre in Pioneer Mall for directions. You might also inquire about the best time to view three particularly interesting examples of nature's oddities located nearby: *Vanishing River, Devil's Bath,* and the *Eternal Fountain* are all accessible only by logging road, and best for hikers or four-wheel-drive vehicles.

Easiest access is to Little Hustan Regional Cave Park, which is about a half hour's drive west off the Island Highway, on the road to Zeballos. Follow the signs (there's a map at the Zeballos turnoff) and don't try to take that Winnebago down the final narrow stretch of road leading to the park. Novices intending to do some serious spelunking should have a guide. (North Island Info centres can arrange one for you.)

Port Alice

The modern community of 1700 was BC's first "instant municipality" in 1965. The original Port Alice is long gone. Most buildings burned to the ground, or were moved to Holberg after the new townsite on Rumble Beach was completed in 1967. Many of the new homes have a spectacular view of Neurotsos Inlet and the coastal mountains across the water. The main industry is forestry, but a small business community offers gas, food, and lodging to the traveller. "Our biggest drawing card," writes Port Alice resident Heather Magnusson, "is the Great Outdoors, with fantastic fishing – an outdoor person's delight!" Golf nuts take note: the *Port Alice Golf and Country Club*, located opposite the Western Forest Products pulpmill past the townsite, has been described as "challenging" and "hilly." We think any course that has periscopes to enable golfers to see the next green certainly qualifies for this description.

Port Hardy

This is it, the end of the road, some three hundred miles north of Victoria. Port Hardy is the northern terminus of the Island Highway, and the jumping-off point for the BC Ferries scenic cruise to Prince Rupert.

This mining town of just over 5,000 owes its start to a 1912 land swindle. The Hardy Bay Land Company placed irresistibly attractive ads in British, American, and Vancouver newspapers, describing Port Hardy – then with a population of seven – as a prosperous seaport. These ads, featuring beautiful but entirely fictitious pictures of stately homes and expansive farms, were very successful in luring prospective immigrants, many of whom parted with their life savings only to discover the sad truth upon arrival. With no other alternative, most decided to stick it out and make the best of a bad situation. By the mid 1930s, when the first logging company was established here, the town was well on its way to steady growth.

Today, logging takes a back seat to mining. Utah Mines Ltd., Port Hardy's largest employer, accounts for 10 percent of all Canadian copper production. The fishing industry is a close runner-up, as one-quarter of the total BC commercial salmon catch is caught in Port Hardy waters.

The growing tourism industry reflects scenic community's efforts to spread the word about the North Island's beauty and diversity.

What to See and Do

Port Hardy's primary appeal is the great outdoors. In fine weather, with the wind gusting in across Hardy Bay and bald eagles soaring overhead, it's hard to imagine a more invigorating place to spend a few days of your vacation. We'll start you off with our choice of outdoor activities, with a few indoor alternatives for the wet days. Remember that the North Island climate, from spring through fall, favours the early riser, as many days start off sunny but turn cloudy by noon.

Beaver Harbour Park and Stories Beach ❖ Stories Beach is one of the few good bathing beaches north of Campbell River. At low tide, the white, sandy beach stretches out forever, ideal for beachcombing. Those large holes in the sand tell you where giant clams are hiding. When you poke your toe into the hole, the retreat of the clam will shoot a geyser of seawater right up your nostrils if you don't move quickly. Adjacent to this beach is a grassy park with picnic facilities, playing fields, a nature trail at the southern end, and washrooms.

The easiest way to find this park and adjoining beach is to start in town and head south on the Island Highway. A few minutes after you pass the Information Stop on the east side of the road, Byng Road veers off towards the east. There is no sign to tell you that you're heading towards Beaver Harbour, Stories Beach, or the Port Hardy Airport (a correctable over-sight, we think!) You will eventually pass the historic com-munity of *Fort Rupert*, where an old stone chimney still stands between the road and the shore to mark the Hudson's Bay Company coal community of 1849. The fort was estab-lished to provide a home for the coal miners, and a trading post for native Indians who sold salmon and furs. It was the only white settlement outside Victoria until fire destroyed it in 1851. The 1912 film "In the Land of the War Canoes," shown at the Provincial Museum in Victoria, was filmed here. Turn left onto Beaver Harbour Road, then bear right onto Stories Beach Road.

The challenging *Tex Lyon Trail* leaders hikers north along the rocky coastline from the Beaver Harbour boat launch to panoramic views of Queen Charlotte Strait at Dillon Point. The full hike is four hours plus, but you can also choose an easy twenty minute stretch only as far as the rock bluffs. *Check tide tables* before starting off to ensure you're hiking on an outgoing tide.

Cape Scott Provincial Park ❖ The history of this wilderness park includes two futile attempts at settlement. In 1897 and again in 1910, hardy Danish pioneers arrived at Hansen Lagoon. Almost eighty families tried in vain to grow crops and to fish. Utter isolation, lack of suitable access routes, and dreadful weather conditions combined to defeat the dreams of these early settlers. In 1972, Cape Scott Provincial Park, accessible only by hiking trails, was established.

The good news about this park is its incredible physical beauty. *Nels Bight* is considered to be the most impressive of the park's nine beaches, a 250-yard wide strip of fine-textured white sand that stretches over a mile and a half. Forests of red and yellow cedar, lodgepole pine, hemlock, and fir adorn the highlands of the park. Remains of the farming settlement can still be seen, and seals and sea lions inhabit the offshore islands.

The bad news—and we do mean *bad*—is the weather. Even in summer prolonged sunny periods are rare. High winds, torrential rain, and generally stormy conditions are to be expected year round. Trails here are often primitive and very muddy. Bring good raingear and a hiking staff to probe quag-mires. There is no such think as a "best time" to visit the park. The visitors' book at the park office testifies to the torture of the trails: "Thank God I'm still alive." The latest report is that the hike to Nels Bight on the north coast takes six hours, and it's another two to the Cape itself, most of this in knee-deep mud. However, before you abandon Cape Scott in favour of something easier, like Everest, we should point out that Jill's eldest son, Stephen, hiked this trail when he was a mere stripling of eleven, proving that you don't necessarily need the stamina and physique of Conan the Barbarian to survive the trip. Interested? Contact the Ministry of Parks, Victoria, 387-5002, for a brochure on the park. Detailed trail maps are available, for a small fee, from Map and Air Photo Sales, 553 Superior, Victoria, 387-1441. Allow an hour down a good gravel road to Holberg to get to the parking lot for the Cape Scott Trail, which starts on Western Forest Products land, a few miles past the village. Happy hiking.

Carrot Park/Seawall/Tsulquate Park ❖ Looking for a pleasant place to stroll along the waterfront? Just off Market Street is a pretty stretch of oceanside park where you can view the panoramic vista of Hardy Bay, with the snow-capped Coastal Mountain range in the background. Stop at the nearby Tourist Information Office at Market and Hastings (949-7622) for a brochure telling the funny tale of how Carrot Park got its name.

Cruising the Inside Passage ❖ This is the poor man's Alaska cruise. You travel from Port Hardy, aboard the BC ferry *Queen of the North*, to Prince Rupert on the mainland. Along the way you pass the same mountains, waterfalls, glaciers, killer whales, sea lions, bald eagles, and marine traffic that the rich folks aboard the high-priced luxury cruise ships see, but at a fraction of the cost. This do-it-yourself cruise will cost you $75 per person one way, plus $155 per vehicle one way. If you're making the round trip, you'll need to rent a cabin; they all have two berths and sinks but prices range from $49 to $117 depending on whether or not you're sharing bathrooms. The ship departs Port Hardy at 7:30 a.m. and arrives at Prince Rupert at 10:30 p.m. If you book one way passage with your car, you can then make a circle tour of the B.C. mainland, driving south through the cattle ranches of the Cariboo and the spectacular Fraser Valley, to Vancouver and the U.S. border. For cruise information and reservations call B.C. Ferries in Victoria (386-3431), Vancouver (669-1211) or Seattle (624-6663).

If you've driven all the way up here to take the mini-cruise and are wondering what to do with your car during your trip, call *Daze Parking and Storage* in Port Hardy (949-7792). For $5 per day they will babysit your vehicle in a fenced compound, with twenty-four hour lighting and security. The lot is in the industrial site just south of the Quatse River bridge, on Highway 19.

Diving ❖ The north end of Vancouver Island boasts some of the world's swiftest tidal currents. Hundreds of islands dot the Inside Passage up the coast, and force the seawater to squeeze through increasingly narrow channels. This makes for excellent diving conditions, rated second in the world for water clarity and colourful marine life. Experienced divers looking for something extra might try wreck diving—but be sure to go with a resident diver who knows the area. Diving charters, including night diving, current diving, photographic diving, or shallow diving for beginners, can be arranged by calling *North Island Diving and Water Sports* on Market Street, 949-7133.

Filomi Days ❖ Try to time your visit to coincide with the second weekend in August when this northern community celebrates Filomi Days in honour of its FIshing, LOgging, and MIning Heritage. Logging displays, salmon barbecues, the World Championship Crab Races, and, of course, the annual Outhouse Race make up part of the crazy festivities.

Fishing and Boating ❖ This is another year-round fishing spot, a major attraction for both locals and visitors from all over the globe. Salmon, trout, red snapper, halibut in the 100-pound range – you name it and Port Hardy claims to have it. Check with the Port Hardy Travel Infocentre, 7250 Main Street, 949-7622 for charter information.

Golf ❖ About twenty minutes south of town, on the Port Alice Highway midway between Port Hardy and Port McNeill, the *Seven Hills Golf and Country Club* is rated at par 70. Residents brag that the view from the clubhouse lounge is "one of the nicest on Vancouver Island." For tee times and course information call Radio Seven Hills, H695009 through the operator.

Port Hardy Museum ❖ It is said that the best collection of Native artifacts on the West Coast is shared by the museums of Alert

Bay and Port Hardy. The Port Hardy Museum is well known for its rotating displays of heritage crafts. There are also travelling exhibits during the summer months. Look for it in the library building, at the corner of Market and Shipley.

Port Hardy Recreation ❖ This is the complex to look for when the rain showers hit. The District of Port Hardy provides facilities for a variety of indoor leisure activities, from roller-skating and floor hockey to swimming. The twenty-five metre indoor pool has six lanes and two diving boards (one and three metres), a water slide, rope swings, sauna, and fitness area. 7360 Columbia. Call for information about public swimming times, 949-6686.

San Josef Bay ❖ Port Hardy is the only town on the east coast of our Island that is within a fifteen-minute drive of the west coast. A deep Pacific inlet called Quatsino Sound cuts into the northern tip of the Island like a skewed fork, its shores dotted with tiny communities. One such place is the village of *Holberg*, which you'll pass through on your way to beautiful San Joseph Bay. On leaving Holberg, go west to a logging crossroad marked "Elephant Crossing." Follow the right fork immediately past this sign.

"San Joe," as Port Hardy residents call it, is an easy daytrip from town, and should *not* be missed if the weather is cooperating. Here is a chance to experience wild, open ocean, crashing surf, and flat, white, west coast sand. You can just feel those negative ions soothing jangled city nerves. Allow about two hours to catch your first glimpse of real Pacific Ocean—an hour down a good gravel road to Holberg, plus an hour on the hiking trail. Take along your own water as the only water supply is another half mile up the beach once you arrive. The beach trail is a well-travelled one, with corduroy sections over the mud, and information signs too. (Take this hike if you've been scared off the Cape Scott Trail.) P.S. If you stop at the logging company's office in Holberg, somebody will radio a message to trucks to watch for you on the roads from there.

Where to Eat

Since you're here to enjoy the great outdoors, you won't even notice the lack of fine restaurants. You'll find the usual number of small-town, quick-bite places, little Chinese restaurants (the oldest is the *Pagoda Gardens* on Granville), and hotel coffee shops. Nothing to write home about, with the possible exception of a restaurant called *Snuggles* next to the Pioneer Inn (see *Where to Stay*). This is a cozy "Olde English Pub" style restaurant, where steaks or salmon are done over alder coals in an open fireplace. When we visited, Snuggles offered Friday evening dinner theatre packages. These are very popular with locals, so call ahead for reservations (949-7575).

Where to Shop

Again, you won't find many shops here that carry anything you can't buy at better prices farther south. There are, however, two stores of interest for visitors who'd like a piece of North West Coast art as a souvenir of their Port Hardy stay.

Cape Scott Gallery ❖ Hand-made pottery, paintings, prints, and photographs of the North Island are offered here, at reasonable prices. 7069B Market Street, 949-7313.

Where to Stay

Port Hardy Inn ❖ You'll find six hotels and dozens of campsites in the Port Hardy area. The hotels are of average calibre, and any one of them should meet reasonable standards. We liked the Best Western Port Hardy Inn because it's the only one in town with an indoor pool. Rates are about $55 double. 9040 Granville Street at the Island Highway, 949-8525.

North Shore Inn ❖ The North Shore Inn is right downtown and has a beautiful view of the harbour and Hardy Bay from every room. Rates start at $60 double. 7370 Market Street, 949-8500.

Pioneer Inn   ❖   A five-minute drive south of town (you'll pass the large sign on the west side of the road on your way into town), the Pioneer Inn is our choice for those who want to be out in the country while still enjoying all the comforts of a modern motel. Good for families, especially if you want a kitchenette. Our gang liked the Nature Trail next door, the playground, and the live bunnies. Rates average $48 double. Box 699, 949-7271. Take the Coal Harbour turnoff from the Island Highway and follow the signs to 4965 Byng.

For more information, call the Port Hardy Travel Infocentre, 7250 Main Street, 949-7622.

The Gulf Islands

A few years ago, Jill went to Mexico for ten days. She returned with a case of Montezuma's Revenge and a number of interesting stories – particularly the one about how her hotel turned out to be a brothel. Two weeks after returning, she was sitting on the beach at Booth Bay Resort on Saltspring Island, wondering why she'd spent $1,700 going thousands of miles when this had been in her back yard all along.

That's the beauty of the Gulf Islands. They're affordable, scenic and easily reached from the Lower Mainland and southern Vancouver Island. You can enjoy either a change-of-scene day trip or a relaxing vacation week. We have concentrated on *Saltspring, Galiano, Mayne* and *Pender* Islands. Lovely *Saturna Island* has been excluded because it is the most difficult to reach and is also the least developed. However, we do recommend Saturna to those who can't bear crowds and city living a moment longer. Hole up at *Boot Cove Lodge*, and let Saturna's peace and tranquility wash over you. This quiet is interrupted annually for the Canada Day lamb bake – a pleasant excuse to visit this island.

The Gulf Islands are generally quite hilly, a challenge for bikers and hikers alike. The many miles of coastline are a mecca for boaters; if you lack even a rubber dinghy, boat rentals by the hour are available at most marinas. Craftspeople are drawn to these islands like bees to nectar – partly for the relaxed pace of rural island life, partly for the mild Mediterranean climate of Georgia Strait and partly for the appeal of making a living within sight of Mother Nature at her best: northern sea lions, harbour seals and giant killer whales are frequent guests in Gulf Island waters. We urge you to view the excellent hand work produced by local artisans, either at home studios or at various retail outlets.

So – go, explore, enjoy our beautiful Gulf Islands.

Saltspring Island

Saltspring was once a refuge for American blacks escaping slavery. Today the largest and most populous of the Gulf Islands is a refuge for those of us who find from time to time that the world is too much with us. The charm of Saltspring is such that some never make it back to the hurly-burly of the rat race again.

The pretty village of *Ganges*, the social and economic heart of the island, wraps around the end of Ganges Harbour, where moored sailboats bob up and down, masts gently clinking. You will be absorbed into the rhythm of Saltspring as you wander through the streets. Most of the island's 7,000 residents live between here and the northern tip of Saltspring.

The Fulford–Ganges Road winds through the centre of the island. It presents a pastoral view of rolling farmlands dotted with sheep, cattle, horses and the odd quaint old church, like St. Paul's, built in Fulford Harbour in 1880. Mounts Tuam and Maxwell form a dramatic backdrop, and the number of houses with craftspeople's signs out front are a reminder that the island boasts a large population of talented artists.

The long, flat stretch of road on the hill above Ganges gives you a panoramic vista of the other Gulf Islands to the east, with Mount Baker in the distance. You *could* circle this island in a two-hour hurry, but we suggest that you explore Saltspring's country roads at leisure and stretch out your visit here as long as possible.

The island is a brief 35-minute ferry ride from Victoria's Swartz Bay to Fulford Harbour. From the mainland it's a longer, more convoluted route, with stops at the other Gulf Islands on the way to Long Harbour. (A reminder: you'll need a vehicle reservation from the mainland. Phone BC Ferries in Vancouver at 669-1211.)

What to See and Do

Personally, when we go to Saltspring we like to beachcomb, walk and generally get away from it all. For excitement we go to the *Inn at Vesuvius*, or the *Blue Heron* at Fulford to exercise our elbow and jaw muscles with a beer and some pub fare. However, we offer the following brief list of activities available on the island:

Beaches ❖ Swimming, we're told is best on the island's more sheltered west side. A popular swimming beach is at **Drummond Park**, near the Fulford Inn. There are several sand and gravel beaches along here – good for collecting rocks, shells and driftwood – as well as an interesting petroglyph. According to Tsaout Indian legend, it is a woman who was changed into a rock to protect Indian land. **Vesuvius Bay** is also recommended for swimming. Find it at the base of a stairway from Langley Street, off Vesuvius Bay Road. Another favourite beach is **Beddis Beach**, at the end of Beddis Road off the Fulford–Ganges road, which offers lovely views of neighbouring islands.

Golf ❖ Golfers should bring their clubs with them so they can play at the public **Saltspring Island Golf Club** on Lower Ganges Road, 537-2121. It's an attractive nine-hole course, open from dawn to dusk every day.

Mount Maxwell ❖ Nerves of steel and a four-wheel drive (or possibly a tank) are recommended for tackling this rocky, dusty, narrow, winding "road" – we use the term loosely. Once you get up this six-mile stretch, however, the panoramic view is utterly stunning, a visual symphony, in summer, of greens and blues soaring off into the distance. Turn off the Fulford–Ganges road onto Cranberry Road, left onto Nobbs and then bear right onto Maxwell Road.

Ruckle Park ❖ At the southeast tip of Saltspring is this beautiful provincial park, with camping and picnic facilities as well as easy hiking trails along the water. **Beaver Point** was an infamous rum-running port during the 1920s, when liquor smugglers did brisk business across the Canada...US border. From the Fulford Harbour area, turn right onto Beaver Point Road, just up the hill from the dock. From Ganges, follow the Fulford...Ganges road and turn left onto Beaver Point Road.

Tennis ❖ Tennis buffs can play on the courts behind the School Board office in Ganges, behind the fire hall on the Fulford-Ganges Road, or in **Portlock Park** at the corner of Vesuvius Bay Road and Ganges Road. At the park, you will also find an adventure playground for kids, a running track and picnic tables.

Where to Eat

Ganges provides a number of soup/sandwich/burger/pizza outlets. When you're in the mood for something a little more interesting, try the following.

The Bay Window ❖ Located in the turn-of-the-century main building at Booth Bay Resort, this restaurant offers a scenic water view and some first-rate cuisine. Emphasis is on seafood at dinner; a number of the reasonably priced lunch options are borrowed from the appetizer roster. Soups and desserts are consistently first-rate. In the summer you can dine outside on one of the two little verandas; in the winter, the long, narrow dining room with fireplace is a cozy, inviting spot. At 375 Baker Road, 537-5651.

Fine Arts Patisserie ❖ How can one resist a cafe which offers a smartie and banana sandwich on multi grain bread with a side of carrot sticks? We hasten to add that there *are* more orthodox menu options, such as the very good chicken salad sandwich, enlivened with a generous handful of fresh tarragon. Vegetarians are well-served here, with plenty of tofu options and a meatless chili. Sweet teeth are also catered to via a showcase full of caloric desserts and breakfast pastries ranging from chocolate croissants to giant cinnamon buns. Breakfast is served all day and the coffee is excellent. Daytime dining only, under the striped awning next to the market on Lower Ganges Road, Ganges.

New Deli Cafe ❖ Chocoholics looking for a quick fix should pop into this waterfront restaurant and order the Dutch chocolate cake. It's a triple layer caloric treat which will have chocolate lovers in nirvana. For the rest of us, there's plenty of fresh salads, homemade soups, and some imaginative sandwiches, such as curried cream cheese and chicken. Sprouts and whole grains abound. Prices are very reasonable and in warm weather you can sit on the deck overlooking the marina. 2104 Grace Point Square, 537-4181.

The Inn at Vesuvius ❖ There are few pleasures that can beat sipping a long cold one on the deck of this neighbourhood pub, watching sailboarders fall into the water of Vesuvius Bay on a sunny summer's day. Simple, tasty, home-style lunches and dinners are available from the Inn's kitchen. Stop by on the weekends for live evening entertainment – and bring along some foreign currency to add to the bill collection behind the bar. Look for the red-roofed building beside the ferry dock at Vesuvius Bay, 537-2312.

Where to Shop

Ganges has seen an explosion of economic activity in the last few years with mini malls, condos and boutiques springing up everywhere. Fortunately, the seaside village atmosphere still prevails over plastic trendiness. Most of our old favourites in Ganges are still thriving, and we've added a few new finds.

Artcraft ❖ For over twenty summers Mahon Hall in Ganges has been the setting for the Artcraft show, a wide-ranging display of handwork created by over 200 Gulf Islands artisans. The diversity is amazing, the prices are competitive and the quality is uniformly excellent. Every price range is covered, from inexpensive potpourri sachets to woven clothing, and includes unique items like sea soap that lathers in seawater (a boon for boaters!), along with hard-to-find pottery containers for ikebana enthusiasts. All work is splendidly displayed. We rate this a must-see for visitors. Mahon Hall overlooks Ganges Harbour.

Embee Bakery ❖ There are always lineups whenever we're here, and no wonder. The bread and buns are fresh and good, with lots of whole grain specialties. Jill's husband is addicted to the bear claws – a great mid-morning snack when you're browsing through the Ganges Farmer's Market on a Saturday. The bakery is located at the foot of Ganges Hill, 537-5611.

Farmers' Market ❖ If you're in Ganges on a Saturday morning, the Farmers' Market, held in the parking lot of the waterfront **Centennial Park**, is a good place to find local crafts, fresh produce, home baking, used books and other browsers' treasures.

Glad's Chocolate Factory & Ice Cream Store ❖ We're glad we went into Glad's, even though we mucked up our clothes by dripping Glad Bars all over them. A Glad Bar is ice cream on a stick, dipped in Belgian chocolate and rolled in ground almonds – and very good it is too, even if it is messy. Also very good (and somewhat less messy) are cones made from Belgian waffles, filled with rich ice cream and topped with whipped cream, maraschino cherries and sprinkles of pure chocolate. Our advice is to skip dessert and head for Glad's handcrafted chocolate novelties, cordial cherries or famous truffles. In Ganges at 112 Fulford-Ganges Road, 537-4211.

Harlan's Chocolate Treats ❖ The gorgeous aroma of fresh roasted coffee draws you into this store of local crafts, cards, brass, china, novelties, bulk tea and coffee beans. The main attraction for us, however, is Harlan's Chocolates. Handmade on the island, they are rich, calorie-laden and utterly decadent. Don't go home without some. 100 Fulford–Ganges Road in Ganges, tucked between a meat market and a pharmacy. 537-4434.

MOUAT'S MALL

This charming multi-level building on the waterfront in Ganges houses a number of interesting shops. Our favourites:

Pegasus Gallery ❖ Here's a showcase for original paintings by West Coast artists (including the famous work of Brian Travers-Smith), as well as intricately carved silver jewelry, soapstone sculpture, porcelain and glassware. The premises are tiny, but every inch is beautifully filled. 537-2421.

Volume II Bookstore ❖ You can learn a lot about an area by prowling through bookstores. for their Saltspring customers, the owners stock a good supply of cooking, gardening and craft books, volumes on how to fix almost everything around the house, lots of travel and guidebooks, plus esoterica from birdwatching to poetry—a pretty fair summation of islanders' lifestyles. There is a good children's section and the adjoining record-and-tape room also carries recordings for kids. 537-9223.

Saltspring Island Art Gallery ❖ You'll find a mixture of style and genre in this gallery, which is run by volunteers from the Gulf Islands FCA (Federation of Canadian Artists) chapter. The paintings, glasswork and sculpture of professional island artists are featured, and profits go toward bursaries for students. Go upstairs, past the accountant's office, to the end of the hall in the Ganges Centre building, adjacent to the Fire Hall.

Waterfront Gallery ❖ Saltspring residents point you towards this co-operatively run shop when you're looking for a special gift made by Gulf Islands artisans. The quality is good and the selection varied, ranging from handmade soaps to quilted clothing—including some sweet little outfits for children. In Ganges at the foot of the hill, 161 Fulford—Ganges Road, 537-4525.

Crossroads ❖ African baskets dominate one corner, Chilean arpilleras hang on the wall, Unicef cards fill a rack...Crossroads is the kind of place where you can feel good, not guilty, about squandering your money since the shop stocks interesting handcrafts of all kinds from third world countries. Shop sponsors include such organizations as Amnesty International, the Sierra Club and the Voice of Women, and there is a reading area well-stocked with informational material. Next to the library at 131 McPhillips, 537-2122.

Heritage Boutique ❖ Woven pillows, inexpensive framed prints, handmade chocolates...find a non-standard Saltspring memento in here. Grace Point Square, 537-2143.

Orcas Gallery ❖ We like the Raku fish swimming along the wall in the back section of this gallery. We also like the selection—and prices!—of the conventional pottery in the same area. The front part of Orcas Gallery displays some excellent local paintings, plus sculpture, carvings and hand-crafted jewellery. It's well worth a look. On Gasoline Alley, which stretches along the waterfront behind (of course) the gas station at the foot of Ganges hill, 537-4004.

Rainbow's End ❖ After you've browsed through Orcas Gallery, check out this boutique for country crafts from dried flower wreaths to handmade soap. In Gasoline Alley, 537-5031

Salt Spring Gems & Art ❖ We found excellent buys on estate jewellery in here. Worth checking out if you appreciate art deco designs of the thirties and forties at prices far lower than you'd find in the city. In Grace Point Square, 537-4222.

Hot Tip: When leaving Salt Spring via the Fulford Harbour ferry terminal, make sure you leave enough time to pay, park, and then run back a few feet to Rodrigo's Restaurant. Buy a container of their homemade salsa, take it home and make nachos. Es muy bueno.

Where to Stay

Saltspring is plentifully supplied with accommodation, ranging from the plush to the pennypinching. The places we mention here do not exhaust the list, but do give you an idea of the choices available in different locations around the island.

Arbutus Court Motel ❖ If our monied friends stay at Hastings House, our budget-minded friends like this place. It's clean and modern and contains kitchenettes if you'd like to do your own cooking. It also has a view overlooking Vesuvius Bay and the ferry terminal. Double rates start at $40. It's on Vesuvius Bay Road, R.R. #1, Ganges, V0S 1E0, 537-5415.

Booth Bay Resort ❖ This is our favourite place to stay, nestled amid trees on the edge of a long finger of water which pokes inland from Booth Bay. The resort consists of comfortable, fully-equipped housekeeping cottages, most with fireplaces. You can dig clams and oysters (rakes and buckets hang outside the cabin doors) and explore the shoreline when the tide is out, or go canoeing when it's in. You could pick fresh blackberries, play checkers on the in-ground board and dine at least once in the excellent *Bay Window* restaurant. Even Jill's husband Colin, a classic Type A personality, manages to relax here. Double rates, including kitchen, start at $57. For reservations write

Box 247, 375 Baker Road, Ganges, V0S 1E0, or phone 537-5651. To find Baker Road, turn off North End Road by the cemetery.

Cusheon Lake Resort ❖ Here's a family-run place that comes highly recommended by a trusted source. Although it's situated on Cusheon Lake, you will have absolute peace and quiet because: (1) there are no pets or television sets, and (2) *no motor boats* are allowed on the lake. Motorless boats are available for rent, or you can swim, fish for trout and bass, hike, dig clams or just loll about in the hot tub. There are eleven fully-equipped housekeeping cabins, some with fireplaces. Double rates start at $85. Write R.R. #2, 171 Natalie Lane, Ganges, V0S 1E0 for reservations, 537-9629. To get there, watch for the Cusheon Lake Road off the Fulford–Ganges Road, and follow the signs.

Hastings House ❖ Hastings House was voted Canadian country house of the year by Hideaway Report in 1984 *and* 1985. We can't afford to stay here, but some of our more affluent friends can and do, along with the well-heeled likes of politicians and celebrities. One of our friends cheerfully but snobbishly pointed out to us that the high prices keep the riffraff out. The "no children under 16, no pets" regulations ensure that you'll have an idyllic, get-away-from-it-all vacation. Situated at the head of Ganges Harbour, Hastings House offers twelve character suites. The one called "Meadowloft," for example, has a larger-than-average bedroom with pastoral views over the gardens and duck pond. "Sealoft" is a smaller bedroom but offers a bird's-eye view of the ocean.

The spacious grounds include a farm garden, orchard, green-house and free-ranging chickens – all of which contribute to the legendary meals. The dining room menu, featured in food magazines, is broadly continental and emphasizes freshness of ingredients. Dinner is a set five-course affair, beautifully pre-sented after cocktails at 7. The luncheon choices include light salads or homemade soups and elegant sandwiches like the grilled shrimp, brie and asparagus. Early each morning, trays appear outside each room, bearing a thermos of coffee and fresh muffins, all part of the room price which starts at $230 double – don't say we didn't warn you! Write Box 1110, 160 Upper Ganges Road, Ganges, V0S 1E0 or phone 537-2362.

Spindrift Resort ❖ Spindrift's cottages perch on a cliff overlooking Long Harbour, where the Vancouver-Salt Spring ferry docks. Local craftwork is incorporated in the decor of the six fully-equipped cottages, and the secluded five-acre grounds offer walking trails and a sandy beach. Highly recommended as an adults only getaway. Double rates start at $70, including kitchen. RR #3, Wellbury Point, Ganges, V0S 1E0, 537-5311.

St. Mary Lake ❖ There are twelve lakes on Saltspring and—here comes another fishing statistic!—the smallmouth bass fishing at St. Mary Lake is said to be the finest in all of British Columbia. There are no fewer than seven lakeside cottage resorts around St. Mary Lake—all provide housekeeping facilities and lake access. Public boat launching is near the Blue Gables Resort at North End Road. Contact the Saltspring Island Travel Infocentre in Ganges (537-5252) for further information about these lakefront resorts.

Bed and breakfast appears to be a growth industry on Salt Spring. Drive any road on the island and you'll see B & B signs on every second driveway. Accomodation ranges from restored farmhouses to ultra-modern architect-designed residences. We suggest you check witht the Travel Infocentre in Ganges for specific information on homes in the particular part of the island in which you wish you wish to stay.

Pender Island

Pender is actually two islands, separated by a narrow canal spanned by a single-lane bridge. The two deep harbour bisected by the bridge—Browning and Bedwell—provide the Pender Islands with many scenic water views, and there are many other little bays and inlets indenting the coastline. Equally lovely are the pretty, rolling valleys and the surprisingly open terrain through much of this hilly island.

What to See & Do

For outdoorsy types, Pender offers a number of possibilities.

Beaches ❖ South Pender's main road changes its name three times as it snakes in a lazy S through the middle of the island. If you follow it right to the end (when it has become Gowlland Point Road) you'll find a pebbly public beach. Our favourite beach, however, is at the end of Craddock Drive, which runs off Gowlland. At low tide you can walk out to the little island just offshore; at any time you can have a living geology lesson in agglomerate rock formations, fascinating for both kids and adults. Those larger islands visible in the south are the American *San Juan Islands*.

Biking ❖ Bike rentals are available at both **Bedwell Harbour Resort** on South Pender and at the very scenic **Otter Bay Marina**, adjacent to the BC Ferries terminal on North Pender. Otter Bay stocks five- and ten-speed bikes, children's bikes, maps and tourist pamphlets. Phone 629-3579.

Community Centre ❖ Just before you cross the canal to South Pender, you'll see the school and community centre complex, where you'll find tennis courts and an adventure playground.

Golf ❖ The *Pender Island Golf and Country Club* has one of the prettiest settings we've ever seen, nestled in a pleasant rural valley. Its nine holes are spread out on either side of Otter Bay Road. Phone 629-6659.

Sort of Golf ❖ Are you up to a challenge? Try playing golf with a frisbee at the *Disc Golf Course*. Be careful—your score could be *disc-usting*. Look for the sign in Magic Lake Estates on Galleon Way.

Hope Bay ❖ The most scenic spot on this most scenic island is at Hope Bay. Drive to the intersection of Clam Bay and Port Washington Roads on the east side of North Pender. Get out of your car in the little parking area and look back at the view of the inlet. It is stunning, especially in the fall when the leaves are changing colour.

Mortimer Spit ❖ East of the canal bridge, on South Pender, is a short gravel road which leads down to Mortimer Spit (look for the sign). This little finger of land pushes out into Browning Harbour and is a great spot for kids—the water is shallow on the inner side of the spit. We were lucky enough to catch sight of seals frolicking quite near shore—maybe you will too!

Prior Centennial Provincial Park ❖ This park provides campsites in a wooded setting, with the usual amenities—toilets, picnic tables—and a trail to a viewpoint overlooking Browning Harbour. Located on Bedwell Harbour Road.

Where to Eat

We like the two pubs, the **Whale Pod**, at Bedwell Harbour Resort on South Pender, and the *Sh-qu-ala* (an Indian word meaning "watering hole") at the much more rustic Port Browning Marina on North Pender. Both have decks overlooking their respective harbours, and both serve very good, reasonably priced pub fare. Also reasonably priced is the continental fare at Bedwell's *Top Sider* restaurant. Entrees average $10 and choices range from an Indonesian sate to tortellini.

There are two reasons to go to the New Improved Driftwood Centre (which, in our opinion, now looks too upscale to look right on rustic Pender).

Campbell's Pender Bakery is one reason. Have a bean pie or a soy sausage roll or a crunchy peanut butter Nanaimo Bar or one of Grandma's scones, loaded with raisins and currants. Very wholesome! Take home a loaf of Real Bread, no namby-pamby white squishy stuff but a round of Frisbee-sized pumpernickel or black bread which will give your teeth and digestive system a healthy workout.

The second reason is **Bob's Driftwood Cafe**. There are fresh flowers on the tables and alfresco dining in the warmer months. Breakfasts are great: eggs and bacon done exactly as requested, thick slices of whole wheat toast, giant wedges of cottage-style French toast. Lunch and dinner choices range from diner classics (fish and chips, BLT sandwiches) to trendier fare (blackened snapper, teriyaki chicken stir fry). Corner of Bedwell Harbour Road and Razor Point Road, 629-6433.

Eagle Nest Restaurant ❖ The menu changes daily (always a good sign) so look for fresh seafood, locally grown vegetables, and innovative soups and desserts. All this and a spectacular view too. Located in Pender Lodge, MacKinnon Road, North Pender, 629-3221.

Where to Shop

If you need the necessities of life, like tonic for your gin or granola bars for the children, *PJ's General Store* at the head of Bedwell Harbour on Aldridge, the all-purpose stores at *Bedwell Harbour Resort, Otter Bay Marina* or the *Driftwood Centre* on Bedwell Harbour Road will supply you.

Pender Crafts ❖ In their new location, a small cedar and glass house complete with water view, Pender Crafts have the room to display lots more work by Co-op members. Plenty of wall space means plenty of paintings are added to the pottery, weaving, jewelry, woodwork and knitted items on view. Open weekends Easter to Thanksgiving, daily during July and August. On Blackberry Lane, adjacent to the intersection of Port Washington and Otter Bay Roads.

Where to Stay

Bedwell Harbour Resort ❖ Jill first came to Bedwell Harbour Resort by boat, but landlubbers can enjoy this first-class operation just as much. The lodge buildings are terraced down the hillside to the water, liked by stairways and ramps lined with cheery red geraniums. The complex includes an outdoor pool, store, the Whale Pod pub, video arcade, a children's play area, a babysitting service and a fine restaurant, the Topsider—plus the marina, of course. The rooms have balconies overlooking the ocean. There are also attractive cabins with kitchenettes if you'd like to be off by yourself. The restaurant and pub boast decks and water views. When you get tired of looking at the water, you can get out on it in a rented boat, or catch something out of it with rented fishing gear. Bikes and scooters are also available here for exploring the rest of the island. Double rates start at $79. Watch for the signs leading you down the hill off Canal Road on South Pender, 629-3212.

Cliffside Inn-on-the-Sea ❖ On North Pender, the Cliffside Bed & Breakfast Inn offers four utterly charming rooms – one, for example, with a brass bed; another with a waterbed – and an enchanting, glassed-in dining room with a view over Navy Channel. Home-cooked meals incorporate produce from the garden. Guests' hearty breakfasts can include peaches in cream, blueberry crêpes or vegetarian quiche. Set price candlelight-and-soft-music dinners (for guests only) offer choice of appetizer, entrée and dessert. You can gather around the fireplace afterwards for conversation, cards or reading. Cruising or fishing charters can be reserved, badminton and horseshoes are on site, there are three secluded waterfront acres, full of flowers and trees, to explore, and buckets and shovels are provided for clam diggers. Or just lie on the deck and work on your tan. The Inn's rates, including breakfast, start at $99 for doubles; plenty of package deals are available. To get here from the ferry terminal, take Otter Bay Road to Bedwell Harbour Road, turn left to Hope Bay, then follow Clam Bay Road to Armadale, Turn right and follow the signs. Phone 629-6691.

Corbett House ❖ Also on North Pender is the heritage Corbett House, which wins raves from B & B fans. This converted farmhouse, with lovely antique and turn-of-the-century furnishings, sits in the middle of a peaceful, pastoral landscape, guaranteed to soothe city-jangled nerves. Breakfast is a full, country-style meal, complete with home-baked bread and freshly ground coffee. No smoking allowed here, folks. Located on Corbett Road, which runs between Port Washington Road and Amies Road. Doubles range from $70 to $85; phone 629-6305 for reservations and current rate information.

Eastridge Chalet ❖ Set amid seven forested acres, complete with walking trails, the Eastridge combines rural charm with modern facilities. The ten units open onto a wrap-around deck; patio chairs are provided so you can sit out and inhale all that healthy country air. There are smoking and non-smoking units available, and one unit is equipped for handicapped guests. Complimentary morning coffee and muffins are included in room rates, which start at $49 for a double. Located adjacent to Prior Centennial Park on Canal Road, North Pender. 629-3353.

Pender Lodge ❖ The comfortable lodge was built as a private residence in 1919 and still retains a homey atmosphere. It overlooks the water and is surrounded by five acres of garden and treed property. Guests can also enjoy the swimming pool and tennis court. There are nine guest rooms in the Lodge, plus housekeeping cottages on the grounds. Lodge rooms with private baths start at $60 double; or try an off-season getaway package for two for one night's accommodation, plus dinner and breakfast in the excellent Eagle Nest restaurant. (See *Where to Eat*). MacKinnon Road, North Pender, 629-3221.

Mayne Island

Mayne is the Islanders' island—the one other islanders visit when they want to get away from it all. Quiet, rural and peaceful, Mayne Island is also of interest to history buffs. *Miner's Bay*, a five-minute drive from the ferry terminal at Village Bay, has always been the centre of Mayne activity. It got its name during the heyday of the 1858 Gold Rush, when miners heading from Victoria to the mainland Mother Lode would stop over here. by the turn of the century, Mayne was a favourite summer resort of Vancouverites, and the island boasted several hotels and boarding houses. Relics of these early days—Indian artifacts and old farm implements—can be seen in the original lock-up building, dating from 1896, which now functions as the *Museum*. Across the road is the *Agricultural Hall*, built about 1900. It is the site of the annual Fall Fair, held on the third weekend in August—the oldest such event on the Gulf Islands. For other stops of interest, read on . . .

What to See & Do

Bennett Bay ❖ Since this *is* an island, you will expect to find beaches. The prettiest, in our opinion, is Bennett Bay, a sheltered swimming spot with warm water plus fine sand for basking or building castles. Unique to this beach are tiny pink shells; we found two of these elusive delights. Alas, we did not sight the resident great blue heron, but a couple of noisy kingfishers made up for him. Peaceful and relaxing—we recommend it. Drive east from Miner's Bay to the end of Fernhill Road, go left onto

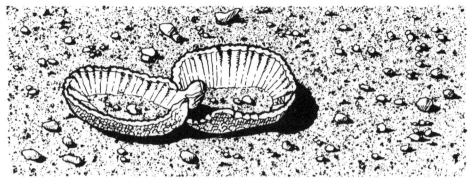

Wilks, and then watch almost immediately for the beach access road on the right.

Campbell Bay ❖ If you're a swimmer, Campbell Bay is for you. It is calm, protected, and warm. The beach is pebbly, but there are lots of big logs and rocks for practising your balancing act to the water. This one is tricky to find because the access is unmarked. Follow Waugh Road until it becomes Campbell Bay Road. Watch for a bit of a fence on the left. That's the beach access. If you see a log house on the right, you've come too far; go back a quarter mile.

Biking Cyclists looking for leisurely miles of country roads across scenic farmland will enjoy Mayne's beautiful terrain and famous King apple orchards – thought to be the first place apples were grown in British Columbia.

Active Pass Lightstation ❖ If you've never seen a lighthouse up close, you're in luck. Visitors are welcomed at the Active Pass Lightstation at Georgina Point from 1 to 3 p.m., daily. This lightstation celebrated its centennial in 1985, and marks the eastern entrance to the narrow, often treacherous Active Pass. You get a nice view of Georgia Strait, and of Sturdies Bay on Galiano Island from this point. You may see killer whales passing by, or the big white BC ferries on their way to and from the mainland. Follow Georgina Point Road from Miner's Bay, right to the end.

Dinner Bay Park ❖ We like this newest addition to Mayne's public spaces. The eleven acres of former farm land contains a large grassy area, edged by a grove of trees, and a short shoaling beach, pebbly but sheltered. There are picnic tables, a covered barbecue facility, a horseshoe pitch, and volleyball net. On Williams Place, off Dinner Bay Road, in the southwest corner of the island.

Sailing and Fishing ❖ If you'd like to see Mayne from the water, several residents offer sailing and fishing charters, some with lunch included. Look for brochures on the ferries or check the notice board at Miner's Bay.

Mayne's small size means that, even if you aren't planning a relaxing overnight – or longer! – stay, you can probably tour the whole island in an easy day-trip.

Where to Eat

Five Roosters Restaurant ❖ Our advice from the first edition still holds true – there's only one place to eat on Mayne and that's the *Five Roosters*. The kitchen is still turning out first-class homestyle fare at reasonable prices in comfortable, non-glamorous surroundings. Hearty homemade soups, thick meaty burgers loaded with extras, and fresh baked desserts. We like it and think you will too. Open from breakfast to dinnertime, but call for dinner reservations first at 539-2727. At Miner's Bay.

Where to Shop

ARTS & CRAFTS

Mayne is dotted with craft workshops and artists' studios. Here is a guide to some local favourites.

Charterhouse ❖ This piece of property is guaranteed to make you want to sell everything and move to Mayne. Follow the past past the flower garden and little pool into the flower-filled foyer, and then turn right into Heather Maxey's little showroom and studio. The emphasis is on fabric crafts, including weaving, with a smattering of jewelry and pottery. Open afternoons in the summer, weekends only in the winter. At Bennett Bay, turn off Arbutus onto Charter Road and follow it, past the tree in the middle, to the Charterhouse sign. 539-2028.

Island Gallery ❖ We keep sending folks into this Gallery, even though we know lots of the stuff is of uneven (bordering on rummage sale) quality, because we keep striking pay dirt—at rock bottom prices. If you're a gambler, you might get lucky too. Open weekend afternoons at the corner of Wilks and Fernhill, part of the Marisol Cabins property; 539-2336.

Greenhouse Studio ❖ When you have some time to wait for the ferry, take a stroll 200 yards along Dalton Drive to #31. Admire the very pretty garden as you walk up the driveway to the tiny studio. Weaving and woodwork are the specialties of the owners, but we like the reasonably priced hand-painted silk scarves too. All items are both designed and produced on Mayne Island. Open afternoons Wednesday to Sunday and holiday Mondays at 31 Dalton Drive, Village Bay. 539-2474.

The House of Taylor ❖ Every nook, cranny, shelf, mantel and piece of antique furniture in this old house seems to be utilized in the owner's quest to display the handiwork of over 100 Island artists. The glasswork is worthy of special mention, as well as the interesting textile crafts. Bookworms take note: the front bedroom is full of used books for sale. At Miner's Bay. 539-5283.

A word of warning: in our experience, open hours listed by craftspeople in their brochures often bear no resemblance to reality. Most artists are happy to make appointments to view, so, if in doubt—phone first.

Stocking Up ❖ The *Mayne Island Centre Store* on Fernhill, and the *Miner's Bay Trading Post* can supply you with aspirins, cold pop, and other necessities of modern life. Newly added to Miner's Bay since the first edition of this book is the *Mayne Street Mall*. It boasts a health food store for the nuts and berries crowd, plus aa bakery and gift shop for chocolates and other caloric delights.

Where to Stay

Your accommodation choices are quite limited on Mayne. Our suggestion is to cultivate a friendship with someone who owns a weekend place here. Failing that, you might try one of the B & B places which have opened in recent years. If you're travelling with kids, we still like the housekeeping cabins (some with fireplaces) at *Blue Vista Resort* overlooking Bennett Bay. Rates start at $40 double. Reservations 539-2463, at the end of Arbutus Drive.

For something completely different, book yourself into *Fernhill Lodge*. The secluded, rambling building contains six "theme" guest rooms – Jacobean, for example, has a 300-year-old oak four-poster bed and period antiques. (Modern ensuite baths replace chamber pots.) The theme idea carries through to dinner, with historical cookery the house specialty. The adventurous can sample Roman (oysters in cumin sauce), Medieval (almond cake with cider syllabub), or Renaissance (cod in rose sauce). Timid diners can enjoy the farmhouse meal, a less exotic but still savoury treat like steak and kidney pie. Breakfast, included in the room rate (starting at $65 double) features fresh muffins, homemade preserves, and herbed scrambled eggs (from the Lodge's own hens). By the way, because of the complexity of the dinner preparation, only one "gastronomic time travel" menu choice is offered nightly. It is chosen by the first party to reserve, so if you have a historical craving, book early by calling 539-2544. No smoking here, please. Located in the centre of Mayne Island on Fernhill Road.

Galiano Island

This mile-wide, finger-shaped island lies northwest by southeast along the Strait of Georgia, with most of the commercial activity – such as it is – located at the south end. The resident population of 775 is augmented by those lucky enough to own holiday retreats in which to unwind from the frenzy and frazzle of city living for a few days. Even a day trip to Galiano is enough to soothe most people. We've attempted to guide you to the highlights of the island, and suggested places where you can take care of more temporal matters – like food and drink!

Enjoy.

Serene, scenic Galiano Island is located halfway between Tsawwassen (on the mainland) and Swartz Bay (on Vancouver Island), and is reached daily by ferries from both terminals. If you're bringing your car over from the mainland, be sure to make vehicle reservations for the ferry–phone 669-1211 in Vancouver.

What to See and Do

Montague Provincial Park ❖ This well-maintained park offers campsites, picnic tables, wooded hiking trails, a beach, warm water for swimming (the harbour is sheltered by Parker Island), and toilet facilities. Be warned: in mid-summer, when forest fire hazard is at its worst, the hiking trails may be closedd. (About 70 percent of Galiano is owned by foresty giant MacMillan Bloedel, which maintains its holdings as a tree farm. Forest fires are a serious threat to the natural beauty of Galiano.) Closure need not be a disappointment, however, because there's plenty of shoreline for beachcombing. An unexpected surprise is the apple orchard near the boat moorage, first recommended to us by radio man Terry Spence of CFAX in Victoria. Montague Park Road, which runs off Montague Road, leads right to the park. P.S. Look for Lovers' Leap, a 150-foot drop from a rocky ledge to the ocean below.

Outings and Sightseeing ❖ Play out your Walter Mitty explorer fantasies ("Here is the intrepid Captain Dionysio Galiano, circumnavigating the island...") with an afternoon aboard a forty-six-foot catamaran chartered from *Southwind Sailing Charters* . Unlike Captain Galiano, who was probably dining on weevily biscuits, you get a seafood picnic included in your charter price. Contact the Hennessys at 539-2930.

Those who prefer to catch rather than eat seafood can head out on a 36-foot sailing vessel from *Fish & Ship* charters. Contact Dave or Krista Barlow at 539-2532.

Eco-tourists (people who travel specifically to enjoy the ecology of special places) can view the Gulf Islands' natural beauty via a kayak trip escorted by *Gulf Island Kayaking*. Suited for both the novice and the seasoned paddler, these trips explore beautiful coastlines, magnificent scenery, and abundant bird and wildlife. Phone 539-2442 for complete info and rates.

If you get seasick in the bathtub, try horseback riding instead; it's a sensible way to tour this very hilly island ("...and here is the intrepid Captain Galiano, about to plant a flag on the top of Mount Galiano..."). Experienced guides from *Bodega*

Resort will lead you over secluded trails. Find them at the corner of Porlier Pass Drive and Cook Road, 539-2677.

Horse make you seasick too? How about staying on terra firma and playing a little golf? The *Galiano Golf and Country Club* welcomes visitors at Ellis Road, 539-5533.

At the northern end of Galiano is *Coon Bay*, a favourite sandy beach for locals. Turn off Porlier Pass Drive onto Cook Road, and follow the unpaved road. At the south end of the island, *Bluff Park*, off Bluff Road, is owned and maintained by islanders, and boasts a superlative view over Active Pass. Masses of wildflowers bloom in profuse splendour here each spring. Stunning vistas are also spread out for those hardy people who hike to the tops of *Sutil Mountain* and neighbouring *Mount Galiano*. While you're enjoying your Captain Galiano fantasies, watch for eagles soaring effortlessly above Active Pass.

There's a scenic lookout high above Trincomali Channel on Porlier Pass Road— a nice spot for a picnic lunch. Warning: not recommended for small children; the drop is far too dangerous for parental peace of mind: There is space for off-road parking but no sign, so keep your eyes peeled about three kilometres north of Retreat Cove Road.

Bellhouse Park ❖ When we first checked out this park, we passed a Dad and two small boys. They were all carrying fishing rods and tackle boxes and wearing the kind of serious expressions which suggested Male Bonding was about to take place. Bellhouse Park, located on a rocky point of land looking southeast to the mainland, is great for kids of both sexes. There's a large expanse of bare rock at the shoreline, perfect for running, kite flying, and, of course, fishing. Walking trails wind through the wooded portion of the park. Look for the blue sign on Sturdies Bay Road, directing you to Burrell Road. Turn on Jack Road and follow it to the end.

Where to Eat

La Berengerie ❖ Nestled amid the trees is this little gem of a restaurant, decorated in charming country style: cedar-panelled walls, beamed ceiling, dark-red tile floors, lace tableclothes, and pottery serving bowls. Evening diners are offered a set four-course dinner, which varies daily. Cost is under $20 per person, and the meals we've sampled have been very good indeed. There are rooms on the second floor here for bed and breakfast fans. Do make sure you have reservations, because it's quite tiny. Corner of Montague and Clanton Roads, 539-5392.

Hummingbird Inn Pub ❖ If touring Galiano has left you with a desparate need for a cold beer, head for the Hummingbird Inn, the island's only pub. The building is a typical example of West Coast cedar and beam architecture; the interior is divided into cozy sitting areas. We like the rounded, brick fireplace nook, down a few steps from the main floor. It features an eye-catching stained glass window created by local artist Paul Hawbolt. The food and the service have been vastly improved since we last reviewed this pub. An expanded menu offers sandwiches, a wide array of burgers (including the popular vegetarian burger named after one of the waiters, a triathlete who represented Canada at the Commonweath Games in New Zealand) pub favourites like the delicious Shepherd's Pie, and salads galore. There are bed and breakfast rooms available above the pub. The Pub Bus makes regular runs to the ferries and provincial park for thirsty travellers—isn't that a good way to handle the ride home after you've had a few? At the junction of Sturdies Bay, Georgeson Bay, and Porlier Pass Roads, 539-5472.

The Pink Geranium ❖ When Ken and Sylvia Mounsey retired to Galiano, they just wanted a little business to run. The legendary Pink Geranium has been successful beyond their wildest dreams. If you want to dine here, particularly in the summer months, reservations are a MUST. The reputation of the P.G. (as locals refer to it) makes this a safe bet for a fine meal. It's only open on weekends, and offers a set four-course dinner for under $20 per person, which includes fresh produce from the garden whenever possible and delights like home-smoked salmon with fresh dill sauce or sourdough bread baked in Sylvia's outdoor brick oven. The dining room is homey and appealing, with its large bay window overlooking the grounds, and lovely silver and china dishes ranged around the plate rails. A special feature is the inglenook, which displays a collection of horse brasses and old books. It's an intimate spot for after-dinner coffee beside the fire. Look for the pink mailbox on Porlier Pass Drive, 539-2477.

Wok on the Run ❖ Yup, Big City living comes to rural Galiano in the form of real take-out Chinese food. In a typically Canadian cross-culinary mix, you can also pick up a deluxe cheeseburger or a pizza. Pick up your vegi-pizza and egg rolls on Porlier Pass Drive (look for the signs north of Gustin Road). Order ahead by calling 539-2141.

Chez Ferrie ❖ If hunger pangs strike when we're waiting for the ferry boat at Sturdies Bay, we look to the white **Chez Ferrie** van parked in the terminal lot for gastronomic relief. The van provides burgers, fish and chips, hot and cold drinks – the usual Fast-Food-In-Parking-Lot stuff. But Chez Ferrie also provides surprisingly good daily specials, like the chicken teriyaki burgers and blueberry cake with whipped cream on our last trip. Beats ferry fare every time.

Where to Shop

Arts and Crafts ❖ Galiano, like many of the other Gulf Islands, hums with the sound of potters' wheels, weavers' looms, artists' brushes, and jewelers' tools. Many of the craftspeople welcome visitors to their studios but, since hours are irregular, our advice is to phone first. Information is available at the Visitors Information booth at Sturdies Bay – or walk around the corner to the *Dandelion Gallery of Fine Art*. On display is an eclectic mix of jewelry, paintings (we especially like the etchings by Ronaldo Norden) and some very distinctive handmade clothes. Look, (and listen) for the tape "Windows" by Galiano guitarist

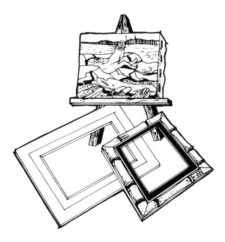

Brad Prevedoros and Mayne Island flautist Mary Reher. Plug it into your car tape deck next time you're stuck in traffic – it's guaranteed to sooth jangled nerves. Find the Gallery on Madrona Drive across from the gas station. 539-5622

The Bookshelf ❖ Running out of vacation reading? If it's Friday, you're in luck. Between 11 a.m. and 2 p.m., volunteers operate a used book store in the North Galiano Community Hall. There are magazines as well as paperback and hardcover books. Prices seem to top out at 25 cents. Look for the Hall on Porlier Pass Road.

Stocking Up ❖ If you're looking for provisions or a quick lunch at the south end of Galiano, stop at the *Corner Store*, Georgeson Bay Road at Studies Bay Road, 539-2986. Or find our favourite, *Burrill Brothers Store*, a homespun general store offering produce in baskets, health foods, fresh meat and cheeses, plus odds and ends like books and cards. Squashed into the back of this tiny space is a coffee room, but don't go in. Only real Galianoers may enter to intigue and potitick in this special place. On Sturdies Bay Road, 539-2611.

The Deli ❖ Just slightly farther along the road, look for a wedgewood blue building, The Deli, for charcoal broiled burgers, sand-wiches, and pizza, as well as imported cheeses and meat – 539-2221.

Trincomali Bakery ❖ This cottage bakery has been a runaway suc-cess, and deservedly so. Natural ingredients are emphasized, as is the lack of preservatives. The sourdough bread has real bite to it, and the cheese and onion buns make tasty sand-wiches. The distressingly caloric goodies are, alas, also irres-tible. All these and a cappuccino machine too! Watche for the sign, about halfway along the island on the water side of Porlier Pass Drive, 539-2004.

The Market ❖ We like The Market, a stationary version of the travell-ing van which used to bring fresh produce to West Coast Island communities. This is the place tp pick up picnic fare, from homemade baked goods to salmon steaks to organically grown apples. There's an excellent selection of cheese, local seafood, bulk supplies like basmati rice and oat bran, and even gourmet delicacies such as fruit spreads, salsas, curries and chutneys. Hippie-turned-entrepreneur Lony Rockafella runs his Market on Georgeson Bay Road near the intersection of Sturdies Bay Road.

Where to Stay

Bodega Resort ❖ The north end of Galiano is the place for people who really want to get away. We like the Bodega Resort, which also has a fine view—over Trincomali Channel this time. You stay in log chalets (these are too sumptuous to be called cabins) complete with stained glass windows, full kitchens, and fire-places. They're set amid twenty-five acres of woods and mead-ows—very relaxing! The resort has several ocean view conference and meeting rooms are available, well used for corporate and educational retreats during the off season. Double room rates start at $60. At Porlier Pass Drive and Cook Road, 539-2677.

Woodstone Country Inn ❖ The Woodstone is a must-stay. We were among the Inn's first guests and fell in love with the place instantly.

Cozy rooms on the south side look out over a pastoral landscape, while rooms on the north share a serene forest view. Most rooms have fireplaces; all have antique furniture, bal-conies or patios, big fluffy duvets, and original art reflecting each room's floral theme (buttercup, lilac, foxglove...)

In the dining room you'll find crisp linens, beautiful flowers, and divine food. Artistic presentation, imaginative use of the Inn's own organically grown herbs and vegetables, and fresh, fresh, *fresh* taste—this entry rates solid raves. Room rates start at $69 double occupancy, which includes a superb country breakfast. Adult-oriented (no pets or smoking please), and wheelchair accessible. It's on Georgeson Bay Road, a few minutes from the Montague Harbour Marine Park beaches. 539-2022.

Reader Reply

We welcome your comments about your favourite out-of-the-way restaurant, shop, park, beach or hotel for future editions of *Island Treasures*. Please send your cards or letters to:

ISLAND TREASURES
Harbour Publishing
Box 219
Madeira Park, BC
V0N 2H0

My favourite _____(restaurant, shop, beach etc.) is:

Name of spot: _____

Address: _____

_____

Why I like it (We encourage specifics here--Best cheese soup in BC! or Oscar de la Renta soap in the bathrooms!):

_____

_____

_____

_____

_____

My name: _____

Address _____

_____

Phone: _____

How's That Again?

(a brief guide to pronouncing the unpronounceable)

arbutus	*ar-BUTE-us*
Chemainus	*shah-MAIN-us*
Esquimalt	*ess-KWY-malt*
Ganges	*GAN-jeez*
Juan de Fuca	*WAHN-duh-FEW-kah*
Kwakiutl	*kwah-CUTE-ill*
Nanaimo	*na-NIGH-mo*
Qualicum	*KWAAH-lick-um*
Saanich	*SAN-itch*
Salish	*SAY-lish*
Sooke	*Sook*
Tofino	*toe-FEEN-o*, or *tah-FEEN-o*
Tsawwassen	*saw-WAH-sen*, or *tah-WAH-sen*
Ucluelet	*you-CLUE-let*

treasure *(TREZH-ur)*, n. any thing that is much loved or valued

230

Index